The
Core Knowledge™
Series

Resource Books for Children
from Year 1 to Year 6

PRAISE FOR THE CORE KNOWLEDGE UK SERIES

'The Core Knowledge Sequence puts knowledge back into primary education. Rich in content, challenging and with clear progression and continuity, it offers an excellent framework to ensure that pupils leave primary school with solid foundations for future learning.'

– Peter Lawson, Head of Primary, Grindon Hall Christian School

'Our recent Core Knowledge lessons on the Arctic have provided our children with a wealth of understanding. The lessons give children the facts, then we are free to create an enjoyable and engaging learning experience. Core Knowledge fuels our pupils' desire to learn more about the world around them.'

– Emma Greaves, Reception Teacher, West London Free School Primary

'It is vital that children receive a solid body of knowledge when they are at primary school because it allows them to expand their comprehension and access a wider field of learning. The Core Knowledge approach does just that. I cannot recommend it enough.'

– Matthew Laban, Headteacher, Kingfisher Hall Primary Academy, London

'Creativity, the arts and design are crucial to the environment and life of every citizen. They should occupy a central place in the curriculum at both primary and secondary levels. The new series published by Civitas, giving examples of how the arts and creativity can play a part in the education of every child, is a real contribution to the teaching of these subjects in all our schools.'

– Sir Nicholas Serota, Director of Tate

'A strong foundation of knowledge gained in the earliest years of education is such an important asset for children, sparking their imagination and providing the cornerstone for their future learning. I welcome the aim of the Core Knowledge books to do just that and I am sure that they will be valued by many parents wishing to help their children to do well at school.'

– Munira Mirza, Deputy Mayor for Education and Culture of London

What Your Year 6 Child Needs to Know

PREPARING YOUR CHILD
FOR A LIFETIME OF LEARNING

Edited by E. D. HIRSCH, JR

General Editors for the Civitas UK edition:
ROBERT WHELAN & TANYA LUBICZ-NAWROCKA

Original illustrations for this edition by MARK BEECH

Published by

Civitas
55 Tufton Street
London SW1P 3QL

First edition published in the USA in 2005 as *What Your Fifth Grader Needs to Know*

UK edition published January 2014

Reprinted with corrections April 2014

Independence: Civitas: Institute for the Study of Civil Society is a registered educational charity (No. 1085494) and a company limited by guarantee (No. 04023541). Civitas is financed from a variety of private sources to avoid over-reliance on any single or small group of donors.

ISBN: 978-1-906837-28-0

Book design and layout by Luke Jefford (www.lukejefford.com)

Printed in Great Britain by Printed Word Publishing, Hastings
(part of the Scantech Group Ltd)

Acknowledgements: US edition

This series has depended on the help, advice and encouragement of more than two thousand people. Some of those singled out here already know the depth of our gratitude; others may be surprised to find themselves thanked publicly for help they gave quietly and freely. To helpers named and unnamed we are deeply grateful.

Editor-in-Chief of the Core Knowledge Series: E. D. Hirsch, Jr

Text Editor: Matthew Davis

Editorial Assistance: Diane P. Castro, Michael Marshall, Susan Tyler Hitchcock, John Holdren, Souzanne Wright, Robert D. Shepherd

Art, Photo and Text Permission Research: Matthew Davis, Susan Tyler Hitchcock, Peter Locke, Emily E. Reddick, Jeanne Siler, The Permissions Group

Writers: This revised edition involved a careful reconsideration and sometimes re-use of material in the first edition of this book, as well as others in the series. In that spirit, we wish to acknowledge all who contributed to either edition. Writers for the revised edition: Rebecca Beall Barnes (music), Matthew Davis, Donna Lucey (American history), Michael Marshall, Michael Stanford (art), Souzanne Wright (maths). Writers for the original edition: Nancy Bryson (science), Bernardine Connelly (history), Tricia Emlet (geography), Marie Hawthorne (science), E. D. Hirsch Jr (science), John Hirsch (maths), John Holdren (history, language and literature), Jennifer Howard (history and science), Blair Longwood Jones (literature), Bethanne H. Kelly (literature), Elaine Moran (visual arts), A. Brooke Russell (geography, science), Peter Ryan (music), Lindley Shutz (language and literature), Helen Storey (language and literature), Steven M. Sullivan (history)

Advisers on Subject Matter: Richard Anderson, Wayne Bishop, Lucien Ellington, Andrew Gleason, Charles F. Gritzner, Eric Karell, Joseph Kett, Michael Lynch, Wilfrid McClay, Joseph C. Miller, Anne Moyer, Kristen Onuf, Mark Rush, Margaret Redd, Gayle Sherwood, Michael Smith, Ralph Smith, James Trefil, Nancy Wayne and others

Advisers on Multiculturalism: Minerva Allen, Barbara Carey, Frank de Varona, Mick Fedullo, Dorothy Fields, Elizabeth Fox-Genovese, Marcia Galli, Dan Garner, Henry Louis Gates, Cheryl Kulas, Joseph C. Miller, Gerry Raining Bird, Connie Rocha, Dorothy Small, Sharon Stewart-Peregoy, Sterling Stuckey, Marlene Walking Bear, Lucille Watahomigie, Ramona Wilson

Advisers on Elementary Education: Joseph Adelson, Isobel Beck, Paul Bell, Carl Bereiter, David Bjorklund, Constance Jones, Elizabeth LaFuze, J. P. Lutz, Sandra Scarr, Nancy Stein,

Phyllis Wilkin, plus all the conferees at the March 1990 conference where the first draft of the curriculum was developed.

Schools: Special thanks to the schools and individual teachers– too many to list here – that have offered advice and suggestions for improving the Core Knowledge Sequence.

Our grateful acknowledgment to these persons does not imply that we have taken their (sometimes conflicting) advice in every case, or that each of them endorses all aspects of this project. Responsibility for final decisions rests with the editors alone. Suggestions for improvements are always welcome, and we thank in advance those who send advice for revising and improving this series.

Acknowledgements: UK edition

General Editors of the UK edition: Robert Whelan & Tanya Lubicz-Nawrocka

Contributing Editor of the UK edition: Nigel Williams

Editorial Assistant: Catherine Green

Author of Visual Arts: Anne Anderson

Design and typesetting of the UK edition: Luke Jefford

Original illustrations for the UK edition: Mark Beech

Maps: Jo Moore, Paul Collicutt and Mark Otton

Owl illustrations: Mark Otton

Compiling the UK edition of a book that has already become an established classic in the United States has been both a privilege and a challenge. Our first thanks must go to E.D. Hirsch, Jr, Linda Bevilacqua and the team at the Core Knowledge Foundation for sharing with us the fruits of their labours over so many years. We fully share their view that all children deserve access to a first-class education, and we hope that the Civitas edition of the Core Knowledge texts will do as much for children in the UK as the US edition has done for thousands of children in the US and abroad.

Many people have helped us. We are especially grateful for the assistance given to the project by Robert Peal in History; Danielle Newman and colleagues at West London Free School in Science; Andrew Phemister in British and European History and Geography; Chris Gray and Margaret Lenton in History; Chris Cull in Music; Peter Clarke in Mathematics; and Matthew Robinson in Language and Literature. Marilyn Brocklehurst of the Norfolk Children's Book Centre shared her passion for children's books and helped us to find titles for the suggested resources sections.

We are grateful to Gail McIntosh for permission to reproduce her excellent original illustrations from the US edition; to Paul Collicutt for adding the dimension of colour to illustrations that were originally black and white and for creating new illustrations and maps; and to all those generous authors, illustrators and copyright owners who have allowed us to reproduce material for this book because they share our passion for bringing to children the very best in words and images.

Thanks to our colleagues past and present at Civitas for their help, especially Emma Lennard, Curriculum Project Director; Matilda Munro, Director of Civitas Schools; Annaliese Briggs for help with the UK Sequence; and Janet Russell for help with the text. Special thanks are due to Anastasia de Waal, Head of Family and Education at Civitas, for her help and guidance.

A Note to Teachers

Throughout the book, we have addressed the suggested activities and explanations to 'parents', since you as teachers know your students and will have ideas about how to use the content of this book in relation to the lessons and activities you plan. To discuss using Core Knowledge UK materials in your school, please contact Civitas at 55 Tufton Street, London SW1P 3QL, 020 7799 6677.

Email: coreknowledge@civitas.org.uk

Companion Website

There is a wealth of additional activities, readings and resources to supplement this book available on the Core Knowledge UK website. This includes a Teacher's Portal with teaching ideas and resources, curriculum planning documents and images from the book that are available for use by teachers and home educators. Please visit our website at:

www.coreknowledge.org.uk

About the Editor

E.D. Hirsch, Jr is a professor at the University of Virginia and the author of *The Schools We Need* and the bestselling *Cultural Literacy* and *The Dictionary of Cultural Literacy*. He and his wife, Polly, live in Charlottesville, Virginia, where they raised their three children.

E. D. Hirsch, Jr receives no renumeration for editing the series nor any other renumeration from the Core Knowledge Foundation.

Contents

Language and Literature

History and Geography

Visual Arts

Music

Mathematics

Science

Foreword to the UK Edition of the Core Knowledge Series

This is the sixth in a series of books for parents who want to help their children do well at school. It describes what every child should aim to have learnt by the end of the school year. It is not a description of everything that could be known but rather a guide to the knowledge that children will need to advance to the next stage of their education. Nor is it primarily a textbook, although it could be used as such – along with other teaching resources – if schools wish.

The Core Knowledge series gives parents the tools to judge how effectively their children are being taught. And it provides teachers with clear aims that can be shared with parents, thereby enlisting them in the common cause of getting the best from every child.

Why publish a British version of a book originally designed for American children? For the last 50 years in both Britain and America there has been no consensus about how and what children should be taught. Sometimes knowledge was dismissed as mere 'rote learning', which was contrasted unfavourably with 'critical thinking skills'. Others argued that education should be 'child centred' not 'subject centred'. Professor Hirsch, who inspired the Core Knowledge series, was among the first to see that the retreat from knowledge was misguided. Above all, he showed that to compare 'knowledge' with 'thinking skills' was to make a false contrast. They are not mutually exclusive alternatives. Thinking skills can be 'knowledge-rich' or 'knowledge-lite'. The purpose of a good education is to teach children how to think clearly – to see through dubious reasoning, to avoid being conned, to learn how to question their own assumptions, to discover how to be objective or to argue a case with clarity. Knowledge does not get in the way of reasoning: it's what we reason with.

The Core Knowledge approach has six main strengths.

- It helps parents to bring out the best in their children. It provides a guide to what young people should be learning and helps parents decide on the school best suited to their child.

- It helps teachers. By providing clear expectations that are shared with parents, teachers are better able to benefit every child. Schools are always at their best when parents and teachers work together.

- It helps children to learn on their own initiative. The books are written in language suitable for each year group, so that children can read alone or with their parents.

● It provides more equal opportunities for everyone. Some children do not receive effective support at home, perhaps because some of us did not ourselves get the best education. A good school can do much to make up for lost ground and the Core Knowledge series is designed for this very task. The books describe what every child can learn if given the chance. What's more, many parents find that they learn as much as their children!

● It encourages social cohesion. Britain today has more cultures, ethnic groups and religions than 50 years ago. If we all share in a common stock of knowledge, social solidarity based on mutual respect for our legitimate differences is more likely.

● It strengthens democracy. A free and democratic society depends on the mass of people being well-informed. We often say that modern societies are 'knowledge-based'. It's true. People who do not share in the knowledge that is regularly used by television news programmes or in our newspapers are at risk of being misled.

We are keen to work with teachers who share our ideals and who hope to play a leading part in developing this new curriculum in Britain. In co-operation with teachers, we have been evolving lesson plans and teacher resource guides, which are available on our website at www.coreknowledge.org.uk.

David G. Green
Director of Civitas

Introduction to the UK Edition of the Core Knowledge Series for Year 6

The concerns that led Professor Hirsch and others to set up the Core Knowledge Foundation in the USA in 1986 are shared by many in Britain. Civitas has acquired direct experience of the problem through its network of supplementary schools. Beginning with a group of children in the East End of London in 2005, Civitas now runs 22 supplementary schools for over 600 children in different parts of the UK. The children attend once a week, either on Saturdays or after school, for help with English and maths. The children are, for the most part, attending full-time schools in areas with higher-than-average indicators of social deprivation, where academic outcomes are not the best in the country. Some children join supplementary schools at the age of seven, eight or even older, unable to read properly and unable to handle simple addition and subtraction. Our approach in the Civitas Schools has been to employ dedicated teachers with high expectations and a commitment to providing solid learning foundations. Children are assessed annually and it has become quite usual to see them make two or three years of progress in their reading and maths ages over the course of one calendar year.

The concepts that Professor Hirsch mentions in his General Introduction such as 'critical thinking' and 'learning to learn' have been just as prevalent in the UK's schools, where the curriculum has become less knowledge-based and more focused on attaining 'skills', as if the two things can be separated. The acquisition of skills requires knowledge, and a knowledge-poor curriculum is one that condemns pupils – especially children from less advantaged backgrounds – to remain outside the mainstream of attainment and fulfilment. The Core Knowledge Foundation believes that all children should be able to unlock the library of the world's literature; to comprehend the world around them; to know where they stand (literally) on the globe; and to realise the heritage that the history of their country has bestowed on them.

Making a reality of this ideal has been the outstanding achievement of the Core Knowledge Foundation in the hundreds of schools across the USA where its curriculum is being taught, and it is why we so admire the work of Professor Hirsch and his colleagues at the Core Knowledge Foundation.

As Professor Hirsch explains in his General Introduction, the project operates within the overarching framework of the Core Knowledge Sequence, produced by dozens of educators over a gestational period of several years. To bring this sequence into the classroom or the home, the Sequence is fleshed out by a book for each year group. We at Civitas were honoured and delighted to be entrusted by the Core Knowledge Foundation with the task of adapting the books for teachers, parents and pupils in the UK. This has entailed some changes to reflect differences between our cultures. For example, Visual Arts looks at the Gothic Revival rather than American painters; our songs include British folk songs like Widecombe Fair and Blaydon Races; British musical nomenclature has been used in the Music chapter and metric measures are given primacy over imperial measures in Science. We have revised the lists of resources to include books and educational materials readily available in the UK. However, for the most part, the US text has been left intact – because knowledge is universal!

We have adapted the Core Knowledge Sequence for the UK and it is freely available online at http://www.coreknowledge.org.uk/sequence.php. This will enable parents and teachers to understand how the grammar of each subject is unrolled over six years of primary school education. The UK Sequence follows the US Sequence very closely, with a few obvious changes. Maths has been slightly revised to reflect the demands of the National Curriculum; and British history and geography replace American. (American history and geography are covered under World History and Geography.)

We share the view of the Core Knowledge Foundation that knowledge is best conveyed through subjects, and so we have followed their division of each book into chapters covering Language and Literature, History and Geography, Visual Arts, Music, Mathematics and Science. We have produced volumes for each year group from Year 1 to Year 6, and these will tie in with the UK version of the Core Knowledge Sequence.

In most states of the USA, children start their full-time education in Kindergarten when they are five rising six, whereas in the UK children of that age would be starting Year 1, having already spent a year in Reception. For this reason, the first book in Civitas Core Knowledge UK series, *What Your Year 1 Child Needs to Know*, represented, with small alterations, the text of *What Your Kindergartner Needs to Know*. The second book, *What Your Year 2 Child Needs to Know*, followed the text of the next book in the US series, *What Your First Grader Needs to Know*. This volume follows the text of *What Your Fifth Grader Needs To Know*, first published in the USA in 1995 and revised in 2005.

Robert Whelan
General Editor, Civitas Core Knowledge UK Project

General Introduction to the Core Knowledge Series

I. WHAT IS YOUR CHILD LEARNING IN SCHOOL?

A parent of identical twins sent me a letter in which she expressed concern that her children, who are in the same grade in the same school, are being taught completely different things. How can this be? Because they are in different classrooms; because the teachers in these classrooms have only the vaguest guidelines to follow; in short, because the school, like many in the United States, lacks a definite, specific curriculum.

Many parents would be surprised if they were to examine the curriculum of their child's elementary school. Ask to see your school's curriculum. Does it spell out, in clear and concrete terms, a core of specific content and skills all children at a particular grade level are expected to learn by the end of the school year?

Many curricula speak in general terms of vaguely defined skills, processes and attitudes, often in an abstract, pseudo-technical language that calls, for example, for children to 'analyse patterns and data', or 'investigate the structure and dynamics of living systems', or 'work cooperatively in a group'. Such vagueness evades the central question: what is your child learning in school? It places unreasonable demands upon teachers, and often results in years of schooling marred by repetitions and gaps. Yet another unit on dinosaurs or 'pioneer days'. *Charlotte's Web* for the third time. 'You've never heard of the Bill of Rights?' 'You've never been taught how to add two fractions with unlike denominators?'

When identical twins in two classrooms of the same school have few academic experiences in common, that is cause for concern. When teachers in that school do not know what children in other classrooms are learning in the same grade level, much less in earlier and later grades, they cannot reliably predict that children will come prepared with a shared core of knowledge and skills. For an elementary school to be successful, teachers need a common vision of what they want their students to know and be able to do. They need to have *clear, specific learning goals*, as well as the sense of mutual accountability that comes from shared commitment to helping all children achieve those goals. Lacking both specific goals and mutual accountability, too many schools exist in a state of curricular incoherence, one result of which is that they fall far short of developing the full potential of our children. To address this problem, I started the non-profit Core Knowledge Foundation in 1986. This book and its companion volumes in the Core Knowledge Series are designed to give parents, teachers – and through them, children – a guide to clearly defined learning goals in the form of a carefully sequenced body of knowledge, based upon the specific content guidelines developed by the Core Knowledge Foundation (see below, 'The Consensus Behind the Core Knowledge Sequence').

Core Knowledge is an attempt to define, in a coherent and sequential way, a body of widely used knowledge taken for granted by competent writers and speakers in the United States. Because this knowledge is taken for granted rather than being explained when it is used, it forms a necessary foundation for the higher-order reading, writing and thinking skills that children need for academic and vocational success. The universal attainment of such knowledge should be a central aim of curricula in our elementary schools, just as it is currently the aim in all world-class educational systems.

For reasons explained in the next section, making sure that all young children in the United States possess a core of shared knowledge is a necessary step in developing a first-rate educational system.

II. WHY CORE KNOWLEDGE IS NEEDED

Learning builds on learning: children (and adults) gain new knowledge only by building on what they already know. It is essential to begin building solid foundations of knowledge in the early grades when children are most receptive because, for the vast majority of children, academic deficiencies from the first six grades can *permanently* impair the success of later learning. Poor performance of American students in middle and high school can be traced to shortcomings inherited from elementary schools that have not imparted to children the knowledge and skills they need for further learning.

All of the highest-achieving and most egalitarian elementary school systems in the world (such as those in Sweden, France and Japan) teach their children a specific core of knowledge in each of the first six grades, thus enabling all children to enter each new grade with a secure foundation for further learning. It is time American schools did so as well, for the following reasons:

(1) Commonly shared knowledge makes schooling more effective.

We know that the one-on-one tutorial is the most effective form of schooling, in part because a parent or teacher can provide tailor-made instruction for the individual child. But in a non-tutorial situation – in, for example, a typical classroom with twenty-five or more students – the instructor cannot effectively impart new knowledge to all the students unless each one shares the background knowledge that the lesson is being built upon.

Consider this scenario: in third grade, Ms Franklin is about to begin a unit on early explorers – Columbus, Magellan and others. In her class she has some students who were in Mr Washington's second-grade class last year and some students who were in Ms Johnson's second-grade class. She also has a few students who have moved in from other towns. As Ms Franklin begins the unit on explorers, she asks the children to look at a globe and use their fingers to trace a route across the Atlantic Ocean from Europe to North America. The students who had Mr Washington look blankly at her: they didn't learn that last year. The students who had Ms Johnson, however, eagerly point to the proper places on the globe, while two of the students who came from other towns pipe up and say, 'Columbus and Magellan again? We did that last year.'

When all the students in a class *do* share the relevant background knowledge, a classroom can begin to approach the effectiveness of a tutorial. Even when some children in a class do not have elements of the knowledge they were supposed to acquire in previous grades, the existence of a specifically defined core makes it possible for the teacher or parent to identify and fill the gaps, thus giving all students a chance to fulfill their potential in later grades.

(2) Commonly shared knowledge makes schooling more fair and democratic.

When all the children who enter a grade can be assumed to share some of the same building blocks of knowledge, and when the teacher knows exactly what those building blocks are, then all the students are empowered to learn. In our current system, children from disadvantaged backgrounds too often suffer from unmerited low expectations that translate into watered-down curricula. But if we specify the core of knowledge that all children should share, then we can guarantee equal access to that knowledge and compensate for the academic advantages some students are offered at home. In a Core Knowledge school, *all* children enjoy the benefits of important, challenging knowledge that will provide the foundation for successful later learning.

(3) Commonly shared knowledge helps create cooperation and solidarity in our schools and nation.

Diversity is a hallmark and strength of our nation. American classrooms are usually made up of students from a variety of cultural backgrounds, and those different cultures should be honoured by all students. At the same time, education should create a school-based culture that is common and welcoming to all because it includes knowledge of many cultures and gives all students, no matter what their background, a common foundation for understanding our cultural diversity.

In the next section, I will describe the steps taken by the Core Knowledge Foundation to develop a model of the commonly shared knowledge our children need (which forms the basis for this series of books).

III. THE CONSENSUS BEHIND THE CORE KNOWLEDGE SEQUENCE

The content in this and other volumes in the Core Knowledge Series is based on a document called the *Core Knowledge Sequence*, a grade-by-grade sequence of specific content guidelines in history, geography, mathematics, science, language arts and fine arts. The *Sequence* is not meant to outline the whole of the school curriculum; rather, it offers specific guidelines to knowledge that can reasonably be expected to make up about *half* of any school's curriculum, thus leaving ample room for local requirements and emphases. Teaching a common core of knowledge, such as that articulated in the *Core Knowledge Sequence*, is compatible with a variety of instructional methods and additional subject matters.

The *Core Knowledge Sequence* is the result of a long process of research and consensus building undertaken by the Core Knowledge Foundation. Here is how we achieved the consensus behind the *Core Knowledge Sequence*.

First we analysed the many reports issued by state departments of education and by professional organisations – such as the National Council of Teachers of Mathematics and the American Association for the Advancement of Science – that recommend general outcomes for elementary and secondary education. We also tabulated the knowledge and skills through grade six specified in the successful educational systems of several other countries, including France, Japan, Sweden and West Germany.

In addition, we formed an advisory board on multiculturalism that proposed a specific knowledge of diverse cultural traditions that American children should all share as part of their school-based common culture. We sent the resulting materials to three independent groups of teachers, scholars and scientists around the country, asking them to create a master list of the knowledge children should have by the end of grade six. About 150 teachers (including college professors, scientists and administrators) were involved in this initial step.

These items were amalgamated into a master plan, and further groups of teachers and specialists were asked to agree on a grade-by-grade sequence of the items. That sequence was then sent to some one hundred educators and specialists who participated in a national conference that was called to hammer out a working agreement on an appropriate core of knowledge for the first six grades.

This important meeting took place in March 1990. The conferees were elementary school teachers, curriculum specialists, scientists, science writers, officers of national organisations, representatives of ethnic groups, district superintendents and school principals from across the country. A total of twenty-four working groups decided on revisions in the *Core Knowledge Sequence*. The resulting provisional *Sequence* was further fine-tuned during a year of implementation at a pioneering school, Three Oaks Elementary in Lee County, Florida.

In only a few years, many more schools – urban and rural, rich and poor, public and private – joined in the effort to teach Core Knowledge. Based largely on suggestions from these schools, the *Core Knowledge Sequence* was revised in 1995: separate guidelines were added for kindergarten, and a few topics in other grades were added, omitted or moved from one grade to another, in order to create an even more coherent sequence for learning. Revised editions of the books in the Core Knowledge Series reflect the revisions in the *Sequence*. Based on the principle of learning from experience, the Core Knowledge Foundation continues to work with schools and advisors to 'fine-tune' the *Sequence*, and is also conducting research that will lead to the publication of guidelines for grades seven and eight, as well as for preschool. (*The Core Knowledge Sequence UK* can be downloaded from the Civitas Core Knowledge UK website www.coreknowledge.org.uk/sequence.php)

IV. THE NATURE OF THIS SERIES

The books in this series are designed to give a convenient and engaging introduction to the knowledge specified in the *Core Knowledge Sequence*. These are resource books, addressed primarily to parents, but which we hope will be useful tools for both parents and teachers. These books are not intended to replace the local curriculum or school textbooks, but rather to serve as aids to help children gain some of the important knowledge they will need to make progress in school and be effective in society.

Although we have made these books as accessible and useful as we can, parents and teachers should understand that they are not the only means by which the *Core Knowledge Sequence* can be imparted. The books represent a single version of the possibilities inherent in the *Sequence*, and a first step in the Core Knowledge reform effort. We hope that publishers will be stimulated to offer educational software, games, alternative books and other imaginative vehicles based on the *Core Knowledge Sequence*.

These books are not textbooks or workbooks, though when appropriate they do suggest a variety of activities you can do with your child. In these books, we address your child directly, and occasionally ask questions for him or her to think about. The earliest books in the series are intended to be read aloud to children. Even as children become able to read the books on their own, we encourage parents to help their children read more actively by reading along with them and talking about what they are reading. You and your child can read the sections of this book in any order, depending on your child's interests or depending on the topics your child is studying in school, which this book may complement or reinforce. You can skip from section to section and re-read as much as your child likes.

We encourage you to think of this book as a guidebook that opens the way to many paths you and your child can explore. These paths may lead to the library, to many other good books and, if possible, to plays, museums, concerts and other opportunities for knowledge and enrichment. In short, this guidebook recommends places to visit and describes what is important in those places, but only you and your child can make the actual visit, travel the streets and climb the steps.

V. WHAT YOU CAN DO TO HELP IMPROVE EDUCATION

The first step for parents and teachers who are committed to reform is to be sceptical about oversimplified slogans like 'critical thinking' and 'learning to learn'. Such slogans are everywhere and, unfortunately for our schools, their partial insights have been elevated to the level of universal truths. For example: 'What students learn is not important; rather, we must teach students to learn *how* to learn.' 'The child, not the academic subject, is the true focus of education.' 'Do not impose knowledge on children before they are developmentally ready to receive it.' 'Do not bog children down in mere facts, but rather, teach critical-thinking skills.' Who has not heard these sentiments, so admirable and humane, and – up to a point – so true? But these positive sentiments in favour of 'thinking skills' and 'higher understanding' have been turned into negative sentiments against the teaching of important knowledge. Those who have entered the teaching profession over the past 40 years have been taught to scorn important knowledge as 'mere facts', and to see the imparting of this knowledge as somehow injurious to children. Thus it has come about that many educators, armed with partially true slogans, have seemingly taken leave of common sense.

Many parents and teachers have come to the conclusion that elementary education must strike a better balance between the development of the 'whole child' and the more limited but fundamental duty of the school to ensure that all children master a core of knowledge and skills essential to their competence as learners in later grades. But these parents and teachers cannot act on their convictions without access to an agreed upon, concrete sequence of knowledge. Our main motivation in developing the *Core Knowledge Sequence* and this book series has been to give parents and teachers something concrete to work with.

It has been encouraging to see how many teachers, since the first volume in this series was published, have responded to the Core Knowledge reform effort.

Parents and teachers are urged to join in a grassroots effort to strengthen our elementary schools. The place to start is in your own school and district. Insist that your school clearly state the core of *specific* knowledge and skills that each child in a grade must learn. Whether your school's core corresponds exactly to the Core Knowledge model is less important than the existence of some core – which, we hope, will be as solid, coherent, and challenging as the *Core Knowledge Sequence* has proven to be. Inform members of your community about the need for such a specific curriculum, and help make sure that the people who are elected or appointed to your local school board are independent-minded people who will insist that our children have the benefit of a solid, specific, world-class curriculum in each grade.

Share the knowledge!

E. D. Hirsch, Jr
Charlottesville, Virginia

Language and Literature

Introduction

This chapter presents poems, stories and sayings, as well as brief discussions of language and literature.

The best way to introduce children to poetry is to read it to them and encourage them to read it aloud so that they can experience the music of the words. A child's knowledge of poetry should come first from pleasure and only later from analysis. However, by Year 6, children are ready to begin learning a few basic terms and concepts, such as metaphor and simile. Such concepts can help children to talk about particular effects that enliven the poems they like best.

The stories in this book are excerpts, abridgements and adaptations of longer works. If a child enjoys a story, he or she should be encouraged to read the larger work. Whilst some of the full texts, such as *Don Quixote* and *Oliver Twist*, might be difficult for Year 6 children, most of these books are also available in child-friendly versions. Good film versions of classic works can help the young reader to appreciate the context of an extract, and musical versions, either on the stage or film, can also make a deep impression. If children are already familiar with such songs as 'Food, Glorious Food' or 'The Impossible Dream', it will enhance their experience of the text.

You can draw children into stories by asking questions about them. For example, you might ask: 'What do you think is going to happen next?' or 'What might have happened if ...?' You might also ask the child to retell them. Don't be concerned if the child changes events: that is in the best tradition of storytelling and explains why we have so many different versions of traditional stories!

The treatment of grammar in this book is a brief overview and should be used in conjunction with a good grammar course, such as Irina Tyk's *Butterfly Grammar*. Some people say that our children already know more about grammar than we can ever teach them, but standard written language does have special characteristics that children need to learn. In the classroom, grammar instruction is an essential part, but only a part, of an effective language arts programme. Year 6 children should also have frequent opportunities to write – and revise their writing – with encouragement and guidance along the way.

The section on familiar sayings and phrases has proved to be one of the most popular features of the Language and Literature chapters. Children will hear these phrases in constant use, without necessarily understanding what they imply unless the meaning is explained. They should be encouraged to come up with their own examples to demonstrate their grasp of the idiom.

Poetry

The Eagle
by Alfred, Lord Tennyson

He clasps the crag with crookèd hands;
Close to the sun in lonely lands,
Ringed with the azure world, he stands.

The wrinkled sea beneath him crawls;
He watches from his mountain walls,
And like a thunderbolt he falls.

The Tiger
by William Blake

Tiger Tiger, burning bright
In the forests of the night,
What immortal hand or eye
Could frame thy fearful symmetry?

In what distant deeps or skies
Burnt the fire of thine eyes?
On what wings dare he aspire?
What the hand dare seize the fire?

And what shoulder and what art
Could twist the sinews of thy heart?
And when thy heart began to beat,
What dread hand? And what dread feet?

What the hammer? What the chain?
In what furnace was thy brain?
What the anvil? What dread grasp
Dare its deadly terrors clasp!

When the stars threw down their spears
And water'd heaven with their tears:
Did he smile his work to see?
Did he who made the Lamb make thee?

Tiger Tiger, burning bright
In the forests of the night,
What immortal hand or eye
Dare frame thy fearful symmetry?

Some Opposites by Richard Wilbur

What is the opposite of *riot*?
It's lots of people keeping quiet.

The opposite of *doughnut*? Wait
A minute while I meditate.
This isn't easy. Ah, I've found it!
A cookie with a hole around it.

What is the opposite of *two*?
A lonely me, a lonely you.

The opposite of a *cloud* could be
A white reflection in the sea,
Or a huge blueness in the air,
Caused by a cloud's not being there.

The opposite of *opposite*?
That's much too difficult. I quit.

Rudyard Kipling.

If by Rudyard Kipling

If you can keep your head when all about you
    Are losing theirs and blaming it on you,
If you can trust yourself when all men doubt you,
    But make allowance for their doubting too;
If you can wait and not be tired by waiting,
    Or being lied about, don't deal in lies,
Or being hated, don't give way to hating,
    And yet don't look too good, nor talk too wise:

If you can dream – and not make dreams your master;
    If you can think – and not make thoughts your aim;
If you can meet with Triumph and Disaster
    And treat those two impostors just the same;
If you can bear to hear the truth you've spoken
    Twisted by knaves to make a trap for fools,
Or watch the things you gave your life to, broken,
    And stoop and build 'em up with worn-out tools:

If you can make one heap of all your winnings
    And risk it on one turn of pitch-and-toss,
And lose, and start again at your beginnings
    And never breathe a word about your loss;
If you can force your heart and nerve and sinew
    To serve your turn long after they are gone,
And so hold on when there is nothing in you
    Except the Will which says to them: 'Hold on!'

If you can talk with crowds and keep your virtue,
    Or walk with Kings – nor lose the common touch,
If neither foes nor loving friends can hurt you,
    If all men count with you, but none too much;
If you can fill the unforgiving minute
    With sixty seconds' worth of distance run,
Yours is the Earth and everything that's in it,
    And – which is more – you'll be a Man, my son!

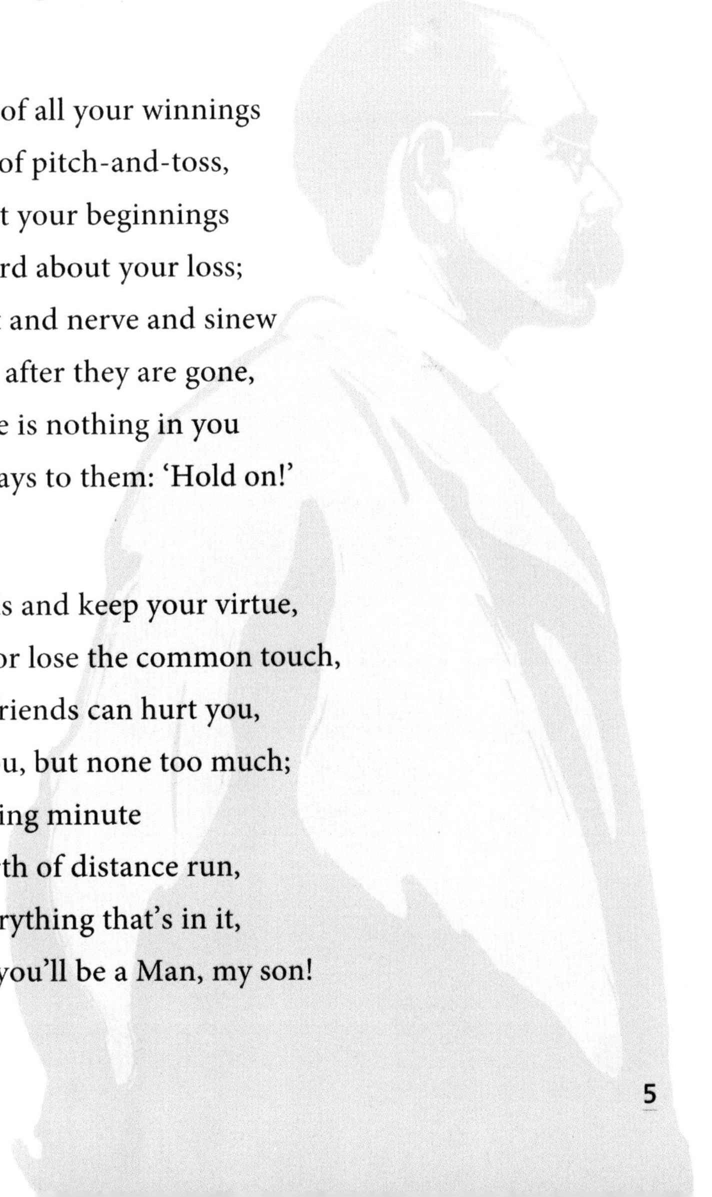

Jabberwocky
by Lewis Carroll

'Twas brillig, and the slithy toves
   Did gyre and gimble in the wabe:
All mimsy were the borogoves,
   And the mome raths outgrabe.

'Beware the Jabberwock, my son!
   The jaws that bite, the claws that catch!
Beware the Jubjub bird, and shun
   The frumious Bandersnatch!'

He took his vorpal sword in hand:
   Long time the manxome foe he sought –
So rested he by the Tumtum tree,
   And stood awhile in thought.

And as in uffish thought he stood,
   The Jabberwock, with eyes of flame,
Came whiffling through the tulgey wood,
   And burbled as it came!

One, two! One, two! And through and through
   The vorpal blade went snicker-snack!
He left it dead, and with its head
   He went galumphing back.

'And hast thou slain the Jabberwock?
   Come to my arms, my beamish boy!
O frabjous day! Callooh! Callay!'
   He chortled in his joy.

'Twas brillig, and the slithy toves
   Did gyre and gimble in the wabe:
All mimsy were the borogoves,
   And the mome raths outgrabe.

This piece of nonsense verse comes from *Through the Looking-Glass and What Alice Found There*. We read part of *Alice's Adventures in Wonderland* in Year 4.

A Ballad of London
by Richard Le Gallienne

Ah, London! London! our delight,
Great flower that opens but at night,
Great City of the Midnight Sun,
Whose day begins when day is done.

Lamp after lamp against the sky
Opens a sudden beaming eye,
Leaping alight on either hand,
The iron lilies of the Strand.

Like dragonflies, the hansoms hover,
With jewelled eyes, to catch the lover;
The streets are full of lights and loves,
Soft gowns, and flutter of soiled doves.

*This London street was painted by
John Atkinson Grimshaw in 1885.*

The human moths about the light
Dash and cling close in dazed delight,
And burn and laugh, the world and wife,
For this is London, this is life!

Upon thy petals butterflies,
But at thy root, some say, there lies
A world of weeping trodden things,
Poor worms that have not eyes or wings.

From out corruption of their woe
Springs this bright flower that charms us so,
Men die and rot deep out of sight
To keep this jungle-flower bright.

Paris and London, World-Flowers twain
Wherewith the World-Tree blooms again,
Since Time hath gathered Babylon,
And withered Rome still withers on.

Sidon and Tyre were such as ye,
How bright they shone upon the Tree!
But Time hath gathered, both are gone,
And no man sails to Babylon.

Time and his moths shall eat up all.
Your chiming towers proud and tall
He shall most utterly abase,
And set a desert in their place.

*In 1872 the French artist Gustave Doré drew this imaginary
scene of a visitor from New Zealand, hundreds of years
in the future, gazing on the ruins of London.*

Macavity – the Mystery Cat

by T.S. Eliot

Macavity's a Mystery Cat: he's called the Hidden Paw –
For he's the master criminal who can defy the Law.
He's the bafflement of Scotland Yard, the Flying Squad's despair:
For when they reach the scene of crime – *Macavity's not there*!

Macavity, Macavity, there's no one like Macavity,
He's broken every human law, he breaks the law of gravity.
His powers of levitation would make a fakir stare,
And when you reach the scene of crime – *Macavity's not there*!
You may seek him in the basement, you may look up in the air –
But I tell you once and once again, *Macavity's not there*!

Mcavity's a ginger cat, he's very tall and thin;
You would know him if you saw him, for his eyes are sunken in.
His brow is deeply lined with thought, his head is highly domed;
His coat is dusty from neglect, his whiskers are uncombed.
He sways his head from side to side, with movements like a snake;
And when you think he's half asleep, he's always wide awake.

Macavity, Macavity, there's no one like Macavity,
For he's a fiend in feline shape, a monster of depravity.
You may meet him in a by-street, you may see him in the square –
But when a crime's discovered, then *Macavity's not there*!

He's outwardly respectable. (They say he cheats at cards.)
And his footprints are not found in any file of Scotland Yard's.
And when the larder's looted, or the jewel-case is rifled,
Or when the milk is missing, or another Peke's been stifled,
Or the greenhouse glass is broken, and the trellis past repair –
Ay, there's the wonder of the thing! *Macavity's not there*!

And when the Foreign Office find a Treaty's gone astray,
Or the Admiralty lose some plans and drawings by the way,
There may be a scrap of paper in the hall or on the stair –
But it's useless to investigate – *Macavity's not there*!
And when the loss has been disclosed, the Secret Service say:
'It *must* have been Macavity!' – but he's a mile away.
You'll be sure to find him resting, or a-licking of his thumbs,
Or engaged in doing complicated long division sums.

Macavity, Macavity, there's no one like Macavity,
There never was a Cat of such deceitfulness and suavity.
He always has an alibi, and one or two to spare:
At whatever time the deed took place – MACAVITY WASN'T THERE!
And they say that all the Cats whose wicked deeds are widely known
(I might mention Mungojerrie, I might mention Griddlebone)
Are nothing more than agents for the Cat who all the time
Just controls their operations: the Napoleon of Crime!

Little Red Riding Hood and the Wolf

by Roald Dahl

As soon as Wolf began to feel

That he would like a decent meal,

He went and knocked on Grandma's door.

When Grandma opened it, she saw

The sharp white teeth, the horrid grin,

And Wolfie said, 'May I come in?'

Poor Grandmamma was terrified,

'He's going to eat me up!' she cried.

And she was absolutely right.

He ate her up in one big bite.

But Grandmamma was small and tough,

And Wolfie wailed, 'That's not enough!

'I haven't yet begun to feel

'That I have had a decent meal!'

He ran around the kitchen yelping,

'I've *got* to have a second helping!'

Then added with a frightful leer,

'I'm therefore going to wait right here

'Till Little Miss Red Riding Hood

'Comes home from walking in the wood.'

He quickly put on Grandma's clothes,

(Of course he hadn't eaten those).

He dressed himself in coat and hat.

He put on shoes, and after that

He even brushed and curled his hair,

Then sat himself in Grandma's chair.

In came the little girl in red.

She stopped. She stared. And then she said,

'What great big ears you have, Grandma.'

'All the better to hear you with,' the Wolf replied.

'What great big eyes you have, Grandma,'

said Little Red Riding Hood.

'All the better to see you with,' the Wolf replied.

He sat there watching her and smiled.

He thought, I'm going to eat this child.

Compared with her old Grandmamma
She's going to taste like caviare.

Then Little Red Riding Hood said, '*But Grandma,*
what a lovely great big furry coat you have on.'

'That's wrong!' cried Wolf. 'Have you forgot
'To tell me what BIG TEETH I've got?
'Ah well, no matter what you say,
'I'm going to eat you anyway.'
The small girl smiles. One eyelid flickers.
She whips a pistol from her knickers.
She aims it at the creature's head
And *bang bang bang*, she shoots him dead.
A few weeks later, in the wood,
I came across Miss Riding Hood.
But what a change! No cloak of red,
No silly hood upon her head.
She said, 'Hello, and do please note
My lovely furry WOLFSKIN COAT.'

The Listeners
by Walter de la Mare

'Is there anybody there?' said the Traveller,
   Knocking on the moonlit door;
And his horse in the silence champed the grasses
   Of the forest's ferny floor;
And a bird flew up out of the turret,
   Above the Traveller's head:

And he smote upon the door again a second time;
   'Is there anybody there?' he said.
But no one descended to the Traveller;
   No head from the leaf-fringed sill
Leaned over and looked into his grey eyes,
   Where he stood perplexed and still.
But only a host of phantom listeners
   That dwelt in the lone house then
Stood listening in the quiet of the moonlight
   To that voice from the world of men:
Stood thronging the faint moonbeams on the dark stair,
   That goes down to the empty hall,
Hearkening in an air stirred and shaken
   By the lonely Traveller's call.
And he felt in his heart their strangeness,
   Their stillness answering his cry,
While his horse moved, cropping the dark turf,
   'Neath the starred and leafy sky;
For he suddenly smote on the door, even
   Louder, and lifted his head: –
'Tell them I came, and no one answered,
   That I kept my word,' he said.
Never the least stir made the listeners,
   Though every word he spake
Fell echoing through the shadowiness of the still house
   From the one man left awake:
Ay, they heard his foot upon the stirrup,
   And the sound of iron on stone,
And how the silence surged softly backward,
   When the plunging hoofs were gone.

15

Stories, Myths and Legends

Tilting At Windmills

Adapted from *Don Quixote* by Miguel de Cervantes

The novel Don Quixote *[DON key-HOH-tay] was written during the Renaissance by the Spanish writer Miguel de Cervantes. The main character, Don Quixote, is a man with a fantastic imagination, who confuses his own experiences with the adventures of a bold and brave knight. Today, if a person believes in things most people view as impossible, we say the person is 'quixotic' [kwik-SOT-ic]. There is a musical version of* Don Quixote *called* Man of La Mancha. *It contains a song called* The Impossible Dream, *which is about how we should all try to make the world a better place, no matter how hard that seems.*

Once upon a time, in a village in La Mancha, there lived a lean, thin-faced old gentleman whose favourite pastime was to read books about knights in armour. He loved to read about their daring exploits, strange adventures, bold rescues of damsels in distress, and intense devotion to their ladies. In fact, he became so caught up in the subject of chivalry that he neglected every other interest and even sold many acres of good farmland so that he might buy all the books he could get on the subject. He would lie awake at night, absorbed in every detail of these fantastic adventures. He often argued with the village priest or the barber over who was the greatest knight of all time. Was it Amadis of Gaul or Palmerin of England? Or was it perhaps the Knight of the Sun?

As time went on, the old gentleman crammed his head so full of these stories and lost so much sleep from reading through the night that he lost his wits completely. He began to believe that all these fantastic tales, full of enchantments, challenges, battles, wounds and wooings, were true histories. At last he resolved to become a knight-errant himself, to travel through the world in search of adventures.

First he got out some rust-eaten armour that had belonged to his ancestors, then cleaned and repaired it as best he could. Although the head-piece of the helmet was intact, unfortunately the visor that would have protected his face was gone. Not to be discouraged, he fashioned another out of some pieces of stiff paper and strips of iron. In his eyes it was the most splendid helmet ever fashioned.

Next he considered what glorious, high-sounding name he might give his horse, who was to bear him on his quest. For though his horse was but a tired hack, practically skin and bones, to him it appeared as magnificent as Bucephalus, the horse of Alexander the Great. After four days of inventing and rejecting various names, he at last settled on Rocinante, which he thought sounded suitably grand.

He then set about choosing a suitable name for himself. After eight days of deep consideration, he decided that he would be known as Don Quixote. Following the example of many knights he admired, he decided to proclaim his native land as well, and so he called himself Don Quixote de la Mancha.

Now he needed to find a lady whom he might adore and serve, for a knight without a lady is like a body without a soul. In a neighbouring village there lived a nice-looking farm girl whom he had admired from a distance. He decided that she would be the lady of his fancy, and that she should be known as Dulcinea del Toboso, a name that to his ears sounded musical and anything but ordinary.

With all these preparations made, Don Quixote was eager to sally forth. A whole world awaited, full of injustices to be made right, and great deeds to be performed. So, clad in his rusty armour, with his improvised helmet tied to his head, Don Quixote mounted Rocinante and started out through the back of the stable yard.

But then he had a terrible thought: he had not yet been dubbed a knight! He took comfort, however, in his memory of the many books of chivalry he had read, and determined that, like many of the heroes in those books, he would simply have himself knighted by the first person that came along. So he rode on until nightfall, when he came upon a simple country inn.

Everything that Don Quixote saw, or thought he saw, came out of the fantastic books he had read; so, when he neared the inn, he saw not a plain inn but a gleaming castle, with turrets thrusting to the sky, and a drawbridge and a moat. He reined in Rocinante and awaited the blast of a trumpet to signal his arrival, for that is what always happened in the books he read. But no trumpet sounded. Just as he was getting impatient, a swineherd came along with a bunch of grunting hogs, which he called together by blowing his horn. With great satisfaction, Don Quixote took this to be the signal he awaited, and rode forth.

The innkeeper, in Don Quixote's eyes, was certainly the keeper of the castle. Don Quixote dismounted and told the innkeeper to take special care of his steed, which was surely the finest horse in the world. The innkeeper looked doubtfully at the bony hack, but decided to humour his guest.

As Don Quixote had not eaten all day, he requested some food. The innkeeper served him a meal of badly cooked fish and mouldy bread, but Don Quixote remained firm in his belief that this was a magnificent castle, and the food a gourmet feast.

When the meal was over, Don Quixote dropped to his knees before the surprised innkeeper. 'Never,' he said, 'shall I rise from here until you have consented to grant me the favour I ask, which will bring you great praise and benefit all mankind. I ask that you dub me a knight.' The innkeeper obliged the Don by whacking him on the shoulder with a sword and mumbling a few words.

The next day, Don Quixote, joyous in having been quite officially made a knight, set forth. His destination was his own village, for he planned to return home for some money and clean clothes (details which had been overlooked in all the books about knights and their adventures). And he planned to find a good man who could serve as his squire.

Don Quixote promised Sancho Panza that one day he would be governor of an island.

With all his powers of persuasion, he set about convincing a labourer, whose name was Sancho Panza, to accompany him. At last, with the promise that Don Quixote would someday make him governor of his very own island, the country bumpkin agreed to leave his wife and children and follow the knight. The tall, lean knight sat upon bony Rocinante, while the plump Sancho Panza climbed astride his donkey named Dapple, a leather wine bottle and well-stocked saddlebags at his side. And so this unlikely pair set off in search of adventures.

Don Quixote and Sancho Panza set off in search of adventure

As they crossed the plain of Montiel, they spied dozens of windmills. 'Fortune has smiled on us,' said Don Quixote to his squire. 'Yonder stand more than thirty terrible giants. I will fight them and kill them all, and we shall make ourselves rich with the spoils.'

'What giants?' asked Sancho Panza.

'Those giants there, with the long arms,' said the knight.

'Be careful, sir,' said the squire. 'Those are not giants, but windmills, and what seem to be their arms are the sails that turn the millstone.'

Don Quixote was thrown off his horse when he tilted at windmills.

'If you are afraid of them, then go say your prayers,' said Don Quixote. 'But I shall engage them in battle.' Immediately he spurred his horse forward, and, paying no attention to Sancho Panza's shouted warnings, he cried, 'Do not run, you cowards, for a lone knight assails you!' Just then a slight wind caused the windmills to begin turning. 'I fear you not, though you have more arms than the giant Briareus,' cried the knight. Covering himself with his shield, and thrusting forth his lance, he spurred Rocinante toward the nearest windmill. His lance pierced one of the whirling sails, which immediately wrenched it with such force that the horse was dragged along and the knight sent rolling across the ground. He lay without moving as Sancho Panza trotted to his side.

'Oh dear,' said Sancho, 'didn't I warn your worship to watch what you were doing when attacking those windmills?'

'I believe,' replied the knight, 'that some evil enchanter turned those giants into windmills to rob me of a glorious victory.'

'As God wills,' said Sancho, helping the knight to his feet. They climbed upon Rocinante and Dapple once more, and continued on their way.

Just as Don Quixote desired, he and Sancho Panza encountered many dangerous and unusual adventures, for so often did the knight mistake shepherds, holy men and peasant girls for miscreant knights, evil enchanters and ladies in distress, that he was continually involved in ridiculous quarrels and brawls. No matter how frantically Sancho urged him to see things as they really were, Don Quixote paid no attention to him. But although these absurd encounters were matters of great seriousness to the knight, many who witnessed them were delighted and amused.

Gradually his exploits became known all over the countryside, and there were few who had not heard of that flower of chivalry, Don Quixote de la Mancha.

The Secret Garden

Adapted from *The Secret Garden* by Frances Hodgson Burnett

Frances Hodgson Burnett's novel The Secret Garden *tells the story of a young orphan girl named Mary Lennox who is sent from India to England to live with relatives. At first, Martha, the housemaid, and Ben Weatherstaff, the gardener, are her only acquaintances. But eventually she discovers a mysterious secret garden and a charming new*

In Year 4 we sang 'On Ilkley Moor Baht 'At', which was in Yorkshire dialect.

friend. Some of the characters speak in a Yorkshire dialect. If you 'sound' the words in your head, it's easy to guess what they mean.

When Mary Lennox arrived in England, everyone agreed she was as sour and cross and contrary a girl as they had ever known. Nothing pleased her, and she would do nothing for herself.

The day she arrived, she asked her nurse, Martha:

'Who is going to dress me?'

Martha stared. 'Can't you put on your own clothes?'

'No,' answered Mary, quite indignantly. 'I never did in my life. My nurse dressed me, of course.'

'Well,' said Martha, 'it's time tha' should learn. It'll do thee good to wait on thyself a bit.'

At first Mary sat inside all the time, moping. Then, one foggy day, Martha said: 'You wrap up warm an' run out an' play you. It'll do you good.'

'Out?' Mary replied in her contrary fashion, 'Why should I go out on a day like this?' But eventually she went out just the same.

While she was outside, a wonderful thing happened. She heard a soft little rushing flight through the air. A bird with a bright red breast landed on the ground near her and burst into song. She stopped and listened to him and somehow his cheerful, friendly little whistle gave her a pleased feeling. The bright-breasted little bird brought a look into her sour little face that was almost a smile.

Mary went a step nearer to the robin and looked at him very hard. She thought his black dewdrop eyes gazed at her with great curiosity.

'I'm lonely,' she said.

She had not known before that this was one of the things that made her feel sour and cross. She seemed to find it out when the robin looked at her and she looked at the robin. Just that moment the robin gave a little shake of his wings and flew away towards a garden that was surrounded by an ivy-covered wall and seemed to have no door. 'He has flown over the wall!' Mary cried out, watching him. 'He has flown into the garden!'

'He lives there,' said old Ben the gardener, 'among th' old rose trees.'

'I should like to see them,' said Mary. 'There must be a door somewhere.'

Ben drove his spade deep and said: 'There was ten year' ago, but there isn't now. None as anyone can find – an' none as is anyone's business. Don't you be a meddlesome wench an' poke your nose where it's no cause to go.' The robin sang loudly. 'It's in the garden no one can go into,' Mary said to herself. 'It's in the garden without a door. He lives in there. How I wish I could see what it is like!' After a few days Mary went out into the gardens again. Ben Weatherstaff caught sight of her and called out: 'Springtime's comin'! Cannot tha' smell it?'

Mary sniffed the air and said: 'I smell something nice and fresh and damp.'

'That's th' good rich earth,' he answered. 'It's in a good humour makin' ready to grow things. In th' flower gardens out there things will be stirrin' down below in th' dark. Th' sun's warmin' 'em.' As they talked, the robin that lived in the locked garden flew to them. Mary asked: 'Are things stirring down below in the garden where the robin lives?' 'Ask him,' said Ben Weatherstaff. 'He's the only one as knows. No one else has been inside it for ten years.'

Ten years was a long time, Mary thought. She had been born ten years ago.

The robin let her come very close as he scratched for worms. After a few moments Mary saw that the robin's scratching had made a hole, and that in the newly turned soil lay a piece of rusty metal. She knelt to pick it up, and found a key. 'Perhaps it has been buried for ten years,' she said in a whisper. 'Perhaps it is the key to the garden!'

She walked to the wall and looked at the ivy growing on it. She could not find a door beneath the dark green leaves. She made up her mind to keep the key with her always, so that if she ever found the door she would be ready.

In the morning, as Mary skipped all around the garden, the robin appeared again and she followed him down the walk with little skips. 'You showed me where the key was yesterday,' she said. 'You ought to show me the door today; but I don't believe you know!' Mary had heard a great deal about magic in stories, and she always said that what happened at that moment was magic.

A gust of wind swept down the walk and swung aside some loose ivy. Mary jumped forward and caught it, because underneath she saw the round knob of a door and a rectangular key plate. Her heart began to thump and her hands to shake a little. The robin sang and twittered as if he, too, were excited. It was the door that had been closed for ten years.

Mary drew out the key from her pocket, put it in the lock, and turned it. She took a deep breath and looked to see if anyone was coming. No one was, so she pushed back the door, which opened very slowly.

Then she slipped through it, and shut it behind her, and stood with her back against it, looking about and breathing quite fast with excitement, wonder and delight.

Mary is experiencing an *adrenaline rush*, which you can read about on page 338.

She was standing inside the secret garden.

It was the most mysterious-looking place anyone could imagine. The high walls that shut it in were covered with the leafless stems of climbing roses. All the ground was covered with grass of a wintry brown and out of it grew clumps of bushes that were surely rose bushes if they were alive. There were other trees in the garden which had climbing roses all over them, swinging down in long tendrils which made light, swaying curtains. Mary did not know whether they were dead or alive, but their thin grey branches looked like a sort of hazy mantle spreading over everything. This hazy tangle from tree to tree made it all look so mysterious. It was different from any other place Mary had ever seen in her life.

'It isn't quite dead,' she cried out softly to herself. 'Some of these roses may be alive. Oh! I can't tell; but so many other things are alive.'

She did not know anything about gardening, but it looked to her as if the small green plants she saw poking through the dirt needed to breathe. She searched about until she found a rather sharp piece of wood and knelt down and dug and weeded until she had made little clear places around all the plants. She went from place to place, digging and weeding, until it was past the time for dinner. She had been actually happy the whole time.

For the next week the sun shone on what Mary now called the Secret Garden. It seemed like a fairy place, different from the rest of Mary's world. Mary was a determined little person, and now that she had something interesting to be determined about, she was very much absorbed. She got a spade and set to work. She dug and pulled up weeds; it seemed to her a fascinating sort of play. Sometimes she stopped digging to look at the garden and tried to imagine what it would be like when it was covered with thousands of lovely things in bloom.

One day as she skipped round the laurel-edged walk, she heard a low, whistling sound, and wanted to find out what it was. It was a very strange thing indeed. A funny-looking boy of about twelve was sitting under a tree, playing a wooden pipe. His cheeks were red as poppies, and never had Mistress Mary seen such round and blue eyes in any boy's face. A brown squirrel was watching him from the tree trunk, a pheasant peeked out from a nearby bush, and quite near him two rabbits were sitting up, as if they and the other animals were drawing near to watch and listen to him. He got up slowly, so as not to frighten the animals, and said: 'I'm Dickon. I know tha'rt Miss Mary.'

Dickon was Martha's younger brother. Mary had heard about him but had never met him, and yet he spoke to her as if he knew her quite well. She felt a little shy. Soon they began to talk about gardening and seeds and plants. She wished she could talk as easily and nicely as he did. He showed her mignonette seeds, poppy seeds and seeds for all kinds of lovely flowers.

'See here,' said Dickon. 'I'll plant them for thee myself. Where is tha' garden?'

Mary did not know what to say. She had never thought of anyone asking her about this. 'I don't know anything about boys,' she said slowly. 'Could you keep a secret, if I told you one? If anyone should find out, I believe I should die!' She said the last sentence quite fiercely.

Dickon looked puzzled, but answered quite good-humouredly: 'I'm keepin' secrets all th' time. If I couldn't keep secrets from the other lads about birds' nests, an' wild things' holes, there'd be naught safe on th' moor. Aye, I can keep secrets.'

'I've stolen a garden,' said Mary, very fast. 'It isn't mine. It isn't anybody's. Nobody wants it, nobody cares for it, nobody ever goes into it. Perhaps everything in it is dead already; I don't know.' She began to feel as contrary as she had ever felt in her life.

'Nobody has any right to take it from me when I care about it and they don't.' She burst out crying.

'Where is it?' asked Dickon softly.

Mistress Mary felt quite contrary still, but she said: 'Come with me and I'll show you.'

She led him to the path where the ivy grew so thickly. Dickon felt as if he were being led to some strange bird's nest and must move softly. When she stepped to the wall and lifted the hanging ivy, he was amazed. There was a door. Mary pushed it slowly open and they passed in together, and then Mary stood and waved her hand round defiantly.

'It's this,' she said. 'It's a secret garden, and I'm the only one in the world who wants it to be alive.'

While Mary watched him, Dickon looked and took in all the grey trees with their grey creepers, and the tangle on the walls. 'I never thought I'd see this place,' he said in a whisper. 'Martha told me about it, once. The nests'll be here come springtime. It'd be th' safest nestin' place in England.'

Mary put her hand on his arm without knowing it. 'These rosebushes – are they alive? Is that one alive – at all?'

Dickon smiled. 'It's as wick as you or me,' he said, and Mary remembered that Martha had said 'wick' meant 'alive'. They ran eagerly from bush to bush, and then Dickon noticed the clearings around the young plants, and asked Mary if she had done that work.

'Yes,' she said. 'But I don't know anything about gardening.'

'Tha' did right,' said Dickon. 'A gardener couldn't have told thee better. Now they'll come up like Jack's beanstalk. There's a lot of work to do here!'

Mary thought that she had never seen such a funny boy, or a nicer one. 'Will you come and help? Oh! Do come, Dickon!'

'I'll come every day if tha' wants me, rain or shine,' he answered. 'But I don't want to make it look all clipped. It's nicer like this, all runnin' wild.'

'Let's not make it tidy,' said Mary. 'It wouldn't seem like a secret garden if it all was tidy.'

Then Mary did a strange thing. She leaned forward and asked him a question she had never before dreamed of asking anyone. And she tried to ask it in Yorkshire dialect because that was his language, and in India a person was always pleased if you knew his or her dialect.

'Does tha' like me?' she said.

'That I does; I likes thee wonderful!'

Then they worked harder than ever, and when it was time for Mary to go, she went slowly to the wall. Then she stopped and went back.

'Whatever happens, you – you never would tell?' she said.

He smiled encouragingly. 'If tha' was a missel thrush an' showed me where thy nest was, does tha' think I'd tell anyone? Not me,' he said. 'Tha'art as safe as a missel thrush.'

And she was quite sure she was.

'Please sir, I want some more!'

Adapted from *Oliver Twist* by Charles Dickens

Oliver Twist was born in a workhouse, which was a place for people who were too poor to support themselves. His mother died soon after his birth and his father was not around, so he was put into the care of a woman who was known as a 'baby-farmer' because she was paid to look after so many children. At the age of nine he was moved back to the workhouse to be put to work. The conditions were harsh, especially for a child, and there was never enough to eat.

The room in which the workhouse boys were fed was a large stone hall, with a large copper container at one end. Out of this container the master of the workhouse, dressed in an apron to protect his clothes and assisted by two women, ladled out the food at meal-times. What do you think these workhouse children had to eat? Some meat, perhaps, or else some nourishing vegetables? No, their meal consisted of only one thing: gruel. 'What is gruel?' you might ask. Nothing very delicious, you may be sure. It is like porridge, but very thin and runny, so that, even when you have had a big bowl of it, you feel as if you have eaten almost nothing. And the workhouse boys certainly didn't have a big bowl of gruel. They were given only one small bowl each and nothing else, except on Christmas Day and a few other important days, when they had two-and-a-quarter ounces of bread as well. The bowls never needed to be washed, because each hungry boy would scrape the bowl with his spoon, trying to get every last morsel of gruel, until the bowls shone as if they had been polished.

When they had done this (which never took very long, as their spoons were nearly as large as the bowls), they would sit staring at the copper container with such eager eyes as if they could have eaten it as well. They would sit sucking their fingers hard, just in case some tiny specks of gruel had splashed into them.

Small boys often have large appetites, and Oliver Twist and his companions suffered the tortures of slow starvation for three months until finally they became so wild with hunger that one boy, who was tall for his age and hadn't been used to that sort of thing (for his father had kept a pie-shop), hinted darkly that, unless he had another bowl of gruel every day, he was afraid he might one night accidentally eat the boy who slept next him. He had a wild, hungry eye and the other boys believed him. They got together to work out a desperate plan of action to get more food, and they decided that one of them would walk up to the master of the workhouse after supper that evening and ask for more. What a terrifying thing to do! Nothing like it had ever happened in the work-house, where people were too weak and afraid ever to challenge the authority of those in charge. No one wanted to be the first, so the boys drew straws for it. Oliver Twist drew the short straw, so it was Oliver who had to ask for more.

'Please, sir, I want some more!'

The evening arrived; the boys took their places. The master, in his cook's uniform, stood beside the copper container; his assistants, who were workhouse boys, stood on either side of him; the gruel was served out; and a long prayer was said over the tiny amount of food. The gruel disappeared; the boys whispered to each other and winked at Oliver; while his neighbours nudged him. Child as he was, he was desperate with hunger, and his hunger made him reckless. He rose from the table and walking towards the master, basin and spoon in hand, said, in a trembling voice:

'Please, sir, I want some more.'

The master was a fat, healthy man; but he turned very pale. He gazed in stupefied astonishment on the small rebel for some seconds, and then leant against the copper container, as if he was about to faint from the shock. The assistants were paralysed with amazement; the boys with fear.

'What!' said the master at length, in a faint voice.

'Please, sir,' replied Oliver, 'I want some more.'

The master aimed a blow at Oliver's head with the ladle; pinned him in his arms; and shouted for the steward, who was called Mr Bumble.

The board of governors of the workhouse were having a very serious board meeting when Mr Bumble rushed into the room in great excitement, and addressing the gentleman in the high chair, said: 'Mr Chairman, I beg your pardon, sir! Oliver Twist has asked for more!'

The men were shocked, as nothing like this had ever happened before. Every face around the table was a mask of horror.

'For *more!*' said the chairman. 'Compose yourself, Bumble, and answer me properly. Do I understand that he asked for more, after he had eaten the whole of the supper that we so generously give each boy?'

'He did, sir,' replied Bumble.

'That boy will be come to a bad end,' said the gentleman in the white waistcoat. 'I know that boy will come to a bad end.'

Nobody disagreed with this, because nobody, in the whole history of the workhouse, had ever asked for more food. It was outrageous! Whatever would happen next? Would all the children start asking for more? A lively discussion took place. The men agreed that if they didn't punish Oliver severely, then the other boys might start rebelling too. This could cause chaos! Oliver was locked up in a small room on his own and a notice was put up on the gatepost of the workhouse, offering a reward of five pounds to anybody who would take Oliver Twist away. In other words, five pounds and Oliver Twist were offered to any man or woman who wanted an apprentice to any trade whatsoever.

'I never was more convinced of anything in my life,' said the gentleman in the white waistcoat, as he knocked at the gate and read the notice next morning. 'I never was more convinced of anything in my life, than I am that that boy will come to a bad end.'

So was the white-waistcoated gentleman right or not? If you read the much-loved story of Oliver Twist *by Charles Dickens you will find out exactly what happens to Oliver as he embarks on an exciting life in London with Fagin, Nancy and Bill Sykes. There have been several films of* Oliver Twist, *and a famous musical called* Oliver! *that you can watch on DVD. You can sing 'Food, Glorious Food' on page 204.*

The Death of Arthur

Adapted from *Le Morte d'Arthur* by Sir Thomas Malory

In previous books we have read about King Arthur and his knights of the Round Table. We learnt how Arthur became king when he was able to pull the sword from the stone; how he received his sword Excalibur from the Lady of the Lake; why the knights sat at a Round Table; what happened to Sir Gawain when he accepted the challenge of the Green Knight; and how the Lady of Shalott brought down the curse upon herself when she gazed out of her window at Sir Lancelot du Lac. In this extract from Sir Thomas Malory's Le Morte d'Arthur, *we read about the death of King Arthur.*

ir Lancelot du Lac was the bravest, the most daring and the most handsome of all the knights. All of the ladies who saw him fell in love with him, but he only cared for Queen Guinevere. Guinevere accepted his service, just as she accepted the service of other knights who fought for right against wrong, but she could not help but fall in love with Lancelot herself.

The way in which Guinevere and Lancelot felt for each other was clear to many at Camelot, even though they tried to hide it, and one of the knights, Sir Mordred, decided to accuse them of betraying the King's trust. Sir Mordred was the son of King Arthur, but he was a bitter man, full of anger, especially towards Sir Lancelot whose famous deeds outshone those of all other knights. And so Sir Mordred provided King Arthur with proof that Guinevere and Lancelot loved each other. Because she was the Queen and was married to King Arthur, by the laws of the land Guinevere was sentenced to death. At the last moment Lancelot helped Guinevere to escape and carried her to safety in his castle. King Arthur led his army to attack the castle, but many of his knights joined the other side and helped Lancelot against him.

las,' said Arthur, 'that I should live to see the day when the fellowship of the Round Table was broken. Now our company is torn apart, with some knights supporting the King and some Sir Lancelot. I fear that Camelot will not survive this bitterness.'

There was much fighting around the walls of Lancelot's castle until the Pope in Rome heard of the terrible struggle which was tearing the fellowship of the Round Table apart, and wrote to order King Arthur to forgive Guinevere and Lancelot. The King obeyed, and indeed he had no wish to see either his beloved Queen or his noblest knight die. Guinevere was allowed to return to Camelot and was treated with all honour, but Sir Lancelot was banished from the kingdom. He had been born in France, and still owned much land there, so he crossed the English Channel to return to his homeland, although his heart was nearly broken by the sorrow of leaving Camelot, Arthur and Guinevere.

And there it might have ended, had it not been for the hatred of Sir Gawain for Sir Lancelot. In the fighting between the knights, Lancelot had killed Sir Gawain's two younger brothers even though they were not armed. It had been an accident, but Sir Gawain could not find it in his heart to forgive Lancelot, and asked Arthur to pursue and kill him. King Arthur took his army to France where he fought Lancelot and his knights. While King Arthur was away, he left Sir Mordred to rule his kingdom. As Mordred was his son, Arthur thought that he could rely on him to behave in an honourable way. Alas, Mordred's wicked nature was soon revealed. He told people that he had received letters from France telling him of his father's death, and that he would now be crowned king himself. When Arthur heard of this, he hurried back from France, only to find, as soon as he landed at Dover, that he and his knights were now facing an army raised by Mordred. They fought on the sea shore, and many of Morded's supporters were killed, although Mordred himself escaped. When Arthur visited his own wounded knights on the battlefield, he was horrified to find the brave Sir Gawain dying.

'Alas, Gawain,' he cried, 'you are my own nephew and the very flower of chivalry. You and Lancelot were the noblest knights of the Round Table, and now I have lost you both.'

'Do not grieve for me, Sire,' said Gawain, 'I have brought this upon myself. I was mad with grief when Lancelot killed my brothers, but now I understand that it was an accident. I have spurred you on against Lancelot, when I should have been bringing you together. But now I am dying, and dying men sometimes see more clearly than those who will outlive them. Heed my words now. You face, in Mordred, a deadly enemy, who will destroy you and all you have tried to create at Camelot. Lancelot, although he has been fighting against you, is a noble knight, and with his help you can retain your crown.

You must make a truce with Mordred that will last for at least one month. That will give Lancelot time to come from France to join forces with you. But whatever you do, you must not fight tomorrow. I see it clearly, as I cross from this world into the next, that you will certainly die if you do. Take heed, uncle, and farewell.'

rthur was filled with sorrow when Gawain died in his arms, but he listened to the warning. He sent messengers to Mordred to agree a truce, even if it meant handing over to Mordred large parts of the kingdom. The truce was drawn up, and both armies met, face to face, the next morning to witness it being signed by Arthur and Mordred. Arthur told his knights that he didn't trust Mordred, and that, if anyone drew a sword, they must be prepared to defend themselves. Mordred said the same thing to his knights, so they met in an atmosphere of deep suspicion. They signed the treaty and called for wine to celebrate, but just at that moment an adder bit one of Morded's soldiers on the ankle. The soldier drew his sword to cut the head off the adder, but Arthur's soldiers thought that he was about to attack the King. They drew their swords, Mordred's soldiers drew their swords, and the most terrible fighting followed. Hundreds of noble knights were slain, and at the end of the day Arthur found that only two of his knights were left alive: Sir Lucan and Sir Bedivere, although Sir Lucan had been badly wounded.

'Alas,' he cried, 'my Round Table is no more. The flower of chivalry has been destroyed. All of my work is undone.'

Then he saw Mordred, leaning on his sword amidst a heap of dead knights. Arthur was so filled with hatred of Mordred, even though he was his own son, that he rushed at him and ran his sword through Mordred's body. Mordred knew that he had received his death blow, but he managed to strike his sword against the side of Arthur's head, inflicting a terrible wound. Both men fell down: Mordred was dead and Arthur very nearly so. Sir Lucan and Sir Bedivere rushed to help Arthur, but as they tried to raise him, Sir Lucan fell down dead of his own wounds.

'This noble knight tried to help me,' said Arthur, 'when he was more in need of help himself. Sir Bedivere, I beg you to carry out my last command. Take my sword, Excalibur, and throw it into the lake which lies on the other side of those trees. Then come back here and tell me what you saw.'

Sir Bedivere took Excalibur, which he saw was a magnificent sword, studded with precious jewels.

'What good will it do, if I throw this sword into the lake?' he asked himself. And so he hid it under a tree. When he returned to Arthur, the King asked him what he had seen.

othing but the waves and the wind,' he replied.

'You are lying,' said Arthur. 'Now do as I told you, and return to tell me what you saw.'

So Bedivere went back to the tree to get the sword, but as he walked towards the lake he thought: 'This is a waste of a beautiful and valuable sword. Why should I throw it away?' And so he hid it under a rock and returned to the King.

'What did you see?' asked Arthur.

'Nothing, Sire, but the waves and the wind.'

'You are still lying, Sir Bedivere. Would you betray me for the value of the sword? Now do as I have told you, or I will kill you with my own hands, wounded as I am. And be quick, for the cold is creeping into my bones.'

So Sir Bedivere took Excalibur and threw it into the lake. A hand arose from the lake, caught the sword, and brandished it three times. Then it sank back into the lake. Sir Bedivere returned to Arthur and told him what he had seen.

'This time you speak truly,' said Arthur. 'Now carry me on your back to the edge of the lake, for I can feel the cold in my bones, and my life is slipping away from me.'

Sir Bedivere carried Arthur on his back to the edge of the lake, where he saw a barge approaching the bank. Upon this barge were a group of noble ladies, including three queens: Queen Morgan le Fay, the enchantress and sister of Arthur; the Queen of North Wales; and the Queen of the Waste Lands. The Lady of the Lake was with them in the barge.

The noble ladies took the body of Arthur from Bedivere, with much crying and sorrow. Morgan Le Fay cradled his wounded head in her lap. 'Alas my brother,' she said, 'you have waited too long to come to us. The cold has entered your bones, and the wound in your head has brought you close to death.'

As the boat moved from the shore, Sir Bedivere cried out: 'My lord Arthur, what shall become of me, now that you are leaving me alone amongst my enemies?'

can no longer help you,' said Arthur, 'for I am going to the vale of Avalon, where I hope that my wound will be healed. If not, I shall die. So farewell, Sir Bedivere, last of the knights of the Round Table of Camelot.'

As the barge sailed away, Sir Bedivere wept, for he felt despair. Then he ran through the forest, he knew not where. All night he wandered, and as the morning came he saw a little chapel in a clearing. Beside the chapel was a tiny building with only one room, called a cell, and in that cell lived a hermit. Hermits were holy men and women who gave up all the pleasures

The hand brandished Excalibur three times then sank back into the lake.

of life and went to live alone in deserted places, passing their time in prayer and thinking about God. When Sir Bedivere entered the cell, he saw an old man with a long beard, kneeling beside a freshly dug grave.

'Who is buried in that grave, old man?' asked Sir Bedivere.

'That I cannot tell you,' replied the hermit. 'I only know that during the night three noble ladies came here with a corpse. They gave me a hundred candles and a hundred gold coins, and asked me to bury the corpse and to pray for his soul.'

'Alas,' said Sir Bevidere, 'I now know that you have buried King Arthur, the noblest king this country ever knew. Those three ladies were queens who took his injured body from me into their barge. They tried to heal the terrible wound in his head, but he has died from it. And now, holy man, I have nothing more to do in this world, for Arthur is dead. May I stay with you here, spending my life in prayer and holy thoughts?'

'You are welcome to stay with me, my son,' said the old hermit, 'and to help me keep watch over the grave of this man who you say was the great King Arthur.'

When Queen Guinevere heard that Arthur was dead, together with all the noble knights of the Round Table, she stole away from Camelot with five ladies and went to a nunnery. There she put on the black and white garments of a nun and spent the rest of her life praying for forgiveness for her part in the events that led to the death of King Arthur and the destruction of the Round Table.

Queen Guinevere became a nun.

That is all I have been able to find out about the death of Arthur from the old books. However, you may have heard some people say that Arthur is not dead at all, but sleeps under the hill at Avalon, waiting to serve his country again in its hour of need. What should we believe? We know that Arthur's wounded body was entrusted to the three queens, and we know that three noble ladies came to the hermit's cell in the night with a corpse. But was the corpse that of King Arthur? Of one thing I am sure, because it is written in all of the old books. Upon that grave, in the hermit's cell in Glastonbury, is a stone engraved with these words:

HERE LIES ARTHUR, THE ONCE AND FUTURE KING.

In 1485 Sir Thomas Malory published Le Morte d'Arthur, *which means the death of Arthur in old-fashioned French. However, this book was not only about the death of the King: it gave an account of everything had happened to him throughout his life, and of all the noble deeds of the knights of the Round Table. In the twentieth century, T.H. White was inspired by* Le Morte d'Arthur *to write his own version of the legend of King Arthur, which he called* The Once and Future King. *This inspired the Walt Disney cartoon film* The Sword in the Stone. Le Morte d'Arthur *also inspired the musical* Camelot. *You can watch both on DVD.*

The Samurai's Daughter

This story is set in feudal Japan around the year 1300. The samurai were the knights of feudal Japan.

Many years ago in Japan, there lived a samurai named Oribe Shima. By some misfortune, Oribe Shima had offended the emperor and been banished to one of the Oki Islands, off the west coast of Japan.

Oribe had a beautiful daughter, eighteen years old, named Tokoyo. When Oribe was sent away, Tokoyo wept from morning till night, and sometimes from night till morning. At last, unable to stand the separation any longer, she decided to try to reach her father or else die in the attempt, for she was a brave girl.

Tokoyo sold everything she owned and set off for the province closest to the Oki Islands. She tried to persuade the local fishermen to take her to the Islands, but no one was allowed to land there.

The fishermen laughed at Tokoyo and told her to go home. But the brave girl was not to be put off. She went down to the beach, found an abandoned boat and pushed it into the water. Then she started rowing. After several hours, Tokoyo reached the Islands. Cold and exhausted, she stumbled ashore and lay down to sleep.

In the morning, she began asking if anyone knew of her father's whereabouts. The first person she asked was a fisherman. 'I have never heard of your father,' he said, 'and you should not ask for him if he has been banished, for it may lead you to trouble and him to death!'

Poor Tokoyo wandered from one place to another, asking about her father but never hearing any news of him. One evening she came to a little shrine near the edge of the ocean. After bowing before a statue of the Buddha and imploring his help, Tokoyo lay down, intending to pass the night there, for it was peaceful and sheltered from the winds.

She was awakened by the sound of a girl wailing. As she looked up, she saw a young girl sobbing bitterly. Beside the girl stood the priest who kept the shrine. He was clapping his hands and mumbling a prayer. Both the man and the girl were dressed in white. When the prayer was over, the priest led the girl to the edge of the rocks and was about to push her into the sea, when Tokoyo ran and caught the girl's arm in the nick of time. The old priest looked surprised, but not angry.

'You must be a stranger to our island,' said the priest. 'Or you would know that this business is not at all to my liking. We are cursed with an evil god called Yofuné-Nushi. He lives at the bottom of the sea, and demands, once a year, the sacrifice of a girl. If we do not do this, Yofuné-Nushi causes great storms that drown many of our fishermen.'

Tokoyo said: 'Holy priest, let this girl go, for I will willingly take her place. I am the sorrowing daughter of Oribe Shima, a samurai of high rank, who has been exiled to this island. I came here to find my father, but I cannot even find out where he has been hidden. My heart is broken, and I have no desire to go on living.'

Saying this, Tokoyo took the white robe off the girl and put it on her own body. She knelt before the figure of Buddha and prayed. Then she drew a small dagger, which had belonged to one of her ancestors, and, holding it between her teeth, she dove into the roaring sea.

When she was young, Tokoyo had spent many days diving with the women in her village to look for pearls. Because of this, she was a perfect swimmer. She swam down, down, down, until at last she reached the bottom, where she found an underwater cave. As Tokoyo peeped in, she thought she saw a man seated in the cave. Fearing nothing, willing to fight and die, she approached, holding her dagger ready. Tokoyo took the man for the evil god Yofuné-Nushi. However, she soon saw that it was not a god, but only a statue of the emperor, the man who had exiled her father.

Tokoyo took hold of the statue and was about to lift it when a horrible creature appeared. It was pale and scaly and shaped like a snake, but with a head and claws like a dragon. It was twenty feet long, and its eyes burned with hatred.

Tokoyo gripped her dagger, feeling sure that this was Yofuné-Nushi. No doubt Yofuné-Nushi took Tokoyo for the girl that was sacrificed to him each year.

When the creature was within six feet of her, Tokoyo ducked sideways and slashed his right eye. Now the monster was half blind, so Tokoyo was able to strike him again, this time near the heart. Yofuné-Nushi gave a hideous gurgling shriek and sank lifeless on the ocean floor. Tokoyo placed her dagger between her teeth, took the monster in one hand and the statue in the other, and swam up towards the surface.

Meanwhile the priest and the girl were still gazing into the water where Tokoyo had disappeared. Suddenly they noticed a struggling body rising towards the surface.

Tokoyo gripped her dagger, feeling sure that this was Yofuné-Nushi.

When the priest realised it was Tokoyo, he climbed down the cliff to help her. He helped lug the hideous monster onto the shore and placed the carved image of the emperor on a rock. Soon other people arrived, and everyone was talking about the brave girl who had killed Yofuné-Nushi.

The priest told the story to the lord who ruled the island, and he reported the matter to the emperor. The emperor had been suffering from a strange disease that his doctors could not cure, but as soon as the statue of him was recovered, he got better. Then it was clear to him that he had been under the curse of someone he had banished to the Oki Islands – someone who had carved a statue of him, put a curse on the statue, and sunk it in the sea. Now the curse had been broken. On hearing that the girl who had recovered the statue was the daughter of Oribe Shima, the emperor ordered the noble samurai released from prison.

Now the islanders were no longer afraid of storms, and no more girls were thrown into the sea. Tokoyo and her father returned to their homeland, where they lived happily ever after.

Learning about Literature

Literal and Figurative Language

When you speak or write, you use language in different ways. Sometimes you use literal language; you say exactly what you mean. But sometimes you use figurative language, which is a more colourful way of expressing yourself when you don't say exactly what you mean. After a really hard game of football or tennis, you might say:

literal: I'm exhausted.

or

figurative: I'm dead.

The game might have worn you out, and you might be lying flat on your back out of breath, but you're still alive! In saying 'I'm dead', you are using figurative language to express how tired you feel.

Look at the verb **floated** in the following sentences. Which use is literal and which is figurative?

(1) The graceful ballerina **floated** across the stage.

(2) The leaf **floated** on the water.

Have you ever heard someone say: 'That's a figure of speech'? A figure of speech is an expression that is not meant to be taken literally. You may know this old joke: 'Why did the man throw the clock out the window? Because he wanted to see time fly.' That's funny because the man in the joke takes a figure of speech literally. What does it really mean to say that 'time flies'?

Scientists always use the literal meanings of words because they need to be clear and precise. Poets and

storytellers often use figurative language to stir our emotions and to help us see things in new ways. The American poet Emily Dickinson used figurative language when she compared a book to a frigate (a sailing ship) that can take us on imaginary voyages:

There is no frigate like a book

To take us lands away…

Imagery

The words writers use to create mental pictures and other imaginary sensations are called *imagery*. The poet A. E. Housman wrote this poem about his longing for the happy days of his youth:

Into my heart an air that kills

From yon far country blows:

What are those blue remembered hills,

What spires, what farms are those?

That is the land of lost content,

I see it shining plain,

The happy highways where I went

And cannot come again.

The title of this poem is its first line, but most people call it 'Blue remembered hills', because this phrase has become so well known. Hills seen in the distance are blue or pale in colour because they are so far away, but when Housman says that he can never go there, he isn't referring to a distance that can be measured in miles. He means that, once we are old, we can never go back to the times when we were younger, because they have gone forever. Time has moved on. The distant hills are an *image* of this.

See a photo of the American Blue Ridge Mountains in Year 5 and learn more about them on page 112.

Simile and Metaphor

When writers use imagery, they often put their images into special kinds of figurative language called *simile* [SIM-ill-ee] and *metaphor* [MET-er-for]. If you've ever said something like 'She's fast as lightning' or 'He's an angel', then you've used similes and metaphors yourself.

Similes and metaphors help us to see things in unusual or imaginative ways by comparing one thing to another. Sometimes they bring together things you normally would not think of comparing. For example, fog might not make you think of an animal, but notice the surprising comparison Carl Sandburg makes in his poem called 'Fog':

The fog comes
on little cat feet.

It sits looking
over harbour and city
on silent haunches
and then moves on.

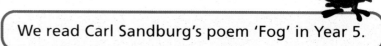

We read Carl Sandburg's poem 'Fog' in Year 5.

A simile is a figure of speech that compares unlike things but makes the comparison obvious by including either the word *like* or *as*. You've probably heard people use common similes in conversation: for example, 'busy as a bee' or 'sweet as honey' or 'proud as a peacock'. The great boxer Muhammad Ali described himself with some vivid similes: he said he would 'float like a butterfly, sting like a bee' in the boxing ring.

Like a simile, a metaphor is a figure of speech that brings together unlike things. But a metaphor doesn't use *like* or *as*, so the comparison is not so obvious. For example, in talking about someone who looks beautiful, you might say:

Simile: *You are as pretty as a picture.*

or

Metaphor: *You are a picture.*

The Victorian writer Christina Rossetti wrote a poem called 'Clouds':

White sheep, white sheep,
On a blue hill,
When the wind stops
You all stand still.

When the wind blows,
You walk away slow.
White sheep, white sheep,
Where do you go?

So, although the poem is called 'Clouds', there is no mention of clouds in it – she talks only about sheep! But we know that she is really comparing the clouds to sheep in a way that makes us look at the clouds in a new way. The metaphor makes the clouds seem more solid, and almost alive.

In Year 5, we read 'Dreams' by Langston Hughes, which contains some powerful metaphors to show what happens when your dreams die.

Sometimes a metaphor may be almost hidden in the words. For example, there's a metaphor lurking in this sentence: *The snow blanketed the dawn.* Do you see how the snow is being compared to a blanket? Now find the metaphor in this sentence: *Darkness swallowed the explorers as they entered the cave.*

Figurative language creates an emotional effect different from a literal statement such as 'The explorers entered the dark cave'. When you use a metaphor to compare the darkness to a hungry animal waiting to 'swallow' the explorers, the cave becomes a place that most of us would rather not enter!

Ready for a metaphor challenge? Richard Le Gallienne's poem 'A Ballad of London' on page 8 describes the city of London as a flower that only opens at night. (Remember that most flowers like the sunlight!) Read the poem several times and see if you can work out what he means by 'human moths'. Who are the 'poor worms that have not eyes or wings'?

You can see this statue of Britannia in Plymouth.

Symbols

A *symbol* is something that stands for or suggests something else beyond itself. You're probably familiar with this lady – she appears on the 50p coins!

She is called Britannia, and symbolises Great Britain. She has the Union Jack on her shield and a lion at her feet, symbolising the power of Great Britain. (The lion is often described as the 'king of the jungle'.) She carries a trident, which she has taken from Neptune, the Roman god of the sea. This symbolises the fact that the Royal Navy was for hundreds of years the greatest navy in the world and essential in the defence of the country. The trident tells us that 'Britannia rules the waves', in the words of the famous song!

We learnt about the symbolic meanings of colours in Year 5. Words, colours and images can all be symbols.

Another familiar symbol is a heart. What does a heart symbolise, especially on Valentine's Day? In contrast, what do the skull and crossbones symbolise on a pirate's flag?

Do you think this pirate might be in love?

Works of literature often contain symbols. In the legend of King Arthur, the sword Excalibur, which Arthur receives from the Lady of the Lake, symbolises his rule over the kingdom. When he dies, Excalibur must be thrown back into the lake, where it is caught by a mysterious hand.

A symbol can mean different things to different people, and things in a work of literature are not always symbols. For example, let's say you're reading a poem about a bird: the bird may be a symbol, suggesting a quality like freedom. Or, the bird may simply be a bird. When you're reading stories and poems, you don't need to search for symbols, but when you do notice them, it's interesting to think about how they enrich what you're reading.

We read the legend of how King Arthur received the sword Excalibur in Year 3.

Personification

Imagine you're trying to sharpen a pencil but the lead keeps breaking. Frustrated, you exclaim: 'This pencil sharpener refuses to work!' Did the pencil sharpener actually refuse? Did it say: 'I won't sharpen your pencil'? Of course not. When you said that the pencil sharpener refused to work, you used a kind of figurative language known as *personification*.

To *personify* is to give the qualities of a human being to a thing or an animal or even an abstract idea, like good luck. 'Fortune has smiled on us,' says Don Quixote to Sancho Panza on page 20, as if there were a lady who could make good or bad things happen to us. Most of the gods and goddesses of ancient Greece and Rome personified things, like forces of nature (Neptune: the sea; Vulcan: fire) or feelings (Venus: love; Mars: war).

Onomatopoeia

Onomatopoeia [ON-oh-mat-uh-PEA-uh] is a Greek word for a special effect that writers use. In a comic book, when something explodes, you read 'BOOM!' Or when a superhero punches a villain, you read 'BIFF!' or 'POW!' Onomatopoeia refers to words that sound like the things they describe. If you drop a coin in a metal bowl, it goes 'clink'. If a car speeds by, it goes 'varroom'. 'Clink' and 'varroom' are examples of onomatopoeia. Try to think of what might produce these sounds: buzz, hiss, clack, gurgle, whoosh.

Now, think of some words that might capture the following sounds: bacon frying, thunder in the distance, windshield wipers going back and forth, a seat-belt fastening, a dog growling.

Alliteration

Another special effect that poets use is *alliteration*. Alliteration means starting several words in a row with the same sound. The first two lines of 'The Eagle' by Alfred, Lord Tennyson, on page 2, are an example:

He clasps the crag with crookèd hands;
Close to the sun in lonely lands

Do you hear the repetition of the hard 'c' sound in the first line? Can you find more alliteration in the second line of the poem?

The story of *Sir Gawain and the Green Knight* that we read in Year 5 first appeared in *alliterative verse* in the Middle Ages. Most of the poet's lines don't rhyme, but the alliteration creates strong sound-patterns in each line. Do you remember the ending?

This is related in the writings of the most renowned romancers,
And ancient chronicles commonly confirm for us
That in Arthur's reign this report was recited.

Drama

A *drama*, or play, is a special kind of story meant to be acted out on stage. Instead of telling you what happened, the dramatist, or playwright, shows you. If you see a play performed in a theatre, the action unfolds in front of you.

The first plays were written by the ancient Greeks as part of religious festivals. At first, a group of men called a 'chorus' sang songs together and danced around the altar of the Greek god Dionysus. Gradually, the performances became more complex. First a single actor from the chorus was allowed to speak as an individual. Then more actors were added, so the characters on stage could talk to each other and act out stories. Eventually these religious ceremonies began to look a lot like modern plays.

Ancient Greek actors used masks for comedy and tragedy. Can you guess which one stands for comedy?

The Greeks developed two kinds of plays: comedies and tragedies. *Comedies* are funny, happy stories, in which everything works out well in the end. *Tragedies* are sad stories, in which things turn out badly. An ancient Greek comedy often ends with a marriage or a celebration; a tragedy often ends with the death of the main character, or with several deaths.

Shakespeare

One of the most famous dramatists was William Shakespeare. His plays are among the most popular of all time and are still performed today. Shakespeare lived near the end of the great age called the Renaissance, which you can read about in the Visual Arts chapter. His plays, written between the 1590s and the 1610s, were performed in theatres around London, including the famous Globe Theatre.

Shakespeare was born in 1564 and he died in 1616. In Year 4, we learnt about centuries. Which century or centuries did Shakespeare live in?

Shakespeare's Comedies

Shakespeare's plays are divided into three groups: comedies, tragedies and histories. His comedies are often about young people who fall in love but find that there is an obstacle of some kind that comes between them. Sometimes the woman's father does not approve of the man she loves, or the lovers' families are enemies, or there is an unfair law that prevents the marriage. Sometimes the woman has disguised herself as a man, for some reason to do with the plot, which causes lots of confusion! The play then tells the story of how the lovers get around these obstacles. The road from thwarted love to happiness and marriage is seldom smooth. Usually there is a period of confusion in which it is not clear who loves whom. Sometimes there are quarrels and breakups, but the comedy usually ends with a wedding – often more than one! One of Shakespeare's most famous comedies is called *A Midsummer Night's Dream*. You can read this play in a version edited for young readers. To really get the feeling of a Shakespeare play, you should see one performed or try to act out some scenes with your friends.

In A Midsummer Night's Dream, *there are two pairs of young lovers who get mixed up in a quarrel between the King and the Queen of the fairies! Here are Helena and Hermia, the two young women.*

One of the greatest things about Shakespeare is his ability to describe all kinds of characters: kings and queens, soldiers, merchants, servants and beggars – and everyone in between! Shakespeare seems to understand all kinds of people: good and bad, heroic and selfish, brave and cruel. He helps us to understand them as well.

Another reason for Shakespeare's greatness is the beauty and power of his poetry. Although the people in his plays think and act like real people, they speak an almost magical language. In *The Tempest*, the character of Prospero, a magician, conjures up spirits to perform a play for his daughter and the young man who has fallen in love with her. When the play has ended, the spirits disappear, and Prospero tells the young people that all the men and women on earth, and everything they know and value, will one day disappear in just the same way:

> *Our revels now are ended. These our actors,*
> *As I foretold you, were all spirits and*
> *Are melted into air, into thin air:*
> *And, like the baseless fabric of this vision;*
> *The cloud-capp'd towers, the gorgeous palaces,*
> *The solemn temples, the great globe itself,*
> *Yea all which it inherit, shall dissolve*
> *And, like this insubstantial pageant faded,*
> *Leave not a wrack behind. We are such stuff*
> *As dreams are made on, and our little life*
> *Is rounded with a sleep.*

How many metaphors and similes can you find in this beautiful speech?

Have you ever spoken of something disappearing into thin air? You might not have known it, but you were quoting from this speech! Many of the phrases that Shakespeare created have become part of our everyday speech, because he expressed things in such a memorable way. The writer Bernard Levin wrote this clever passage which is almost entirely composed of phrases from Shakespeare's plays:

Quoting Shakespeare by Bernard Levin

If you cannot understand my argument, and declare **'It's Greek to me'**, you are quoting Shakespeare; if you claim to be **more sinned against than sinning**, you are quoting Shakespeare; if you recall your **salad days**, you are quoting Shakespeare; if you act **more in sorrow than in anger**, if your **wish is father to the thought**, if your lost property has vanished **into thin air**, you are quoting Shakespeare; if you have ever refused to **budge an inch** or suffered from **green-eyed jealousy**, if you have **played fast and loose**, if you have been **tongue-tied, a tower of strength, hoodwinked** or **in a pickle**, if you have **knitted your brows, made a virtue of necessity**, insisted on **fair play**, slept **not one wink**,

---

> **stood on ceremony, danced attendance** (on your **lord and master),
> laughed yourself into stitches,** had **short shrift, cold comfort** or **too
> much of a good thing,** if you have **seen better days** or lived in a **fool's
> paradise** – why, **be that as it may, the more fool you,** for it is a **foregone
> conclusion** that you are (**as good luck would have it**) quoting
> Shakespeare; if you think it is **early days** and clear out **bag and
> baggage,** if you think it is **high time** and that that is **the long and short
> of it,** if you believe that the **game is up** and that **truth will out** even if
> it involves your **own flesh and blood,** if you **lie low** till the **crack of
> doom** because you suspect **foul play,** if you have your **teeth set on edge**
> (at **one fell swoop**) **without rhyme or reason,** then – **to give the devil
> his due** – **if the truth were known** (for surely you **have a tongue in your
> head**) you are quoting Shakespeare; even if you bid me **good riddance**
> and **send me packing,** if you wish I were **dead as a door-nail,** if you
> think I am an **eyesore,** a **laughing stock,** the **devil incarnate,** a **stony-
> hearted villain, bloody-minded** or a **blinking idiot,** then – **by Jove! O
> Lord! Tut, tut! for goodness' sake! what the dickens! but me no buts** –
> **it is all one to me,** for you are quoting Shakespeare.

As well as making up these brilliant phrases, Shakespeare would often make up a word if he could not find one to serve his purpose. Many words make their first appearance in the English language in Shakespeare's plays, including words we still use today like *gloomy, generous, countless, hurry, assassination, monumental* and many more. Shakespeare probably had more influence on the English we speak than any other writer, and he has greatly influenced many writers since his own day. Once you have read his beautiful poetry, you may feel his influence too!

Learning about Language

Categories of Nouns

You know what a noun is, but do you know how many different categories of nouns there are? There are four: *common* nouns, *proper* nouns, *abstract* nouns and *collective* nouns.

Collective nouns, which we looked at in Year 5, represent a group of people, animals or things, like a herd of cattle, a collection of stamps or a team of players. Collective nouns always take singular verbs, so we say:

*The **team** is winning,* not

*The **team** are winning*
(because there is only one team).

Proper nouns are the names of individual people, places and organisations. Titles of books, plays and films are proper nouns. They always begin with capital letters.

Elizabeth   Jamal   Great Britain   British Broadcasting Corporation

Metropolitan Police   Hollywood   Newcastle   Snow White

Abstract nouns are the names of thoughts, ideas, feelings and qualities: things that you cannot see or touch.

*Don Quixote loved to read books about **chivalry**.*

*Dickon felt great **tenderness** for all living things.*

*There is a sense of **mystery** about the house in Walter de la Mare's poem 'The Listeners'.*

*You should never show **fear** if you come across a wild animal.*

***Music** can often lead to **romance**.*

Common nouns are all the nouns that don't come into any of the other three categories – the things that you can see and touch all around you.

In the following passage, all of the nouns are printed in purple. Make a table with four columns headed: Common Nouns, Proper Nouns, Collective Nouns and Abstract Nouns. Copy each noun into one of the columns. How many nouns are there in each column? How many altogether?

Our **teacher**, **Mrs Goswami**, took us to the **theatre** to see **Antony and Cleopatra**. It was written by **William Shakespeare** and is set in **Egypt**. We had a long **journey** to get there, travelling on a **train** for over two **hours**, then transferring to a **coach**. We had all been told to take a packed **lunch**, which we ate as soon as we had left the **station**. My best **friend**, **Monisha**, was feeling such **excitement** that she could hardly eat any of her **sandwich**, but any **nervousness** she might have felt disappeared when we went into the brightly-lit **auditorium**. The **seats** were so comfortable that, although no one felt any sense of **boredom**, one or two **children** did give way to **tiredness** and fell asleep during the **performance**, although only for a brief **period**. The **play** showed how **Mark Antony** was torn between his **feelings** of **love** for **Cleopatra** and **duty** towards the **people** of **Rome**, which are both strong **emotions**. The whole **class** applauded at the end, and the **audience** rose to its **feet** to show the **cast** how much their **performance** had been appreciated. Before leaving **Stratford-upon-Avon**, we visited the **house** where **Shakespeare** was born and the **church** where he is buried. The **congregation** of this **church** realises that the **admirers** of the great **playwright** form a large **fan-club**, and that they will receive **visitors** from all over the **world**.

Verbs and Objects

What do you need to make a sentence? A verb! There must be someone, or something, doing something. The subject of the verb is doing the action of the verb, so in the sentence:

The train was running late.

The **train** is the subject of the verb, because it is doing the running. In the sentence:

Susanna tries her best.

Susanna is the subject because she is doing the trying.

Some sentences add another element to their subject and verb – a *direct object*. The object is on the receiving end of the action of the verb. In the sentence *Dad cooked the beefburgers*, **beefburgers** is the direct object of the verb 'cooked'. It is called a direct object, because the verb acts directly on it: the beefburgers are *being cooked*.

Michelangelo painted the **ceiling** of the Sistine Chapel.

Queen Victoria opened the **Great Exhibition** at the Crystal Palace.

To find a direct object, first find the subject and the verb. Then ask yourself who or what the verb is acting on.

Sometimes, when a sentence has a direct object, it also has an indirect object. The indirect object answers the question to *whom?* or to *what?* An indirect object is the person or thing that receives the direct object from the subject.

Jim threw Tina the ball.

In the sentence above, **ball** is the direct object and **Tina**, who received the ball, is the indirect object. Here's another example. If you had lived in 1918, you might have read this headline:

Parliament gives women the vote!

To find the indirect object in this sentence, remember to find the direct object of the verb first. You would ask 'gives what?' and the answer would be 'the vote'. And then you would ask, 'gives the vote to whom?' The answer would be 'women'. So **vote** is the direct object and **women** is the indirect object.

Interjections

An interjection is a word added to a sentence to convey emotion, as in this passage from *Oliver Twist* on page 28:

Oliver rose from the table and walking towards the master, basin and spoon in hand, said, in a trembling voice: '*Please, sir, I want some more.*'

'*What!*' said the master at length, in a faint voice.

'What!' is an interjection, because the master of the workhouse isn't really asking Oliver what he said – he heard it only too well! Here are some more interjections:

Help! I'm late for work!

Hey, come back here!

Ouch! That hurt!

Use interjections in your own writing when you are trying to capture the way people talk in everyday life.

Personal Pronouns

Pronouns take the place of nouns. There are several kinds of pronouns, but the kind we use most often is the personal pronoun – the pronoun that can replace the name of a person or thing in a sentence:

*When Louis Armstrong played **his** trumpet, **he** moved **our** hearts with **his** rhythm and shattered glasses with **his** pitch.*

Using personal pronouns makes our sentences shorter and less cumbersome. But how do you know which pronoun to use? Most people use the pronoun that fits without knowing its name or the rule for its use. They say, 'Give me the book', not 'Give I the book'. But the rule for choosing personal pronouns is easy to learn: the personal pronoun must agree with the noun it replaces in case, gender and number. Let's see what that means.

Agreement in Case

Think of the various pronouns you can use to refer to yourself: *I, me, my* or *mine*. Which form of pronoun you use depends on how you use it in a sentence. A pronoun takes the place of a noun, and the particular form a pronoun takes – that is, the *case* of the pronoun – must agree with the function of the noun that the pronoun replaces in the sentence. There are three cases: nominative, objective and possessive. Let's look at the nominative and objective cases by considering the following sentence:

The nurse held the babies.

If you were to replace 'the nurse' with a pronoun, which one would you use? Here are the pronouns you could choose, each in a different case:

nominative case: **she**

objective case: **her**

What is the function of 'the nurse' in the sentence? It is the subject. When the noun acts as the subject, you replace it with a pronoun in the nominative case:

***She** held the babies.*

Now, what pronoun would you use to replace 'the babies' in that sentence? Here are your choices:

nominative case: **they**

objective case: **them**

What is the function of 'the babies' in the sentence? It is a direct object. When the noun to be replaced is either a direct object or an indirect object, the pronoun must be in the objective case.

*She held **them**.*

Here are the personal pronouns in the nominative case: **I, we, you, he, she, it, they**. Any of these nominative pronouns will work as the subject of a sentence like the following:

_____ *danced to the music.*

Here are the personal pronouns in the objective case: **me, us, you, him, her, it, them**. Any of the objective pronouns will work as the object in a sentence like the following:

He threw the ball at _____

Often you will use the nominative and objective case correctly without thinking about it, although there are some tricky cases to watch out for. Sometimes people use the objective case when they should use the nominative case:

*My brother and **me** are going to the market.*

What is the function of the word **me** in that sentence? It's part of the subject. If you take away the other part of the subject – my brother – you'll see how odd it sounds to say '**Me** am going to the market'. So the correct form is the nominative:

*My brother and **I** are going to the market.*

Be on the lookout for the mistake people occasionally make when they use a nominative pronoun instead of an objective pronoun, as in the following:

*Dad is taking Mark and **I** to see the parade.*

You wouldn't say: 'Dad is taking I to see the parade'. So use the objective pronoun:

*Dad is taking Mark and **me** to see the parade.*

Possessive Case

Here are the personal pronouns you use when the noun is showing possession: **mine, ours, yours, his, hers, its, theirs**. These are called the possessive pronouns.

Jane's story is more exciting than _____

Mine, ours, yours, his, hers, its and **theirs** will all fit in the blank.

But we can also change Jane's story to **her** story. The possessives that come before a noun are a little different from those that stand by themselves. The ones that come before a noun are **my, our, your, his, her, its** and **their**.

_____ story is more exciting than mine.

The **her** in 'her story' is still called a possessive personal pronoun. But you see that it doesn't stand alone. It is a word that modifies the noun 'story', just as an adjective would. Notice that you can use **mine, ours, yours, his, hers** and **theirs** all by themselves, but **my, our, your, her** and **their** always come before the thing they possess, as in 'my dog' or 'her book'. **His** can be used all by itself or to modify a noun.

Agreement in Gender

Pronouns also need to agree in _gender_ with the noun they replace – whether female, male or neither. If you were describing the shocking thing that Oliver Twist did, you wouldn't say: 'She asked for more'. You would say: 'He asked for more', because Oliver Twist was a boy, and **he, him** and **his** are the pronouns we use for nouns that are masculine. Do you know the pronouns we use for feminine nouns?

Objects such as a table or a door have no gender. **It** is the pronoun we use for things that are gender-neutral, such as a heart, a painting or a hammer. For instance, when describing the heart, we might say: '**It** is an amazing muscle'.

Agreement in Number

Agreement in _number_ means the pronoun must be singular or plural like the noun it replaces. Use singular pronouns when talking about one thing and plural pronouns when talking about more than one thing.

Here are the singular pronouns we use for one person:

nominative	objective	possessive
I	me	my, mine
you	you	your, yours
he	him	his
she	her	her, hers
it	it	its

Here are the plural pronouns we use for more than one person:

nominative	objective	possessive
we	us	our, ours
you	you	your, yours
they	them	their, theirs

The Versatile Comma

You know how to use a full stop (.) at the end of a sentence that makes a statement, a question mark (?) at the end of a sentence that asks a question, and an exclamation mark (!) at the end of a sentence or phrase that is exclaimed or shouted out, like 'My foot hurts!' You have also learnt to use commas in certain situations, such as when you want to separate items in a list (but not between the last two items if they are separated by a conjunction like 'and' or 'or'):

Lemonade is made from water, sugar and lemon juice.

You also need a comma when you write a sentence with a co-ordinating conjunction such as 'but', 'and', 'or', or separating two phrases that could otherwise stand on their own:

We went to the shop, but they didn't have any bread.

I took the test, and I think I did well.

Commas are used after the words yes and no:

Yes, I can hear you, my dear!

No, I don't want another slice of pizza.

Commas are used in addresses to separate the names of cities, counties and countries:

Our trip took us to Paris, France.

Golden Hill is in Shaftesbury, Dorset.

Commas are also used to separate *subordinate phrases* or *clauses* from the main clause in the sentence. For instance, look at the following sentence.

*My best friend, **Susan Scott**, is coming to my house tonight.*

'Susan Scott' tells us more about 'my best friend', but the sentence would still make sense if the words were removed. Therefore, we call it a subordinate phrase and we use commas to separate it from the rest of the sentence.

What is the difference between a subordinate phrase and a subordinate clause? A clause contains a verb, whereas a phrase does not. Subordinate clauses can be quite long, as in this case:

*Don Quixote, **a poor, skinny man who comes from an insignificant town somewhere in Spain**, thinks he is a knight in shining armour.*

Once again, the words in purple could be removed and the sentence would still make sense, so we use commas to separate them from the rest of the sentence. Can you see the verb in this part of the sentence? It is 'comes', so this is a subordinate clause, rather than a phrase.

Brackets

Another way in which you can separate words that are not essential to the structure of the sentence is by using brackets. The words in brackets give us a bit more information, but they are not as important as the rest of the sentence:

*The children **(who were already tired)** did not want to do another hour of maths.*

*The Crystal Palace **(which was the popular name for the Great Exhibition of 1851)** stood in Hyde Park in London.*

*Manchester United **(the home team)** can always be sure of support from the crowd at Old Trafford.*

Now write out these sentences, putting brackets around the words that need to be separated from the rest of the sentence:

The twins noisy as ever were running around the garden.

Charlie's dog Tigger always ready for a game caused havoc by chasing the football around the pitch.

I tried my hardest in spite of the rain to sweep the leaves from my grandparents' drive.

Prefixes

A prefix is a set of letters that can be attached to the front of a word to make a new word. For instance, you probably know that **unfriendly** means 'not friendly', and a **replay** is what happens when a football match in the FA Cup ends in a draw and has to be played again. Here are some more prefixes that will help you make sense of unfamiliar words.

anti- means 'against', 'in opposition to' or 'opposed to'

An **antibacterial** soap fights against bacteria.

inter- means 'between' or 'among'

International trade is trade between nations, and an **intercity** train runs between two or more cities.

co- means 'together with' or 'joint'

If your sports team has **co-captains**, it has two captains who serve jointly. When two groups don't like each other but try to get along, they try to **co-exist**.

mid- is short for 'middle'

Midnight is the middle of the night.
Shakespeare's play *A **Midsummer** Night's Dream* takes place in the middle of the summer.

fore- means 'before' or 'the front part of'

A **forefather** is someone from an earlier time or an ancestor.
If you **forewarn** a friend, you warn her ahead of time. (But if your friend has **foresight**, she won't need to be **forewarned**!)

post- means 'after'

A **postgraduate** student is continuing his studies after taking a degree.
A **postmortem** examination is carried out on the body of someone who has died.

il-, *ir-*, *in-* and *im-* are four prefixes that mean 'not'

Illegal parking is not legal.
An **irregular** edge is not regular.
An **intolerant** person is not tolerant or understanding towards other people.
An **immature** person is not mature.

semi- means 'half', 'incomplete' or 'partial'. In some cases, it can also mean twice within a period of time.

A **semicircle** is half a circle.

A **semi-annual** event happens twice a year.

Suffixes

A *suffix* is a set of letters that can be attached to the end of a word. The suffixes *-ly* and *-ily* can be added to adjectives to make adverbs, like **desperately** and **angrily**.

-ist is a suffix that is very useful when you want to describe what somebody does or believes. It can be added to nouns to indicate a person associated with that noun:

A **pianist** is someone who plays the piano

An **artist** is someone who creates art

A **biologist** is someone who studies biology

A **Buddhist** is a person who follows the teachings of the Buddha

An **idealist** is someone who has high ideals.

-ish is a suffix that is often added to nouns to make them into adjectives.

Is your brother a fool? Then he is **foolish**.

Does your best friend have style? Then she's **stylish**.

Sometimes this suffix can also mean 'approximately' or 'somewhat', as when we say something is not exactly green, but **greenish**.

-ness is a suffix that indicates the state, condition or quality of something.

Redness is the state or quality of being red.

Sadness is the condition you experience when you are sad.

-tion and *-sion* are two suffixes that are often used to make verbs into nouns.

If you decide to do something, you make a **decision**.

If you react to a referee's decision, you have a **reaction**.

If you tense up, you experience **tension**.

Writing

Nobody is born knowing how to write, and the only way to get good at it is to practise. Here's a list of different kinds of documents you can create in your own writing:

- A letter to a friend or relative
- A description of a person or place
- A summary of what you did yesterday
- A short story
- A poem
- A report

> In Year 5 we outlined how we would write a report about Australia. What else could you write a report about?

Why not try some of the kinds of writing you haven't already tried?

Informative Writing

In informative writing, the author provides information about a person, place or thing. It can be a bit like writing a report and sometimes you will need to conduct research to understand a topic better. For instance, if you are writing an encyclopaedia entry or a non-fiction book, you might need to do some research first to make sure your facts are correct before sitting down to write.

Informative writing can also explain what something is or how it works. You may know already about the subject, so you will not have to research it. For example, you could write a letter to someone about the members of your family, or about your day. You could also write a magazine article about your town or city, or a guide for a tourist visiting it. These are different types of informational writing that use slightly different styles. If you go to your local library and look at a travel guide and some magazines, you will see that they are written in different styles. The travel guide will provide practical information about what to see and do, where to eat and sleep, and how to get around a place. A magazine article might focus on a few main highlights of things to do in a town or city and explain an experience the author had (for instance, finding the best ice cream shop in town). Informative writing usually presents unbiased information that is impartial and doesn't give the author's judgement about something.

Try writing your own informational piece. You could explain the rules of a game, write an encyclopaedia entry, draft a guide to your town or write a magazine article about local landmarks. Think about how you would use a slightly different style of writing for each of these.

Persuasive Writing

Persuasive writing is used to persuade, or convince, others of something. Therefore, it presents biased information that describes the author's beliefs or feelings. Examples of persuasive writing are a leaflet or flyer trying to persuade someone to come to an event, an advert for a business, a book review, a letter to someone influential or a speech to voters during an election. Can you draft a leaflet or a poster trying to persuade people to come to your school play or concert? What types of things would you say to convince them that it will be a good event that they should attend? What information would you leave out?

You could also write a letter to the newspaper to convince others about something you feel strongly about, or you could write and deliver a speech to an audience to convince them of your ideas. Here are some topics you could write about:

● Do you think school uniform should be compulsory?

● Are summer holidays too long?

● What would you do to improve something in your community?

For the first two questions, don't just write 'yes' or 'no'; you need to persuade others by saying why you believe what you believe. You can either write down your views, to be read by others, or you can write a speech that you could read in front of an audience. Try it! Did you convince them of your point?

Sayings and Phrases

In this section we introduce a handful of common sayings and phrases that can be difficult to understand if you have never heard them before. As you study these phrases, try to imagine a situation in which you might use each one.

Birthday suit

When you were born, you weren't wearing any clothes. When we say someone is wearing his or her 'birthday suit', we mean that person is naked.

Bite the hand that feeds you

An ill-tempered dog might bite his master, even though he depends on his master for food. When you harm someone who supports you, you are 'biting the hand that feeds you'.

Forty winks

To 'have forty winks' is to take a nap.

Chip on your shoulder

When someone has 'a chip on his shoulder', it means that he seems eager to pick a fight.

Count your blessings

People use this saying to mean 'be thankful for what you have'.

Eleventh hour

This phrase means 'at the last possible moment'.

Eureka!

People use this word when they have solved a problem. 'Eureka' is a Greek word that means: 'I've found it!' The Greek mathematician Archimedes was sitting in his bath when he realised that he could calculate the volume of the King's crown by measuring the water it displaced. He was so excited, he jumped out of the bath and ran through the town shouting: 'Eureka!'

Every cloud has a silver lining

Even bad things usually have a hidden good side.

Few and far between

Things that are 'few and far between' are rare or not easily available.

The grass is always greener on the other side of the hill

This saying is often used to console a person, who feels that what other people have is better than what she has. It points out that appearances can be deceiving.

Kill two birds with one stone

When you do one thing but manage to accomplish two goals, you are 'killing two birds with one stone'.

Lock, stock and barrel

The lock, the stock and the barrel were the essential parts of guns in earlier times. If you bought the whole gun, you would want the lock, the stock and the barrel. The phrase 'lock, stock and barrel' has come to mean 'the whole package' or 'every last bit'.

Make a mountain out of a molehill

When someone makes a big deal out of something that is not very important, we often say the person is 'making a mountain out of a molehill'.

A miss is as good as a mile

This saying reminds us that missing by a little bit is of no more use to you than missing by a whole lot.

It's never too late to mend

There is always time to improve yourself or change your ways.

Out of the frying pan and into the fire

This expression describes what happens when you go from a bad situation to an even worse one.

A penny saved is a penny earned

When you save money instead of spending it, it is almost the same as earning money, because you'll have extra cash instead of an empty pocket.

Read between the lines

When you 'read between the lines', you go beneath the surface of what someone says to find out what that person really means.

Sit on the fence

To 'sit on the fence' is to avoid taking sides in a debate or argument.

Steal his/her thunder

If you are planning on doing something that will impress other people, but another person does it first, that person is 'stealing your thunder'.

Take the bull by the horns

This phrase means to stop hesitating and take action.

Till the cows come home

Cows may sleep in their pastures and not come home to the barn until the very end of the day. When we say that something will go on 'till the cows come home', we mean that it will go on for a very long time.

Time heals all wounds

When people say 'time heals all wounds', they are usually talking about feelings. Sometimes after something bad happens, you feel better only when a lot of time passes.

Tom, Dick and Harry

If you invite 'every Tom, Dick and Harry' to a party it means you are inviting just about everyone, instead of choosing your guests carefully.

Vice versa

When people use this Latin term, they mean something is exactly the same but the other way round. 'He's angry with her, and vice versa' means both are angry with each other.

A watched pot never boils

When you wait anxiously for something to happen, it always seems to take longer.

Well begun is half done

If you start something off well, it will be easier to finish.

What will be will be

Some things are beyond our control, so there's no point in worrying about them.

Suggested Resources

Poetry

Revolting Rhymes by Roald Dahl (Jonathan Cape) 2012

Old Possum's Book of Practical Cats by T. S. Eliot (Faber) 2010

The Oxford Treasury of Classic Poems, edited by Michael Harrison and Christopher Stuart-Clark (Oxford) 2011

Because a Fire Was In My Head: 101 Poems, edited by Michael Morpurgo (Faber) 2013

Classic Poetry: An Illustrated Collection, selected by Michael Rosen (Walker) 2009

Stories

King of Shadows by Susan Cooper (Red Fox) 2010. A young actor appearing in *A Midsummer Night's Dream* travels back in time to the Globe Theatre in 1599 where he meets Shakespeare.

Arthur, High King of Britain by Michael Morpurgo (Egmont) 2013

The Once and Future King by T. H. White (Harper Voyager) 1996

Learning About Language

Oxford Primary Grammar, Punctuation and Spelling Dictionary (Oxford University Press) 2013

Oxford Junior Illustrated Dictionary (Oxford University Press) 2011

Improve Your Grammar by Rachel Bladon (Usborne) 2000

Usborne Guide to Better English: Grammar, Spelling and Punctuation by Robyn Gee and Carol Watson (Usborne) 2004

Junior Dictionary and Thesaurus by Cindy Leaney and Susan Purcell (Miles Kelly) 2011

Perfect Pop-Up Punctuation Book by Kate Petty and Jenny Maizels (Bodley Head) 2006

Grammar: You Can Do It! by Andy Seed and Roger Hurn (Hodder) 2011

The Butterfly Grammar by Irina Tyk (Civitas) 2008

Films & DVDs

Camelot, directed by Joshua Logan (Warner Home Video) 1967; 2006, U. Musical based on T. H. White's *The Once and Future King.*

Cats by Andrew Lloyd Webber (Universal) 1998. Musical based on T. S. Eliot's *Old Possum's Book of Practical Cats.*

Man of La Mancha, directed by Arthur Hiller (Twentieth Century Fox) 1972; 2005, PG. Musical version of *Don Quixote.*

Oliver Twist, directed by David Lean (Carlton) 1948; 2008, U. The classic film adaptation of Dickens's novel.

The Sword in the Stone, directed by Wolfgang Reitherman (Walt Disney) 1963; 2008, U. Disney cartoon based on T. H. White's *The Once and Future King.*

Shakespeare in Performance

Shakespeare's Globe, on London's South Bank, and the Royal Shakespeare Company, in Stratford-upon-Avon, both offer a range of educational activities to make Shakespeare's plays accessible to young people. See www.shakespearesglobe.com/education/ and www.rsc.org.uk/education/

History and Geography

Introduction

This chapter covers geography, world history and British history. Geography has been described as the study of what's where, why it's there and why we should care. It looks at how humans are challenged by, adapt to, use and change the natural environments in which they live. By Year 6, students should know the rudiments of world and British geography. They should be able to read and colour maps, and make simple maps of their own. They can be shown maps of their own town and county and be invited to study maps during field trips and family holidays. As their skills develop, they can be allowed to navigate on car journeys or to find their way around a city using a map. Our study of regions of the British Isles that began in Year 4 continues in Year 6 with Scotland, Wales, the North East and the North West of England.

The world history and geography topics for Year 6 build on those introduced in Year 5. In Year 5, students studied early American history including the Revolutionary War, American independence and the slave trade. In Year 6, they learn about the American Civil War and the geography of the United States of America, Canada and the countries of Central and South America. British history covers the period of the Industrial Revolution of the late eighteenth century through the Victorian era of the nineteenth century, including the many social and political reforms made at that time. Our approach to history is chronological and narrative: we have tried to show how the events of one era have led to those of the next. In the case of British history, it is particularly important for children to grasp the sequence of events that contributed to the industrial revolution and the growth of the British economy during the nineteenth century, together with the creation of the largest empire the world has ever known, the empire 'on which the sun never set'.

Parents and teachers are encouraged to build on the foundation provided here by discussing history with children; by visiting historic houses, monuments and sites; by visiting museums and galleries; and by seeking out additional resources, including the many excellent TV programmes on historical subjects which are often also available on DVD. There are many good books, DVDs and online resources suitable for Year 6, listed at the end of this chapter.

World Geography

Arctic and Antarctic

Geographers use latitude to divide the earth into bands that run parallel to the equator. These bands tell us a lot about the climate of those regions. The further from the equator in either direction, the colder the climate tends to be.

Far to the north, at about 67° N latitude, there is an imaginary boundary called the *Arctic Circle*. Why 67°? The earth tilts 23° on its axis. Above 67° there will be at least one

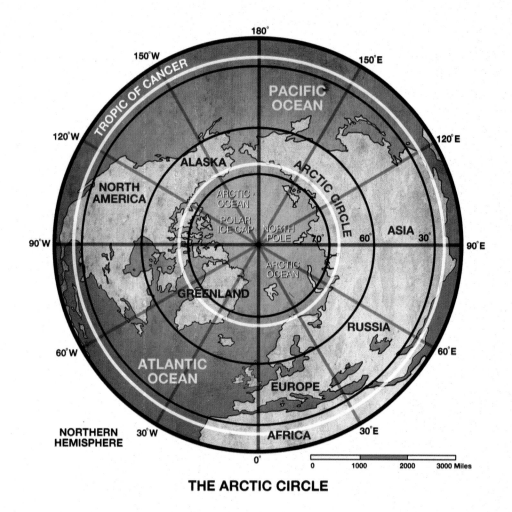

THE ARCTIC CIRCLE

day in summer when the sun does not set and one day in winter when it does not rise. The closer to the pole, the more such days there will be.

The lands and waters north of the Arctic Circle are called the Arctic Region. You can see the lands inside the Arctic Circle as if you are looking from above the North Pole on the map opposite. Notice that these lands form a ring around the Arctic Ocean. Much of this ocean is frozen in a thick pack of ice called the polar ice cap.

In the Southern Hemisphere, there is another imaginary circle called the *Antarctic Circle*, located at about 67° latitude. The Antarctic climate is even colder than that of the Arctic. Most of Antarctica is buried under a permanent ice cap sometimes as much as three miles thick! This southern polar ice cap contains more fresh water than all the world's streams, rivers, lakes and clouds put together.

23° from the equator are the tropics. The Tropic of Cancer is in the northern hemisphere and the Tropic of Capricorn is in the south. Between the tropics, the sun can pass directly overhead at midday.

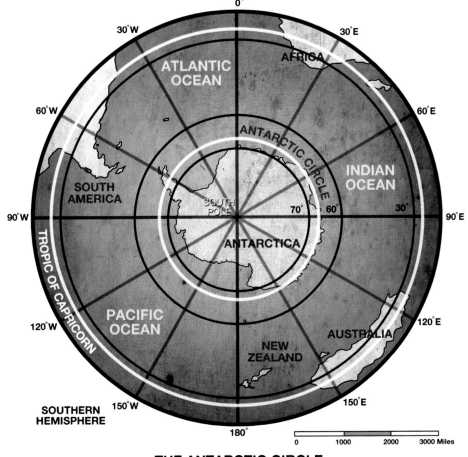

THE ANTARCTIC CIRCLE

Longitude and Time Zones

Longitude is connected with time of day. As Earth rotates (spins) on its axis, different parts of Earth point towards the sun. Only half of Earth faces the sun at any given time. That half experiences daytime, while the other half experiences night-time. When it's noon at the prime meridian, it is midnight at the 180° meridian on the other side of Earth.

Suppose you are following a cricket match in Australia, played in Brisbane. They start playing at 11 AM but they are a long way east of Greenwich, by about 150°. As the earth spins, the sun appears to travel 15° across the sky in an hour, so 11 AM in Brisbane is ten hours earlier than 11 AM in the UK. The first ball will be at 1 AM Greenwich Mean Time (GMT). You might prefer to wake up early and hear the evening session. What time will that start in Britain if it is 4 PM there?

Just as the prime meridian is the reference point from which distance east and west is measured, it is also the reference point for measuring time. Using the prime meridian as the starting point, we could divide the world into 24 hourly time zones, to match the 24-hour cycle of Earth's rotation on its axis. In fact, countries do not always set their clocks by the sun. Many countries use daylight saving schemes which involve putting the clock forward or back at certain times of the year to get lighter mornings in the winter, or longer evenings in the summer. Sometimes countries that trade with each other find it easier if they are all on the same time, even if they might really be in different time zones.

Find the 180° meridian on the Time Zones map on the next page. This line is halfway around the world from the prime meridian. Now look at the sometimes zig-zagging line that generally follows the 180° meridian: this is called the international date line. If you cross the date line going east, Monday becomes Sunday. If you cross it going west, Sunday becomes Monday.

Round Earth, Flat Map

Have you ever compared a globe and a flat map, noting the differences in size of the world's landmasses? If you do, you will notice that some landmasses seem larger on the flat map than on the globe. For example, the island of Iceland looks very large on some maps. Sometimes it looks larger than Italy. But in fact, Italy is about three times the size of Iceland. What's going on?

These differences in size result from distortions that occur when mapmakers represent our round Earth on a flat piece of paper. Here's one way to understand this: take a large

World Time Zones

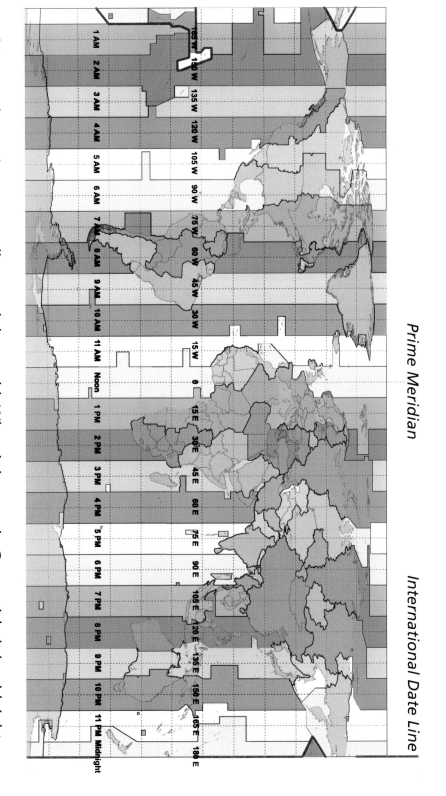

Prime Meridian

International Date Line

This map shows time zones all around the world. When it is noon in Greenwich, it is midnight in New Zealand according to the sun and the stars. Can you see the international date line where today becomes tomorrow – or yesterday?

1 AM · 2 AM · 3 AM · 4 AM · 5 AM · 6 AM · 7 AM · 8 AM · 9 AM · 10 AM · 11 AM · Noon · 1 PM · 2 PM · 3 PM · 4 PM · 5 PM · 6 PM · 7 PM · 8 PM · 9 PM · 10 PM · 11 PM Midnight

165 W · 150 W · 135 W · 120 W · 105 W · 90 W · 75 W · 60 W · 45 W · 30 W · 15 W · 0 · 15 E · 30 E · 45 E · 60 E · 75 E · 90 E · 105 E · 120 E · 135 E · 150 E · 165 E · 180 E

sheet of paper and wrap it around the globe so that the paper touches the globe along the equator. The paper forms a tube or cylinder that does not touch the globe at the poles. Now, pretend your globe is hollow and made of clear plastic. On the plastic are opaque outlines of the world's landmasses. If you put an electric light in the middle of this hollow, clear globe, the light would cast the shadows of the globe's features onto the tube. Where the paper fits fairly closely to the globe, the sizes and the shapes of the shadows would be accurate. However, where the paper is far away from the globe, there will be some distortion.

Think in particular about how areas near the poles are represented on the globe and the tube. On the globe all the lines of longitude meet in a single point at the pole, but on the paper tube the lines of longitude are stretched apart to look vertical and parallel. That's why Greenland, Iceland and Scandinavia look so big on many flat maps.

Mapmakers are known as *cartographers*. They use the mathematics that go along with simple geometric shapes – such as the sphere, cylinder, cone, or plane – to draw maps on flat pieces of paper. Different kinds of maps are called 'projections'.

On what part of the cylinder will the shadows cast by the light most accurately represent the globe's features? Where will there be the most distortion?

The Mercator Projection

The Flemish cartographer Gerardus Mercator was the first to project Earth's surface onto a flat map. Made in the 1500s, his is still the best-known map projection of the world. Mercator's projection was made onto a cylinder like the one in the description above.

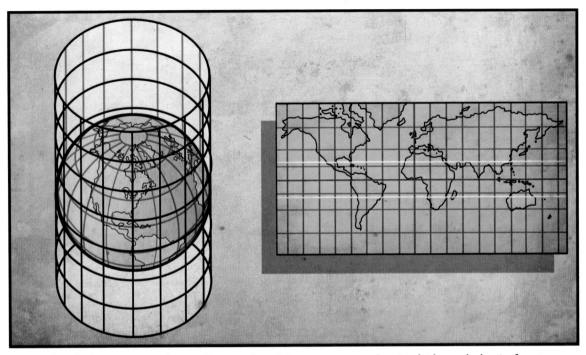

On the left you see how Gerardus Mercator projected the globe's features onto a cylinder. On the right, a finished Mercator projection map laid out flat.

Generally speaking, you can trust the Mercator projection for the area between the Tropics of Cancer and Capricorn. Direction on Mercator's map is also accurate, so the map is helpful in ship navigation. However, the Mercator projection makes landmasses near the poles look larger than they are. Thus, Greenland looks larger than Australia on the Mercator projection shown above, when in fact Australia is much larger.

Conic and Plane Projection

If you twisted a piece of paper into the shape of a cone and put it over a part of a globe, you would end up with a conic projection. This projection is most accurate where the cone touches the sides of the globe. As you move away from places where the cone touches the paper, however, distortion increases, so conic projections are rarely used for world maps. Instead, they focus on smaller parts of the globe, such as single countries.

If you put a flat piece of paper against the globe, it would touch the globe at one point only, like the polar projection in the diagram overleaf. This method is called plane projection. Maps of this sort are accurate only in the centre, near where the plane touches the globe.

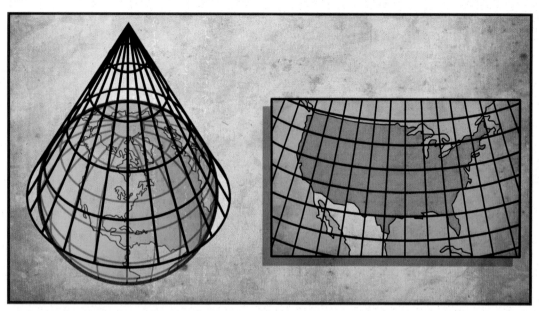

Look back at the diagram of the Mercator projection map. Notice that the meridians and parallels on that map run vertically and horizontally. Compare that to the conic projection maps here and on page 109. How are the maps different? How are they similar?

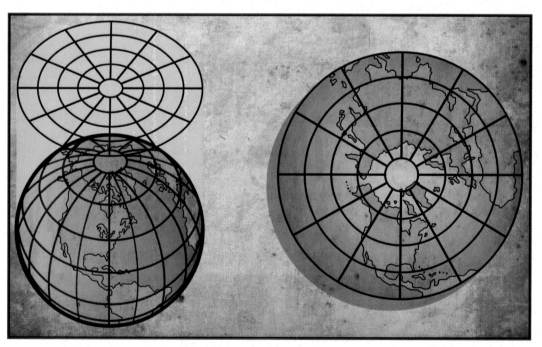

Would this polar projection be your first choice if you wanted to learn about the geography of Africa? Why or why not?

British Geography

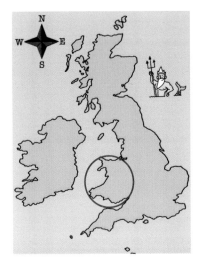

Let's Explore Wales

Wales is bordered to the east by England; its other borders are all with stretches of water – the Irish Sea, the Celtic Sea and the Bristol Channel.

When the Romans left Britain in the fifth century, Wales was an independent kingdom until it was conquered by Edward I. Apart from a short time of independence in the fifteenth century, Wales has been ruled by the English monarch ever since. Edward I built a series of castles around Wales to make sure that the Welsh did not rebel against English rule. One of the largest of

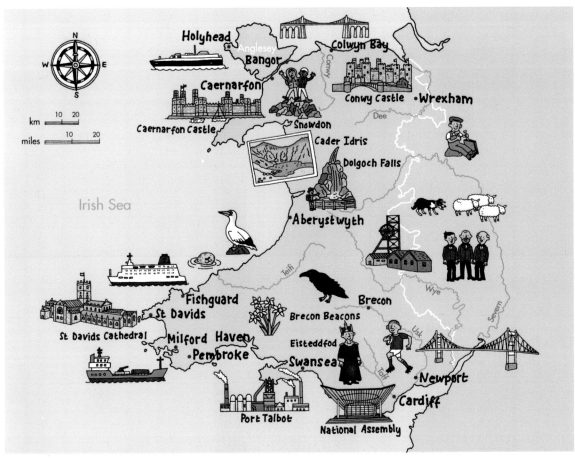

these.was Caernarfon Castle, where Edward's son was born. He was also called Edward and succeeded his father as Edward II. When he was a teenager, Edward II was given the title 'Prince of Wales' by his father, to create a link between the Welsh and the English people. Ever since then, the oldest son of the monarch has held the title of Prince of Wales. Prince Charles, the present Prince of Wales, was *invested* (meaning he was presented with the official title) at Caernarfon Castle in 1969.

Caernarfon Castle

Wales is one of the four countries that make up the United Kingdom. The other three are Scotland, England and Northern Ireland. As part of the United Kingdom, Wales is governed by laws passed by the Houses of Parliament in Westminster, but Parliament has devolved, or transferred, certain powers to the Welsh Assembly in Cardiff. This means that Welsh people can vote for people to represent them in the Assembly where they make their own decisions about some things.

What Language is Spoken in Wales?

Wales is a *bilingual* country. This means that there are two official languages: English and Welsh. All of the signs that you see in public places are in both languages. If you went to school in Wales, you would learn Welsh and might even have some of your lessons in Welsh.

The Welsh language sounds very different from English and has some very long words.

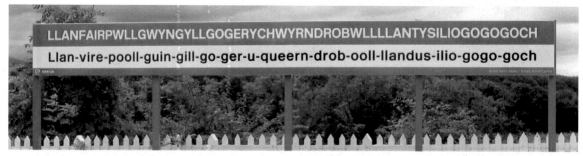

This railway station has the longest name in Britain, and perhaps the world!

Llanfairpwllgwyngyllgogerychwyrndrobwllllantysiliogogogoch, a town which has the longest place name in Britain, is perhaps the most famous! The name means: *Saint Mary's Church in the hollow of the white hazel near the rapid whirlpool and St Tysilio's Church of the red cave.* In one place name you get two churches and two colours, one tree, a hollow, a cave and a whirlpool!

The Land of Song

Music is so important to Welsh people that Wales is known as the 'land of song'. Welsh choirs are famous for their magnificent voices and Wales has produced many famous singers who perform everything from opera to popular music. Rugby is also an important part of Welsh culture, and

You can find another rugby song to sing on page 200.

fans of the sport often sing songs at rugby matches. English people might recognise the tune 'Cwm Rhondda', which is known as the hymn 'Guide me O Thou great Redeemer', but the favourite Welsh rugby song is 'Calon Lân'. Here it is in Welsh and English:

Nid wy'n gofyn bywyd moethus,
Aur y byd na'i berlau mân:
Gofyn wyf am galon hapus,
Calon onest, calon lân.

Not for me, the life of grandeur.
Gold and pearls have no appeal.
But a heart of joy and candour,
And a heart, sincere and real.

Chorus
Calon lân yn llawn daioni,
Tecach yw na'r lili dlôs:
Dim ond calon lân all ganu
Canu'r dydd a chanu'r nos.

Chorus
Hearts of pure and loving kindness
Like the fairest lily known.
They can sing, sincere and guileless,
Dawn till dusk and dusk till dawn.

A new bard is chosen at the National Eisteddfod.

Wales holds special arts festivals called Eisteddfods [aye-STED-fods] where people enter competitions in which they perform poetry, play music or sing, all in Welsh. The winners of the competitions are called *bards*. The biggest festival is the National Eisteddfod, held every year at the beginning of August. There are eight days of competitions and it takes place in a different town each year. If you entered an Eisteddfod, what would you like to perform?

77

Mountains and Rivers

What is the landscape like in Wales?

Wales is a mountainous country. Its highest mountains are in Snowdonia, a region in the North West, and the highest of these is Mount Snowdon, at 1,085 metres high. Snowdonia is the third largest National Park in Britain and many people go there every year to enjoy its spectacular scenery. The Brecon Beacons are a ridge of high hills in the South and this area is also a National Park. Further west are the imposing Black Mountains and the steep cliffs of the Pembrokeshire Coast. It is a good area to visit if you want to see unusual wildlife, such as seals, gannets and ravens. It is difficult growing crops on steep hills so farmers choose to keep sheep instead. The sheep like to eat the grass on the hills and farmers use sheepdogs to round up the sheep for them. They hold sheepdog trials, which are competitions to see which dogs do the best job.

The only flat part of Wales is the island of Anglesey. Its biggest town is Holyhead, where you can take a ferry across the Irish Sea to Dublin.

Rain falls abundantly on the mountains in Wales, and runs into lakes, rivers and waterfalls. The biggest rivers in Wales are the Wye, the Severn and the Dee. They flow eastward, so a lot of Welsh water flows into English rivers.

The Industrial Revolution in Wales

The Industrial Revolution made a big difference to the work that Welsh people did. It created a demand for coal to power all the machinery, and large seams of high-quality coal were found under the ground in South Wales. This coal was needed to fire the furnaces that were used in creating metals like steel. Huge coalmines were dug to mine the coal and many people worked there. A large steel industry developed in South Wales, because there was lots of coal available for the furnaces. Port Talbot became an important centre for steel-making. Because of the mining, the steel-works and other industrial activities, great cities grew up in South Wales like Newport, Swansea and Cardiff, the capital city. These are still the biggest cities in Wales. Today there is less coal-mining and steel-making, but large tankers bring oil to Milford Haven where it is refined into petrol. *Light industry*, like working in offices and public services, is now more important than *heavy industry*, which is the name people give to the traditional industrial processes like steel-making. Tourism is also now important and brings money to the country. Many people like to visit the castles built by the Normans, Edward I and others to stop the Welsh from rebelling against English rule!

In the north of the country, the rocks are different to those in the south, and there was less industrial development. The mountains of Snowdonia are made of slate, which can split

A slate quarry

into large, flat sheets. Welsh slate makes very good tiles to cover roofs, as well as worktops, flooring and gravestones. In the last part of the nineteenth century the slate industry was very important in north Wales, which had the largest slate quarries in the world.

The smallest city in Britain is St Davids in south-west Wales. The country's patron saint is buried in the cathedral there.

Now you have read about Wales, can you answer these questions?

What lies across the borders of Wales to the north, south, east and west?

What would you see if you visited the Brecon Beacons?

How does Welsh water end up in English rivers?

How did the Industrial Revolution change Wales?

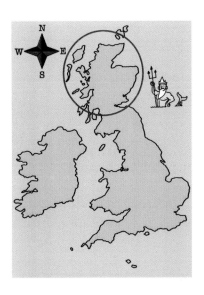

Let's Explore Scotland

For hundreds of years, Scotland was an independent country with its own king. Then, in 1603, Queen Elizabeth I of England died without leaving

We learnt about the Act of Union in Year 5.

any heirs to the throne. James VI of Scotland was asked if he would like to be king of England as well, so he became James I of England. Although he was king of both England and Scotland, they were still separate kingdoms. Then, in 1707, the Act of Union was passed, joining Scotland and England together to make the Kingdom of Great Britain.

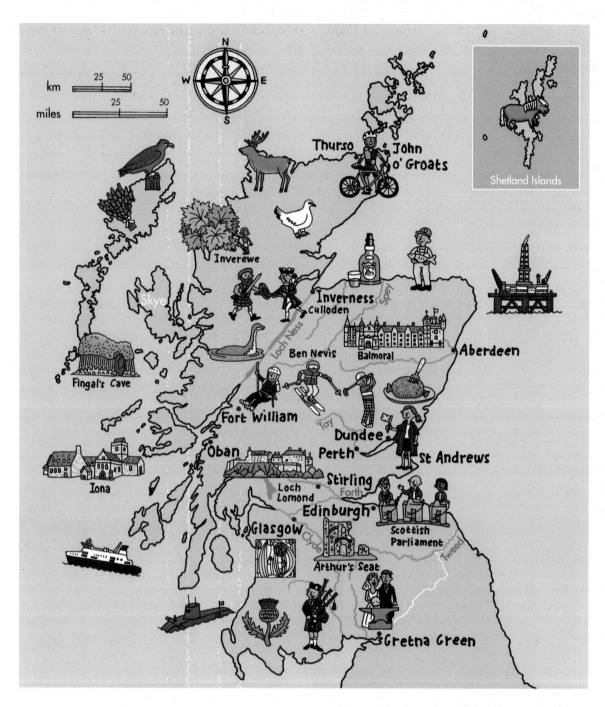

Like Wales, Scotland is now one of the four countries that make up the United Kingdom, and, also like Wales, it has had some powers devolved to it by the British Parliament in Westminster. Since 1999, people in Scotland have been able to vote for

Members of the Scottish Parliament (MSPs) to represent them in Edinburgh and pass laws on some things related to their own country.

Scotland lies in the northern part of the British Isles. It has a border with England to the south, the North Sea to the east, the Atlantic Ocean to the North and the Irish Sea to the south-west. As well as the mainland, Scotland has nearly 800 islands.

Can you see John O' Groats, at the very northern tip of Scotland on the map? Because it is so far north, it has become popular with people who do sponsored walks and cycle-rides for charity. They often start or finish at Land's End on the very south-western tip of England, so the expression 'from John O' Groats to Land's End' has come to mean 'from one end of Britain to the other'.

Highlands and Islands

Beyond John O' Groats are two groups of islands: the Orkneys and Shetlands. They were once ruled by Vikings from Scandinavia, on the other side of the North Sea. Shetland, famous for its breed of small, long-maned ponies, is so far north that it is usually put on a small extra map, inset in one corner (just like we have done!). If you went there in summer, it would hardly get dark, even at midnight. In winter, daylight only lasts for a few hours. Can you use a globe to explain why?

Off the west coast, you can see two groups of islands that are called the Inner Hebrides and the Outer Hebrides. The largest island of the Inner Hebrides is Skye, where Bonnie Prince Charlie fled with Flora MacDonald after his defeat at the Battle of Culloden in 1746. Now it has a bridge to the mainland, but Bonnie Prince Charlie had to travel by boat.

A Shetland pony

We sang 'The Skye Boat Song' in Year 5.

The island of Staffa has a cave formed out of volcanic rock columns, called Fingal's Cave. It is made from rocks that look like those of the Giant's Causeway in Northern Ireland. Some people say that this was the other end of the causeway built by Finn MacCool to link Ireland and Scotland.

Fingal's Cave

Another island in the Inner Hebrides is Iona. It is tiny, but many people regard it as a special and holy place. St Columba founded a community of monks there in the sixth century, and people still like to visit the Iona Abbey to take time from their busy lives to think about things.

We read about Finn MacCool and the giant Benandonner in Year 4.

Further out in the Atlantic Ocean are the Outer Hebrides. They have a very low population density, which means that a small number of people live in a large area. In 1831 some chess pieces were discovered on a beach on the Isle of Lewis in the Outer Hebrides. The chess pieces are very old, probably from around 1200, and are made from walrus ivory and whale tooth. They were probably made in Norway and may have been buried by a traveller from Scandinavia. You can see these at the British Museum in London and at the National Museum in Edinburgh.

These chess pieces are about 800 years old.

Highlands and Lowlands

Scotland is a country with many mountains, including the Grampians. Ben Nevis, the tallest mountain in the British Isles at 1,344 metres, is part of the Grampian range. The mountainous area of Scotland, in the North West of the country, is known as the Highlands.

Big birds of prey, like ospreys and golden eagles, live wild in Scotland.

Most of the large towns in Scotland are in the Lowlands, because life in the Highlands was always hard, so not many people can live there. The Highlands has one of the lowest population densities in Europe. Farming is difficult in mountainous areas, and people have struggled to produce enough food locally to live on. Fishing and weaving have been important through the centuries. There are many ancient trackways (routes) between the Lowlands and the Highlands, the best known ones being Causey Mounth and Elsick Mounth.

Highlanders, the name given to people living in the Scottish Highlands, developed their own unique way of life. They lived as members of clans, led by clan chieftains. Every clan had its own tartan pattern, so people could tell which clan you were from by looking at the tartan.

Cities and Towns of Scotland

Edinburgh is the capital city of Scotland, and the second largest city in the country. Edinburgh is in the Lowlands in the South, although there are still hills and even a large outcrop of volcanic rock, right in the middle of the town. It is called Castle Rock because Edinburgh Castle stands on the top of it.

Edinburgh Castle

Edinburgh has many beautiful buildings laid out in wide streets and squares, some of them designed by the famous Scottish architect Robert Adam. Princes Street is one of the most popular shopping streets in the country. Edinburgh is home to the largest annual arts festival in the world: the Edinburgh Festival, which takes place in August and involves hundreds of plays, concerts, operas, dance events and exhibitions. It is also home to Holyrood Palace, the official residence of the Queen when she is in Scotland. It faces Edinburgh Castle down a long street called the Royal Mile that is lined with important and historic buildings. The new Scottish Parliament building is beside Holyrood Palace on the Royal Mile.

Outside Edinburgh, there are other Lowland cities, such as Stirling, the ancient capital, and St Andrews, known both for its university and its golf course beside the sea.

Glasgow is Scotland's biggest city. It lies in the west of the Lowlands beside the river Clyde. It grew from being a small settlement to being one of the largest seaports in the world, from which many ships left for America and the West Indies. Glasgow became famous for its shipbuilding, as well as other industries. During the Victorian period, Glasgow was called 'the second city of the Empire' – after London.

The third largest city in Scotland is Aberdeen. Aberdeen has always been famous for its granite – a very hard stone that is ideal for buildings in cities, where there is a lot of pollution. It was used to build the Houses of Parliament in London. Aberdeen's traditional industries were fishing and weaving, but in the 1970s oil was discovered in the North Sea. Aberdeen became the centre of the European petroleum industry and is known as the oil capital of Europe. Huge oil rigs were constructed in the North Sea where people have to live for weeks at a time, drilling for oil. Aberdeen has the largest heliport in the world to carry them there and back by helicopter.

Scotland is famous for producing whisky, a very strong alcoholic drink which is made in *distilleries*. There are many of these distilleries around the river Spey.

In the south of Scotland, very close to the border with England, is a village called Gretna Green, which is famous as a place where people go to get married. This is because in the eighteenth century it was not possible for people under 21 to get married in England if their parents objected. As a result, young couples started running away from home to get married in Scotland, where the law was different. The first village they came to, as their stage coach crossed the border, was Gretna Green. Scottish

Many people still travel to Gretna Green to be married at the anvil.

law did not even require that marriages should be performed by ministers of religion, as long as there were witnesses, so a lot of people got married in the blacksmith's shop. The blacksmith performed the ceremony over his anvil, so the Gretna Green anvil has come to symbolise marriages that people enter into in places where they don't live. In spite of the fact that marriage laws have changed in both England and Scotland, Gretna Green is still a very popular place to get married.

What Languages do People Speak?

Scotland has three languages: English, Scots and Scots Gaelic. Scots Gaelic is a Celtic language that originally came from Ireland. Only a small number of Scottish people can still speak it, and they mainly live in the Outer Hebrides and the Highlands. The Scots language is more like English. The most famous poet to write in Scots was Robert (or Robbie or Rabbie) Burns, who lived from 1759 to 1796. Like other poems, songs and stories that are written in a dialect (for example 'On Ilkley Moor Baht 'At' in Year 4 and 'Blaydon Races' on page 202), you can usually understand them if you say the words out loud. Here is the first verse of a poem that Burns wrote when he saw a nest of mice which had been disturbed by a plough:

To a Mouse, on Turning Her Up in Her Nest with the Plough

Wee, sleekit, cow'rin, tim'rous beastie,
O, what a panic's in thy breastie!
Thou need na start awa sae hasty
Wi' bickering brattle!
I wad be laith to rin an' chase thee,
Wi' murd'ring pattle.

Can you say the words out loud and work out what they are? It may be a little tricky but the picture will help!

Burns is sometimes described as the national poet of Scotland and Scottish people like to gather together to celebrate Burns Night on his birthday, 25 January, wherever they are in the world. Some people say that Robert Burns wrote the famous song 'Auld Lang Syne' that is sung on the stroke of midnight on New Year's Eve, or Hogmanay as it is called in Scotland, but Burns said he only wrote down a song that he heard an old man singing.

Other famous Scottish writers include Robert Louis Stevenson, the author of popular adventure stories for young readers like *Treasure Island* (that we looked at in Year 5) and

J. M. Barrie, who created the magical character of Peter Pan. Carol Ann Duffy's poems are widely read in schools, and she is the first Scot to be appointed as Poet Laureate by the Queen.

Beware of the Monster!

The valleys between the mountains in Scotland are called glens. These glens contain large lakes, called lochs, some of which are open to the sea, and therefore have salt water, and some of which are filled by rainfall, which is fresh water. Saltwater lochs and freshwater lochs have different wildlife, but rumour has it that there is a very strange creature indeed in one particular loch – Nessie, the Loch Ness Monster! Some people have photographed and filmed a mysterious long thin object rising above the surface of the loch, and there is a legend that a dinosaur surviving from prehistoric times is living at the bottom of the lake. It may be just an old tree floating up from the bottom but they like to think it is a monster. Do you think they could be right?

Now you have read about Scotland, can you answer these questions?

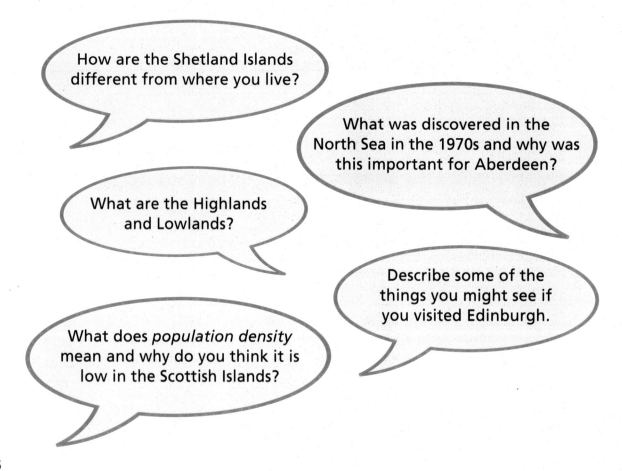

How are the Shetland Islands different from where you live?

What was discovered in the North Sea in the 1970s and why was this important for Aberdeen?

What are the Highlands and Lowlands?

Describe some of the things you might see if you visited Edinburgh.

What does *population density* mean and why do you think it is low in the Scottish Islands?

Let's Explore the North West

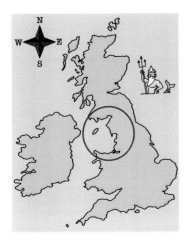

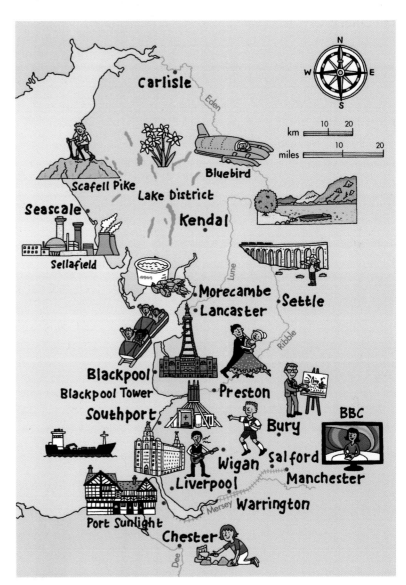

The counties of Lancashire and Cumbria form the North West of England.

West of the Pennines and north of the River Dee, the North West of England has two big cities and an outstanding area of countryside. Liverpool and Manchester are centres of much of the area's employment and culture. The Lake District has England's highest mountain, deepest lakes and some of its most beautiful views.

How the Lakes Were Made

The spectacular scenery of the Lake District was created by the movement of glaciers in the ice age, hundreds of millions of years ago. When the ice age was coming to an end, glaciers, which were enormous blocks of ice, began to melt slowly and to slide between mountains. The glaciers were so large and heavy that they carved out deep valleys with long, narrow lakes in the bottom. Unlike liquid water, glaciers cannot easily go around corners. Where a river might change course to go around a protruding rock, a glacier may eventually bulldoze through it. Glaciers move so slowly that you can't see the movement, but all that frozen water is heavy and can push its way through anything! The mountains there have sharp ridges where two glaciers started off in different directions, one on each side. The largest lakes are Ullswater, Windermere and Derwentwater. Windermere is England's longest lake; Wastwater is the deepest.

Can you see the way in which glaciers have carved valleys in this landscape, leaving a sharp peak?

In 1967 Donald Campbell tried to break the water speed record with his boat Bluebird on Coniston Water. He was trying to travel at 300 miles per hour, but the boat crashed and he died.

The Lake District is very popular with people who enjoy going for long walks in beautiful countryside. The highest mountain in England is Scafell Pike, which is 978 metres high.

Writers in the Lake District

For hundreds of years, people found the idea of wild nature quite frightening. They didn't want to explore the wilderness! That changed in the eighteenth century, at the beginning of what was called the Romantic Movement. People started to think that scenes of nature could inspire people who looked at them with noble thoughts and a love of beauty.

They began to write about their thoughts and the feelings they had when they were exploring this beautiful landscape. One of the most influential was the poet William Wordsworth. He went to live in the Lake District and he wrote many poems which helped people to appreciate the unique beauty of the place. One of his most famous poems is called 'Daffodils', and it begins like this:

> *I wander'd lonely as a cloud*
> *That floats on high o'er vales and hills,*
> *When all at once I saw a crowd,*
> *A host of golden daffodils,*
> *Beside the lake, beneath the trees*
> *Fluttering and dancing in the breeze.*

You can visit Dove Cottage in Grasmere where the poet William Wordsworth lived.

What do you imagine when you hear these words? Other poets went to live in the Lake District so that they could be inspired by its beauty, and they became known as the Lake Poets.

In 1810 Wordsworth published *A Guide to the Lakes*, encouraging people to visit the Lake District and to preserve it. He described it as: 'a sort of national property, in which every man has a right and an interest who has an eye to perceive and a heart to enjoy'. Other people agreed with him, and in 1951 the whole area was created The Lake District National Park. This means that all development is very strictly controlled so that people in years to come will be able to enjoy the beautiful landscape.

Many other writers have been inspired by the Lake District, especially those who worried about the effect that the Industrial Revolution was having on Britain. John Ruskin, who lived in a house on the edge of Coniston Water, encouraged people to appreciate the beauty of nature and not to allow factories and railways to cover the whole country. In the twentieth century, Arthur Ransome wrote *Swallows and Amazons*, about a group of children who have adventures while sailing their boats on the lakes. Beatrix Potter wrote about Peter Rabbit, Jemima Puddleduck, Jeremy Fisher and other animal characters while she lived at Hilltop Farm in Near Sawrey, which you can still visit.

Beatrix Potter lived at Hilltop Farm in the Lake District.

How did Liverpool and Manchester become cities?

About 100 miles south of the Lake District are the cities of Liverpool and Manchester. Both grew large and wealthy as a result of the Industrial Revolution. Manchester became the centre of the cotton industry and was known as Cottonopolis. Liverpool stands at the mouth of the River Mersey and had always been an important port, with ships sailing to and from America, Ireland and Europe, but the volume of manufactured goods produced in factories in the north of England during the Industrial Revolution made the port much bigger and busier. By the early part of the nineteenth century, it is estimated that 40 per cent of world trade went through Liverpool. On page 133 you can read about the railway that was opened between Manchester and Liverpool in 1830.

Like other industrial cities, Liverpool and Manchester grew very quickly in the early part of the nineteenth century, as thousands of people moved from the countryside into the towns to work in factories. The conditions under which these people lived were often very bad. Some factory owners began to think that their workers deserved something better, and they built 'model villages'. One of the most successful of these was Port Sunlight, to the south-west of Liverpool. It was created by William Lever, who made his fortune by manufacturing soap. He bought some land in Cheshire, south of the River Mersey, and moved his factory there from Warrington. He built hundreds of pleasant houses with gardens and open spaces, as well as community buildings such as schools, a hospital, a theatre, swimming pool and art gallery. The buildings were designed in an old-fashioned style to remind people of the days before the Industrial Revolution, when employers and employees were more friendly with each other. The new development was called Port Sunlight, after the company's most successful soap.

These lovely houses were built for people working in the Lever Brothers soap factory.

Where did people go on holiday?

In the nineteenth century, factories and mills in Lancashire would close for one week in the year in order for the machinery to be thoroughly cleaned. The workers got time off, although they weren't paid whilst the factories were shut. Many people decided to use this time off to go on holiday. The building of the railways allowed them to travel easily to different places for their holidays, and many people enjoyed going to the seaside. Don't forget, people at that time could not jump on an aeroplane and fly off on holiday. People who lived in the North West were able to travel to Southport, which has flat sandy beaches, or to Morecambe, with its famous bay full of shellfish, especially shrimps. However, the most famous seaside town of all is Blackpool, which grew in the nineteenth century from being a small resort where wealthy people went to bathe to being the biggest seaside resort in the country, accommodating thousands of factory

The Blackpool Illuminations contain so many bulbs they turn the seafront into 'The Golden Mile'.

workers on their holidays every year. It had a promenade, which is a walkway along the seafront, three piers reaching out into the sea, a ballroom, a funfair, a circus and the biggest opera house outside London. In 1879 Blackpool became the first town in the world to have electric street lighting, and this led to the famous Blackpool *illuminations*: a series of huge, illuminated displays along seven miles of seafront. People would visit Blackpool for the beach in the summer, but also to see the lights when the weather was colder. A tramway was built all along the seafront to let people see the lights. You can still ride on it today: it is the oldest surviving tramway in the country.

Blackpool has seen many changes in the last 50 years as people started to go abroad for their holidays. Manchester and Liverpool have changed over time too. *Heavy industry*, which means work in places like mines, factories and shipyards, has been in decline ever since the last part of the twentieth century. As factories and mines have closed, people have had to find work in areas such as health care, education, communications, tourism, technology, banking and insurance. These are known as *light industry.*

Entertainment and the arts are important in both cities. In the 1960s a famous band called the Beatles were performing at the Cavern Club in Liverpool. At the time, most pop music came from America, but the Beatles became the most successful group in the world, and paved the way for more British singers and groups. Because so many of them came from Liverpool, this musical revolution was known as the Mersey Sound, after the River Mersey. The Tate Gallery in London opened another gallery, the Tate Liverpool, in the restored Albert Dock in 1998 to display works of art from its collection. In 2008, Liverpool was the European Capital of Culture. Tourism is now one of the most important industries in the city.

The Albert Dock in Liverpool was named after Prince Albert, the husband of Queen Victoria, who opened it in 1846. For many years it received precious cargoes of silks, cotton, tea, tobacco and sugar from countries as far apart as America and China. Now you can see paintings hanging in the Tate Gallery there.

The people of Manchester, who are called Mancunians, have also had to change the sort of work they do as heavy industry has declined. Manchester is a busy modern city where people work in engineering, scientific research, education and communications. The BBC has moved a lot of its staff and programmes to a site on the Manchester Ship Canal in Salford called MediaCityUK. Manchester United is one of the most famous football teams supported by people from around the world.

Use your knowledge of the North West of England to answer these questions:

Which counties form the North West of England?

Why did the cities of Liverpool and Manchester grow in the early part of the nineteenth century?

Which area of the North West has England's highest mountain?

What is Port Sunlight and why was it built?

What are glaciers and how have they shaped the landscape in the Lake District?

Where did factory workers go while the factories shut once every year?

Let's Explore the North East

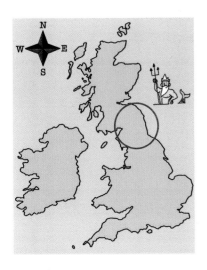

The counties of Northumberland and Durham form the North East of England.

Have you ever thought that the map of Britain looks a bit like a person sitting down? If we use our imaginations, we can see that there is a range of hills called the Pennines that is in the position the spine would be in, if Britain were a person. For that reason, the Pennines are called 'the backbone of England'. From the Peak District in the Midlands, almost to the Scottish border, the Pennines divide the North West from the North East and Yorkshire. On the East side, several fast-flowing rivers run towards the North Sea. Can you see them on our map?

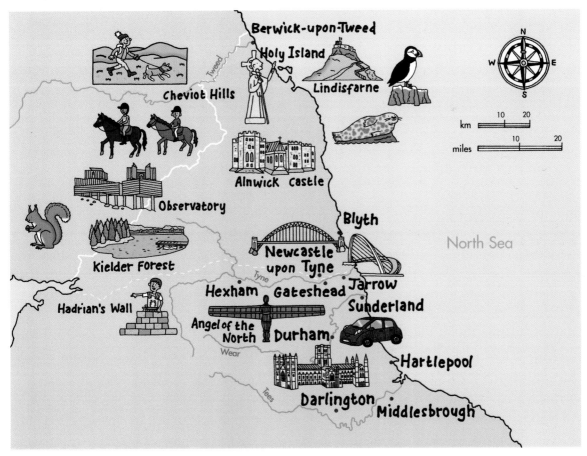

The Scenery of the North East

The landscape of the Pennines is so beautiful that the northern part of it has been designated an Area of Outstanding Natural Beauty. It is home to many animals and birds like owls, grouse, red squirrels and otters, as well as rare plants and England's biggest waterfall, called High Force. The area is very popular with walkers, who can walk along a track called the Pennine Way for 268 miles, if they have the energy!

More beautiful scenery can be found in the Kielder Water and Forest Park, near the border with Scotland. The forest is the largest in England and is an excellent wildlife habitat, home to red squirrels and nesting ospreys. Because Kielder Park is in a part of the country that is not near to any towns or cities, the sky at night is really dark – in fact, it is darker than the night sky anywhere else in England. For that reason, it is perfect for star-gazing. On winter nights you can study 'deep sky' objects such as galaxies, while in summer you can view the beautiful Milky Way, passing comets and shooting stars. There is an observatory where astronomers use powerful telescopes to study the stars and planets. You can look through them too, if you visit at certain times.

Do you remember learning about the Roman invasion of Britain in Year 2? The first attempt to conquer Britain in 55 BC was a failure, but the Romans came back in 43 AD and were more successful. The southern and eastern parts of England quickly became parts of the Roman Empire. The Romans travelled further, conquering Wales and northern England. However, when they came to the part of the British Isles that we now call Scotland, and which was then known as Caledonia, they had a struggle on their hands. Caledonia was inhabited by tribes of Picts, who were very fierce and did not want the Romans to rule them. Eventually, the Romans decided that it was too much trouble to hold on to this part of their Empire, so the Emperor Hadrian ordered a wall to be built right across the country, stretching for 80 miles from one end to the other.

It was an amazing achievement, stretching across hills and valleys and crossing rivers. All along the wall were forts and towers, where soldiers would guard the frontier. You can still see the remains of this amazing wall today. It is the greatest Roman monument in Britain. Can you spot Hadrian's Wall on the map on page 93?

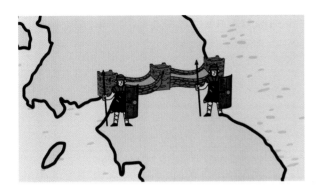

These are the remains of a fort on Hadrian's Wall at Housesteads

Today the border between Scotland and England is further to the north, with its eastern end meeting the River Tweed. Berwick-upon-Tweed is England's most northerly town but it has changed between being in England and Scotland several times. After it finally became English in 1482, they built a set of protective walls around it.

Lindisfarne and the Islands

A page from the Lindisfarne gospels.

A short distance to the south of Berwick-upon-Tweed, there is a causeway to the island of Lindisfarne, which is also known as Holy Island. A causeway is a raised road over wet ground that often, as here, gets covered by the sea at high tide, so you can only get to Lindisfarne when the tide is out. St Aidan, who brought Christianity to Northumbria, built a monastery on Lindisfarne in 635 AD and lived there between visits to the surrounding area. St Aidan and his monks set up the first school in the area and taught reading and writing so that people would be able to read the Bible and other holy books, then write beautiful copies of them. These books are called *illuminated manuscripts* because they were written by hand and then illuminated, or illustrated, with beautiful pictures and designs. The most famous illuminated manuscript produced at Lindisfarne is the copy of the gospels. It is now in the British Library.

Beyond Lindisfarne are some even smaller islands which are inhabited by no one except thousands of grey seals, rabbits, puffins and other birds. People who visit the islands by boat are warned to wear hats as some of the birds, like the arctic terns, will attack anyone who comes too near their nests.

The Towns of the North East

Most of the large towns and cities in the North East are on the coast or near it. For a long time, there were two heavy industries that employed most of the working people in the area: coal mining and ship-building. The rich seams of coal in the North East became important in the Industrial Revolution. So much coal was mined there that, by the beginning of the twentieth century, a quarter of all Britain's coal came from the North East. 'Taking coals to Newcastle' became a saying that meant offering people something they already had. The area was also a centre for ship-building, with big shipyards like Swan Hunter on Tyneside employing thousands of men. Sunderland, on the River Wear, was described as 'the largest ship-building town in the world', with over a third of the town's workforce busy in the shipyards. These shipyards produced both ocean liners to carry travellers in luxury and warships to defend the nation. The shipyards were very busy during both the first and the second world wars, but after that there was not enough work for everyone. Many men were told they no longer had jobs. Most of the shipyards and coalmines have now closed.

Many people now work in light industries such as retail (which means working in shops), office work, health, education and working for the government. In 1986 the Japanese car manufacturer Nissan opened a factory in Sunderland which has been very successful.

Newcastle has a monument to Charles, the second Earl Grey, who was Prime Minister when the Great Reform Act of 1832 was passed, giving more people the right to vote. You can read more about the Act on page 144.

Above: *This painting by William Bell Scott is called:* In the nineteenth century the Northumbrians show the world what can be done with iron and coal. *It shows engineering, railways and coal (in the barge on the river), the main industries of the North East.*

◀ Bottom left: *The Ark Royal, for 30 years the flagship of the Royal Navy, was built at the Swan Hunter shipyard on the River Tyne. This photograph shows it being launched*

◀ Bottom right: *Grey's Monument in Newcastle*

There are modern landmarks too. The most famous of the bridges that link Newcastle and Gateshead on opposite sides of the river are the Tyne Bridge and the Millennium Bridge. The Millennium Bridge, which is smaller, lifts to allow ships underneath. Newcastle is a centre for arts and education, with theatres, concert halls, museums and galleries. Every year, thousands of runners take part in the Great North Run between Newcastle and South Shields.

The Millennium Bridge

The Angel of the North

People arriving in the North East by the main road, the A1, see the *Angel of the North*, a giant winged statue designed by the sculptor Antony Gormley that has come to symbolise the North East. The wings of the Angel are curved slightly forwards to welcome people to the area. Antony Gormley has said that one of the things he wants his statue to make people think about is the change from an industrial age to an information age.

Now use your knowledge of the North East to answer these questions:

Why are the Pennines known as the *backbone of England*?

What is the Angel of the North?

What were the two main industries in the North East during the industrial revolution?

How and when can you travel to the island of Lindisfarne from the mainland?

What main industries do people in the region work in now?

American History

The United States of America

Think about the word 'united'. What do you think it means? You may have heard it before; some football teams have the word 'united' in their name. United means 'joined together'. North America has many states within it. A state is similar to a country; some of the states in America are bigger than the UK. If we put these two words together, we get United States. Now we can see that the United States of America is made up of many different states that have joined together to create one nation.

You can see from the map below that there are 48 states in North America. Alaska and Hawaii are also part of the United States, so there are 50 states in the USA altogether. The states you can see on the map have not always been united in the way they are today. The history of the United States is complex; battles and wars have been fought over land and power. Let's find out more about the history of the United States of America.

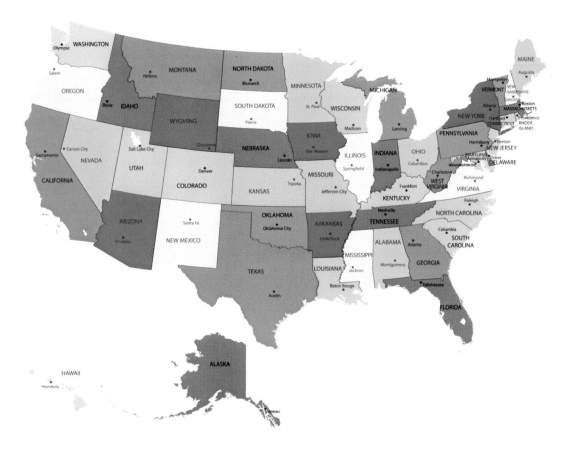

American Expansion

In 1776, the thirteen British colonies in North America decided to break away from British rule and they formed the United States of America. At first, this new nation was made up only of these thirteen states running down America's Atlantic coastline.

> We learnt about the American War of Independence in Year 5.

During the years that followed, the United States of America rapidly took on new lands. We call this *expansion*. In 1803, the country doubled in size when President Thomas Jefferson bought a large area of land from France's leader Napoleon Bonaparte for $15 million in a deal named the Louisiana Purchase. Explorers began to venture into these new lands, recording what they discovered and making their way to the Pacific Ocean. People built towns and cities in this new land.

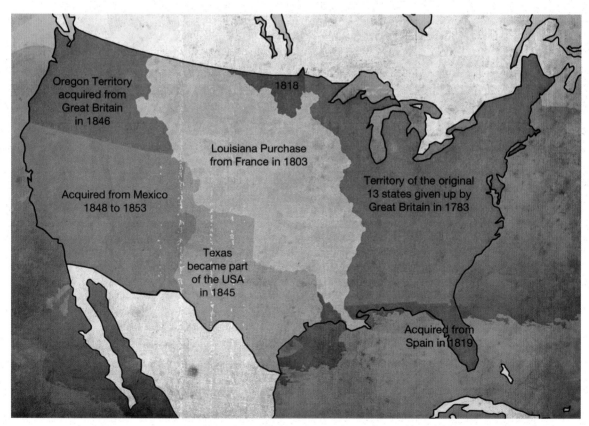

The Louisiana Purchase doubled the size of the USA.

The Lewis and Clark Expedition

President Jefferson wanted to learn all he could about the new, unexplored lands to the West so, in 1804, the year after the Louisiana Purchase, he sent an expedition to explore and map the land west of the Mississippi River. From 1804 to 1806, a group of explorers led by two men, Meriwether Lewis and William Clark, walked and canoed all the way to the Pacific Ocean and then back to Virginia.

Meriwether Lewis and William Clark were assisted in their expedition by Native American guides.

Lewis and Clark made maps and wrote down their observations concerning weather patterns, rocks, soil types, plants and animals. They found the bones of a fifteen-metre-long dinosaur, and they recorded 200 new species of plants.

In Year 3 we sang 'Clementine', a song about 'a miner, forty-niner, and his daughter Clementine'.

Many people arrived in California in 1849 to mine gold, and they were called the 'forty-niners'. However, they did not all become rich, as they had hoped.

America kept on growing, or *expanding*. In 1845, the Republic of Texas became the twenty-eighth state. The following year, President Polk persuaded the British to hand over their land in the Pacific Northwest (now the states of Washington, Oregon and Idaho). America wanted to control the whole of the Pacific coastline, and in 1846 war broke out with Mexico. America won the Mexican War and controlled land covering what are now the states of California, Nevada and Utah. This was very good timing, as in 1848 gold was discovered in California. Tens of thousands of Americans moved west to make their fortune. People rushed to California to dig for gold, so this time became known as the Gold Rush.

For all of those people travelling west, the journey was expensive and dangerous. Their belongings would be loaded into canvas-covered wagons called prairie schooners and pulled for up to 2,000 miles by oxen and horses. The trip could last for six months, through rain, hailstorms and attacks from Native American tribes. Many *pioneers*, which is the name given to people exploring the west, died before making it to their destination.

Pioneers travelled in covered wagons like this one.

The pioneers wanted to explore and rule over all of the land stretching from the Atlantic to the Pacific Ocean. However, this land was not uninhabited, as Native American tribes had lived there for thousands of years. At first, relations between the Native Americans and white settlers were friendly. However, Native Americans soon grew unhappy. European settlers killed off the buffalo herds on which they depended and brought diseases such as cholera, smallpox and measles that wiped out entire tribes. The American government and the Native Americans signed agreements called treaties stating who had the right to live in certain places. These treaties were often broken and this caused a series of wars between the American settlers and the Native Americans, which would end forever the Native American way of life.

Causes of the American Civil War

Do you remember studying the British slave trade? In 1833, slavery was abolished, or ended, throughout the entire British Empire. In the United States of America, things took a bit longer. The government of each individual state could decide whether or not to allow

In Year 5 we learnt about British abolitionists like William Wilberforce and Thomas Clarkson.

slavery. In the North, people made their living as small farmers, shopkeepers, craftsmen, merchants or factory workers. The economy of the North was becoming industrial, which meant more machines were used and slaves were no longer needed. However, the states in the South relied on slaves to work on their large farms (often harvesting cotton). Most of the northern states abolished slavery. The states in the South did not.

To *abolish* means to stop something, or ban it. The abolition movement was a campaign to stop slavery. One of the most important campaigners of the northern abolition movement was a journalist named William Lloyd Garrison. He published a newspaper called *The Liberator*. Another important abolitionist was Frederick Douglass. Douglass was born into slavery on a plantation in Maryland around 1818. As a young man he was sent to work in the home of Hugh Auld in Baltimore. Auld's wife Sophia ignored a ban on teaching slaves to read and write, and she gave Douglass the education that would allow him to become famous in later life. In 1838, Douglass escaped from his slave master and travelled to the free state of New York.

Frederick Douglass

Douglass talked to people and wrote articles about slavery. In 1845, he wrote his autobiography, which became a bestseller in the United States. He spent two years living in Britain where money was raised to buy his freedom. Douglass returned to America a free man and launched *The North Star*, a newspaper dedicated to ending slavery in the South.

Uncle Tom saved the life of Little Eva, but later in the story he is treated very cruelly and dies.

Abolitionists like Garrison and Douglass persuaded some people, but nobody stirred up opposition to slavery more than Harriet Beecher Stowe. In 1852, Stowe published a novel called *Uncle Tom's Cabin*. The novel tells the story of Uncle Tom, a kind and religious slave who saves the life of a white girl but later is sold to a cruel master. When Tom refuses to tell where two escaped slaves are hiding, the master whips him until he dies.

Over 300,000 copies of *Uncle Tom's Cabin* sold in one year, an amazing number for that time. Some Northerners felt so outraged they wanted to force the South to end slavery.

Slaves on southern plantations also did what they could to oppose slavery. Some ran away. Others deliberately broke tools. Some tried to fight back. Some even tried to kill themselves. Many slaves suffered quietly. Most slaves became Christians and some made a new kind of music, songs called spirituals. These songs brought together African music and the Christian religion and were often based on stories in the Bible about how the people of Israel were delivered from slavery in Egypt.

You can learn more about spirituals on page 199.

In 1858, a man named Abraham Lincoln ran for election to the Senate (the American version of Parliament). He was an intelligent and upright man, nicknamed Honest Abe. During his campaign, he gave an important speech against slavery, in which he stated: 'A house divided against itself cannot stand. I believe this government cannot endure, permanently half slave and half free.' Lincoln lost the election, but he gained national attention for speaking out against slavery.

One of the most important things about American politics is that states make their own decisions and the President in Washington has only limited power over them. Southern states claimed that, as the American Constitution did not forbid slavery, each state had the right to decide whether to allow it or not. They threatened to leave the union and become an independent country if any president tried to outlaw slavery.

The War

In 1860, Abraham Lincoln was elected President. In December 1860, South Carolina left the United States. By February 1861, six other southern states had left too, and these states joined together to form their own country named the Confederate States of America, or the Confederacy. These states demanded that US soldiers leave the South. Lincoln did the opposite, and sent supply ships to reinforce a fort in South Carolina named Fort Sumter. When the Southerners heard this, they began shelling Fort Sumter. On 12 April 1861, the Civil War began.

More of the Southern states left the United States and joined the Confederacy. This new group of states chose their own president, had their own flag and built up their own army.

The commander of the Confederate army was General Robert E. Lee. He was a hero of the Mexican War, and had served the United States army for more than thirty years. He was asked to command the Union forces, but, being from the South, he decided to

This statue of Abraham Lincoln is in the Lincoln Memorial in Washington D.C.

The Confederates attacked the Union stronghold of Fort Sumter.

command the Confederate army instead. Lee was a good leader and the Confederates won most of the major battles from 1861 to the summer of 1863.

Ulysses S. Grant had fought in the Mexican War, but then left the army to work in his father's leather shop in Illinois. He entered the war as a colonel on the Unionist side. He was soon promoted to general and, in 1864, Lincoln placed Grant in charge of the entire Union army. Grant was not as experienced as Lee, but he soon became his match on the battlefield.

Lincoln wanted slavery to end, but first he wanted to hold the nation together. He was careful how he expressed opposition to slavery because some states fighting for the Union – the border states of Delaware, Maryland, Kentucky and Missouri – allowed slavery. Lincoln was concerned that if he took too strong a stand against slavery, the border states would join the Confederacy.

However, Lincoln was under enormous pressure from his supporters to take a firmer stand against slavery. In 1862, the Union won their first major battle at Antietam in Maryland. Lincoln saw this as the ideal opportunity to make an important speech about freedom. The Emancipation Proclamation announced that all slaves in areas under Confederate control were free, beginning 1 January 1863. Of course,

Learn how to write a persuasive speech on page 59.

Lincoln could not force Southerners to free their slaves, but news of the *Emancipation Proclamation* brought hope and joy to African-Americans.

At first, neither the Union nor the Confederacy allowed black people to be soldiers. Prejudice still led many to believe that black people were not clever or brave enough to be good soldiers. However, as the Union army needed more soldiers, in 1862 the law was changed to allow African-Americans to fight in the army, and they rushed to volunteer to fight against the Confederacy.

Gettysburg

By the summer of 1863, the Union was attacking the Confederacy from all sides. They were closing in on the South, so General Lee made a last attempt to fight back. He led 75,000 soldiers into Pennsylvania and, on 1 July 1863, the two armies met just outside a place called Gettysburg. There were 90,000 Union troops there and for two days Lee attacked again and again. The Union troops had the advantage of being on hilltops, and each time the Confederates charged, cannonballs and bullets rained down on them. On 4 July 1863, Lee began his long retreat back to Virginia. Each side had suffered over 20,000 casualties.

The Battle of Gettysburg

On 19 November, Lincoln delivered a speech at Gettysburg to honour the fallen soldiers. It only took two minutes, but is remembered as one of the greatest speeches in American history. It began: 'Fourscore and seven years ago, our fathers brought forth upon this continent a new nation, conceived in liberty, and dedicated to the proposition that all men are created equal.' This was an important reminder that the United States had been founded on principles of freedom.

Surrender

By 1864, Union troops controlled part of every Confederate state and they were very close to winning the war. Jefferson Davis and the Confederate Government fled their capital of Richmond, burning down much of the city as they left. On 3 April 1865, Union troops

The Room in the McLean House, at Appomattox C.H., in which GEN. LEE surrendered to GEN. GRANT.

*General Robert E. Lee (sitting on the left in the centre) surrenders
to General Ulysses S. Grant (sitting on the right in the centre)
at Appomattox Court House, ending the American Civil War.*

led by black soldiers marched into the city, where crowds of cheering African-Americans, many of them slaves, greeted them.

Lee and his weary soldiers retreated to a small town called Appomattox, where they were surrounded by Union troops. General Grant allowed Lee's soldiers to surrender and return to their homes. As General Lee rode away, Grant removed his hat to show his respect for Lee. Union soldiers started to celebrate, but Grant ordered them to be quiet. Grant did not want the Southern soldiers to feel even worse. 'The war is over,' Grant said. 'The rebels are our countrymen again.'

Northerners were very happy when they heard the news of General Lee's surrender, but the celebrations would soon end. Only five days after Lee surrendered, President Lincoln and his wife attended a play at Ford's Theatre in Washington, not far from the White House. As Lincoln watched the play, an actor named John Wilkes Booth, who supported the Confederate army, crept up behind the President and shot him. The Civil War had ended, but so had the life of President Abraham Lincoln.

American Geography

How Big is the United States of America?

Have you travelled by car, train or bus to different cities in the UK? Did it take several hours to get there? Britain is about 600 miles long, from the north of Scotland to the south of England, and 300 miles wide. The United States of America is about 1,500 miles from top to bottom, and 2,600 miles from the east side to the west side. It is about 38 times larger than the UK, so if you thought it took a long time to travel across the UK, it would take a lot longer to travel across the United States of America!

What is New England?

In Years 4 and 5, we learnt about early English settlers who set up colonies in North America. One of the first groups of settlers was called the Pilgrims, who set up a colony in Massachusetts in 1620. Massachusetts is now one of the five states in the region called New England, named after the country the settlers had come from.

The Pilgrims arrived in Massachusetts in search of religious freedom.

Boston is the largest city in New England, and it is a key city in the history of the American War of Independence. Do you remember learning in Year 5 about Paul Revere? He rode his horse crying 'the Redcoats are coming!' during the beginning of the War of Independence to warn his fellow Americans about the British soldiers. Paul Revere was from Boston, which is one of the most historic cities in North America, with cobblestone streets and many old buildings.

In Years 4 and 5 we learnt about the universities of Oxford and Cambridge in the UK. The important American university, Harvard, was modelled on them and is also one of the most *prestigious* (meaning it has a high status) in the world. This university was named after John Harvard, who had gone to Cambridge University before moving to the United States, and is located in the American town that is called Cambridge. Cambridge lies on one side of the Charles River, opposite Boston. Cambridge is also home to another

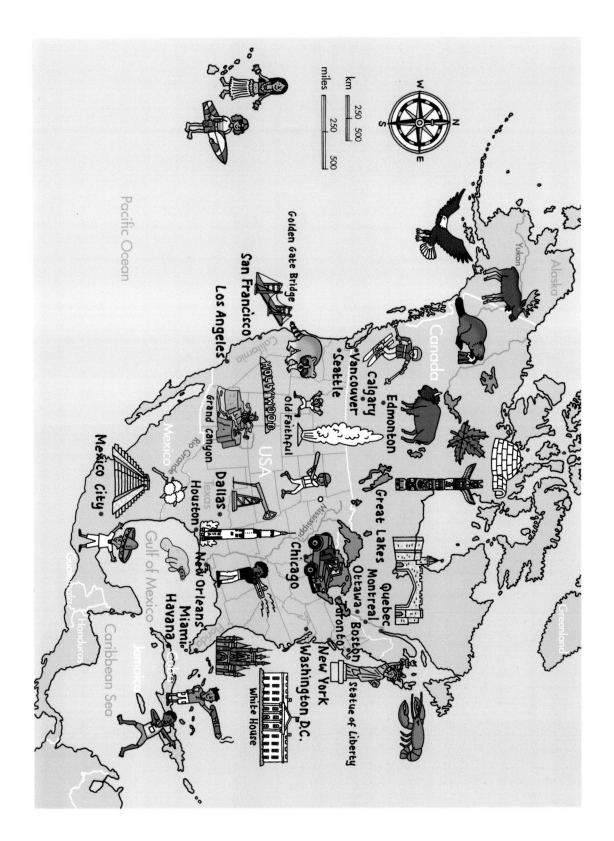

important university: the Massachusetts Institute of Technology (called MIT), which is known for being one of the best in the world for its research and teaching about science and technology.

North of Boston and the state of Massachusetts, you can reach the states of Maine, New Hampshire and Vermont. Many people in New England go skiing in these states because they are cold in the winter. Vermont produces lots of maple syrup from its maple trees and Maine, on the coast, is known for its delicious lobster. Many people enjoy hiking in the forests of these states, as well as in the White Mountains of New Hampshire which is home to the largest mountain in the region: Mount Washington, named after George Washington, the first American president. In the autumn, the White Mountains and much of New England are covered with colourful orange, yellow and red trees that are about to lose their leaves. Americans call autumn 'the fall', because it is when the leaves fall from deciduous trees.

The Charles River

We found out about the difference between deciduous and evergreen trees in Year 1.

The Mid-Atlantic

New York City is famous for its tall buildings which are called skyscrapers. In the late 1800s and early 1900s, many immigrants from Europe travelled by boat to the United States to begin their new lives. Ellis Island in New York Harbour was the largest port where these immigrants would have to pass inspection before being allowed to enter the country. Because of the high number of immigrants who came to live in the United States, the country is sometimes called a 'melting pot' of people from all over the world. The Statue

The Statue of Liberty

of Liberty in New York Harbour is one of the icons of the United States of America, and each of those immigrants coming to Ellis Island would have seen it. The statue was a gift from the people of France, who admired the way in which the USA had become 'the land of the free'. They felt that America was the kind of free nation they had tried to create during the French Revolution (which we read about in Year 5).

The Guggenheim Museum in New York was designed by the American architect Frank Lloyd Wright. Compare its architecture to that of the Guggenheim Museum in Bilbao, which we saw in Year 3.

People from all over the world come to visit, live and work in New York City. There are famous museums, such as the Metropolitan Museum of Art (called the Met), the Museum of Modern Art (called MOMA [MOH-ma]) and the Guggenheim Museum. The city is also known for its 'Broadway shows' that take place at forty different theatres in New York City's Theatre District, near the famous street called Broadway. Apart from theatre shows, you can also see musical performances at Carnegie Hall, which is a large concert hall in Manhattan near Central Park.

New Jersey and Pennsylvania are other states in the mid-Atlantic region. New Jersey is known for its seaside, the 'Jersey shore'. In Pennsylvania, the city of Philadelphia played an important part in American history because it is where the Declaration of Independence was signed. Pennsylvania is known for its factories: cities like Pittsburgh are large manufacturing centres.

> In Year 4 we learnt how Alexander Graham Bell demonstrated his new invention, the telephone, in Philadelphia in 1876.

The South

Many battles of the American Civil War were fought in the South Atlantic states, especially those along the border between the Union (the North) and the Confederacy (the South). Delaware, Maryland, Virginia and West Virginia are South Atlantic States. Washington D.C. (or Washington, District of Colombia) is the capital of the United States of America. It is a district, not a state, and it was built as the capital since it was roughly halfway between the North and the South, and it was near the Atlantic Ocean. The president of the USA lives in the White House in Washington.

The Capitol building in Washington D.C.

The Appalachian Mountains run all the way from Maine in the North to Georgia in the South. This mountain range goes through fourteen states. Each year, many people try to hike the entire Appalachian Trail, which is a hike that covers over 2,000 miles and takes about six months! Most people start in the south in Georgia in early spring and then hike north, through sections of the Appalachian Mountains called the Great Smoky Mountains and the Blue Ridge Mountains in Georgia, North Carolina and Virginia. Hikers travel along the ridges of the mountains that

overlook valleys where some people live. As they go farther north, they enter into deep forests in southern New England and then reach the steep and rocky peaks of the White Mountains in New Hampshire. Hikers must

> We learnt about the Appalachian Mountains in Year 5.

try to reach the end of the trail in Maine before the winter weather sets in.

Florida is the southernmost state in the South Atlantic region. Florida is a peninsula that juts out and separates the Atlantic Ocean and the Gulf of Mexico. Can you find it on the map on page 109? This state is known for its beaches and warm climate. In the Everglades National Park, you can find interesting animals such as alligators, crocodiles and manatees.

An alligator

Some southern states, referred to as the 'Deep South', were the main Confederate states during the Civil War. The states of Alabama, Georgia, Louisiana, Mississippi and South Carolina (along with parts of Florida and Texas) are sometimes called the 'Deep South' because they are the most southern. During the days of early American history they were sometimes called the 'cotton states' because their plantations produced large amounts of cotton, mainly through the work of slaves before the Civil War. Cotton grew well in the Deep South because of the temperate winter climate and the hot summer weather.

Other states in the South include Kentucky, Tennessee and Oklahoma. They are inland states in the centre of the United States of America. Kentucky is known as the 'Bluegrass State' because of the bluegrass that grows in its fertile soil. It is also known for its horseracing, including the Kentucky Derby horserace. Famous American musicians Elvis Presley and Johnny Cash lived in the city of Memphis, and the state of Tennessee has played an important role in the development of many forms of American popular music, including rock and roll, blues and country music.

Texas is an extremely large state: the whole of the United Kingdom could easily fit inside it! The neighbouring state of Oklahoma is known for its extreme weather, including very cold winters, extremely hot summers and tornadoes.

> We learnt about the power of tornadoes in Year 5.

The Mid-West

North of Texas and Oklahoma are many other states that are part of the Great Plains, including Kansas, Nebraska, Montana, South Dakota, North Dakota, other American states and even three Canadian provinces. The Great Plains contain land that is prairie and grassland. A prairie [PRARE-ree] is an ecosystem with grasslands and shrublands where, rather than trees, many types of grasses and shrubs grow well in the temperate climate. On average, the grasses that grow in the Great Plains are about two metres high – which is taller than you! This is a very fertile region of the United States that is known for its agriculture because the area produces lots of corn and wheat, and farmers also raise cattle and other animals.

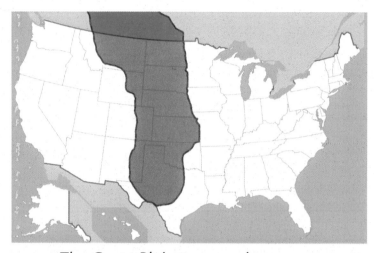

The Great Plains cover a large area of the United States of America.

The Great Plains lie between the Rocky Mountains of the West (which we'll read about in the next section) and the Mississippi River. The Mississippi is the main river of the largest drainage basin in North America. Starting in Minnesota, the Mississippi River grows bigger and bigger with many tributaries joining it as it flows south to its delta at the city of New Orleans in Louisiana.

To the east of the Mississippi River are the other Mid-Western states of Wisconsin, Michigan, Illinois, Indiana and Ohio. Each of these states, together with the state of

New York and the Canadian province of Ontario, borders the Great Lakes. These are five extremely large lakes that are close to each other. On the small strip of land that separates Lake Ontario and Lake Erie, you can see a massive waterfall called Niagara Falls. On one side of the falls is New York state, and Canada is on the other side. The large American city of Chicago ('the windy city') lies on the shores of Lake Michigan. Lake Huron and Lake Superior are two of the northern lakes that also border Canada.

Niagara Falls

Which Mountains Can You Find in the West?

In Year 5, we started learning about the Rocky Mountains, which cover many states in the American West. 'The Rockies' stretch for over 3,000 miles from the state of New Mexico, through parts of Colorado, Wyoming and Montana in the United States and then into Canada. When the Lewis and Clark expedition travelled west, the Rockies presented them with a challenge since it was very difficult for the explorers to cross over this rugged and steep mountain range. Nowadays, much of the Rocky Mountains is protected as National Parks which are popular tourist destinations where people come to enjoy hiking, camping and mountaineering.

Yellowstone is home to the largest collection of geysers in the world including the famous 'Old Faithful' geyser. Yellowstone was America's first National Park, and it was created to preserve these geysers and the ecosystem existing here. In Year 4 we learnt how living things depend on each other and how, when one creature dies out, an entire web of living things is affected. Yellowstone National Park has protected an ecosystem that includes forests, meadows, lakes and valleys. Many animals live in this ecosystem, including grizzly bears, wolves, bison, elk and even swans.

> In Year 5 we learnt that the Rockies are taller and 'younger' than the Appalachian Mountains.

> Geysers form in areas with lots of volcanic activity under the Earth's surface, as we read in Year 5.

If you are lucky, you can spot bull elk in Yellowstone National Park.

Further north, in the western part of Montana on the border with Canada, there is another large, protected natural area called Glacier National Park. As you would expect, there are glaciers here, and the park is home to grizzly bears, moose and mountain goats, as well as rare or endangered species such as the wolverine and Canadian lynx.

This geyser in Yellowstone National Park erupts so regularly that it is known as 'Old Faithful'.

Which States Have Coastlines on the Pacific Ocean?

The states of Washington, Oregon and California are the three states that are on the Pacific Coast. The largest city in Washington is Seattle. South of Seattle are the large volcanoes of Mount Rainier and Mount St Helens. In Year 5 we learnt how Mount St Helens erupted and blew its top off in 1980, which devastated the area.

South of Washington and Oregon is the state of California. The Californian city of San Francisco is known for its beautiful Golden Gate Bridge. Los Angeles is home to Hollywood where many popular films and TV programmes are produced. Surfers come to the cities of Los Angeles and San Diego and also enjoy surfing all along California's long coastline, particularly in the southern half of the state where the air and water temperatures are warmer.

California is the state with the largest population. Alongside the well-known tourism and entertainment industries, California also has a strong technology industry with computers, tablets, phones and other devices being developed in Silicon Valley and elsewhere. In addition, California's warm climate and fertile soil make it ideal for agriculture. Many different fruits and vegetables are grown here, including strawberries, oranges, grapes, lemons, broccoli and artichokes.

The Golden Gate Bridge in San Francisco

Forty-eight of the American states, including all of the ones you have learnt about here, are located in the main landmass of the United States of America, but there are also two additional states that make up the fifty states. The largest American state is Alaska. It is also the northernmost state and can be extremely cold, so few people live there. In south-central Alaska and the interior of the state, there is a sub-arctic climate and short, cool summers. In the extreme north of Alaska there is an arctic climate with long, very cold winters and short, cool summers. If you look at the map of the Arctic Circle on page 68, you can see that part of Alaska is within it, just like parts of Canada and Scandinavia.

Alaska

Temperatures are very cold in Alaska, but you can find very warm temperatures and a tropical climate in the state of Hawaii. This small state is very far away from other landmasses of the USA. In fact, if you were to row from San Francisco in California to Hawaii, it would take you at

In Year 5 we learnt about the South Pacific and how Hawaii is a set of islands in Polynesia.

least a month! Many people enjoy going to Hawaii on a special tropical holiday, spending time on its beaches, seeing its volcanoes and exploring the rainforests.

The Many Climates of North America

At the beginning of this section, we read about how large the United States of America is compared with the UK. As you have seen, the US has many different regions and many different climates. Even within one state there can be large variations in climate. New England is usually very hot in summer (with temperatures up to about 30 degrees Celsius) and very cold in winter, with lots of snow and ice. The further south you go, the warmer it gets, and the Deep South is usually extremely hot throughout the summer.

Canada

Like the United States of America, Canada is a very large country that stretches from the Atlantic Ocean to the Pacific. In fact, Canada is even larger than the USA and is the second largest country in the world (after Russia) in terms of its area.

Canada's harsh climate makes it difficult for people to live in the northernmost areas of the country. There are over one million Aboriginal or native peoples in Canada including the First Nations tribe, the Inuit and

These children are wearing traditional fur clothing to keep them warm while they prepare to ride on this dog-sledge.

Many Inuit people use modern vehicles and technologies, such as snowmobiles.

the Métis. They live in all parts of Canada, but particularly in the northern territories. Although many people think of igloos and traditional sledges when they think of Canadian Aboriginal peoples, nowadays many tribe members live in modern houses and use snowmobiles to help them get through the long winters in remote areas.

Most Canadians live in the South where the climate is warmer. Like Seattle in the United States, the city of Vancouver in Canada is located on the West Coast and has a temperate, oceanic climate with wet weather. Vancouver is the most densely populated city in Canada, with the highest number of people for its area. It is also a diverse city with many people from around the world coming to visit and live there.

Calgary has been called the world's cleanest city and Canada's most eco-friendly (or 'green') city. Calgary is located inland near the Rocky Mountains that extend from the United States north into this area of Canada. Because of the mountainous area, the city has a high elevation. The winters are long, cold and dry and the summers are short, moderately warm ones. The city has many parks for people to enjoy, as well as a large network of paths for walking and biking.

Toronto is Canada's largest city, and it is located on the shores of Lake Ontario which we read about on page 115. The city of Toronto is only about 200 years old, and this somewhat new city has its streets laid out in a grid system to make it easier for people to find their way around.

Canada's government is a parliamentary democracy which is based on the government of the UK. In the days of the British Empire, Canada was a British colony. It is now an independent country but it is a member of the Commonwealth of Nations and Queen Elizabeth II is the Queen of Canada.

Parliament Hill in Ottawa is home to the Canadian Parliament buildings.

Ottawa, in the eastern province of Ontario, is Canada's capital city. It is home to the Parliament of Canada and attracts many visitors each year. Ottawa is the fourth-largest Canadian city and is located along the banks of the Ottawa River.

The maple leaf is the symbol of Canada and is part of the Canadian flag. Can you see it in the map on page 109?

To the East of Ottawa is the large city of Montreal. Montreal, Ottawa and Toronto all tend to have humid continental climates. Therefore, winters are cold and snowy and summers are pleasant and warm. From November until about March, Montreal usually receives over 200 centimetres of snow each year. Can you measure that amount with a tape measure to see how much it is?

The beaver is the national animal of Canada.

Montreal and Quebec City are both in an area called Quebec. This province was originally a French colony, and many families are French-Canadian. In Montreal, just over half of residents speak French at home and, in Quebec City, roughly 95 per cent of citizens learn French as their first language. Many people are *bilingual* (speaking two languages) and speak both French and English. Quebec City is one of the oldest European settlements in North America. It is a World Heritage Site, and many of its historic buildings are protected.

Central and South America

South of the United States of America are Central and South America. While the British and French colonised much of North America, the Spanish and Portuguese gained colonies in Central and South America. Bordering the US to the south is the country of Mexico. The country has many factories that produce manufactured goods, electronics and cars. Many North American tourists, in particular, enjoy the beaches of Baja California and Cancun in Mexico.

Mexican food is well-known around the world. In Mexico, food can be very different in each region. Many people have tasted Mexican food such as tacos and burritos, which can sometimes be spicy. Cocoa beans, from which chocolate is made, grow in Mexico. *Mole poblano* [moll-LAY po-BLA-no] is a rich Mexican sauce made from cocoa powder and peppers, as well as many other ingredients. It takes hours to make and is served over other dishes such as enchiladas.

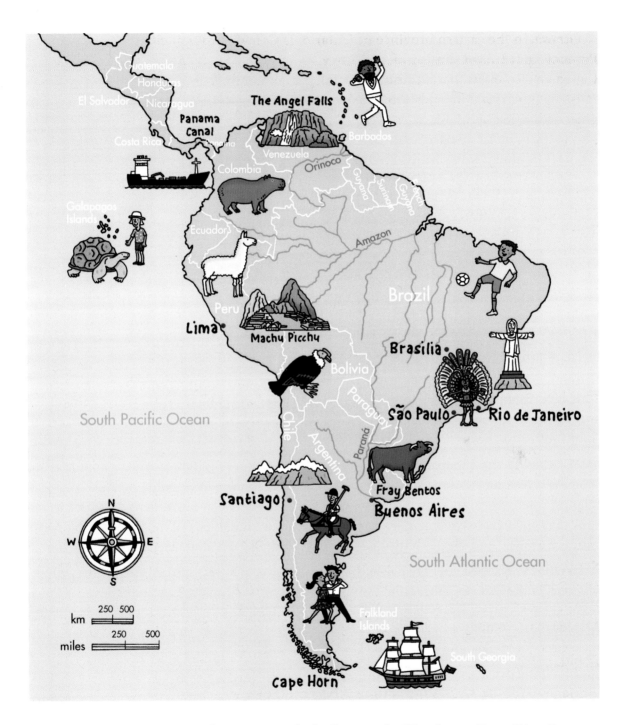

Other countries in Central America include Guatemala, Honduras, Costa Rica, Panama and others. Do you remember reading in Year 4 how the explorer Francis Drake travelled up the western coast of the Americas, looking for a passage so that he could sail back to England? He never found one because it didn't exist, but four hundred years later a passage was created between the Atlantic and the Pacific Oceans by digging a canal. It was dug in Panama, because the most obvious place to link the two great oceans was across the narrowest part of the *isthmus* – a narrow strip of land – joining North with South America. Although the French first tried to build a canal in Panama and failed, the United States of America bought out the French and started to build their canal in 1904. The canal was very expensive to build and many workers lost their lives while working on this project. After ten years, in 1914, the Panama Canal successfully opened. Roughly 14,000 ships pass through the Panama Canal each year. This saves them from having to sail all the way around the southern tip of South America.

Boats enter these locks to travel through the Panama Canal between the Atlantic and Pacific Oceans.

We read about Darwin's finches in Year 5.

There are twelve independent countries on the continent of South America. Bordering Panama is Colombia, south of which is Ecuador. Off the coast of Ecuador are the Galapagos Islands, where Charles Darwin studied the differences between finches and tortoises to see how they had evolved and adapted to life in the different habitats of the islands. *Galapagos* means tortoises, and the giant tortoises Darwin studied can still be seen there.

Brazil is the largest country in South America. Most people in Brazil speak Portuguese, whereas in the rest of Central and South America most people speak Spanish.

The Amazon rainforest stretches across nine different countries in South America, including Brazil, Peru, Chile and Ecuador. The Amazon rainforest has the largest number of different species of animals and plants living there compared with any other tropical rainforest in the world. You can find scarlet macaw birds, tree frogs, monkeys, jaguars and electric eels. Because parts of the Amazon rainforest have suffered from *deforestation*, or having many trees cut down, the ecosystem has been affected. People have become aware of the problem and are working to protect the rainforest, as well as the many different plants and animals that live there.

The Amazon Rainforest

Do you remember how we learnt about different mountain ranges in Year 5? The Andes Mountains in South America are extremely tall and they are the longest mountain range in the world. There are many different climates and ecosystems within the Andes. The tropical Andes includes tropical forests and cloud forests, and it extends through Venezuela, Colombia, Ecuador, Peru, Bolivia, Chile and Argentina. In Chile and Argentina, there are other parts of the Andes that are either very wet or very dry. The tallest mountain in South America, Mount Aconcagua, is in the Argentinian Andes. It is also the tallest mountain in the world outside of Asia, being 6,962 metres above sea level.

The Andes

We learnt in Year 5 how the Inca people built Machu Picchu nestled in the Andes in Peru.

British History

Why Was Queen Victoria So Popular?

George III, George IV and William IV

Queen Victoria reigned for longer than any other British monarch so far. She is remembered as having been a wise Queen and a good wife and mother during her 63-year reign. This made her very different from some of the kings who came before her.

   Last year, you learnt about George III, whose attitude towards the thirteen British colonies in America led them to break away from the British Empire and form the United States of America. As George grew older, he became better at sharing his power and was popular among the British people. He was nicknamed 'Farmer George' because he loved working on his farm near Windsor Castle. In 1810, George III was struck with a terrible illness. His urine turned purple and he began to see things that weren't there and to say things that didn't make sense. People at the time said he was insane, but it is now thought that he was suffering from a disease called porphyria. None of his doctors knew what his illness was or how to cure it, so the last ten years of his reign were spent at Windsor Castle, playing an old harpsichord, which looks similar to a piano, and speaking gibberish.

   During this period, George III's son, the Prince of Wales, took over as monarch. He was the 'Regent', meaning that he reigned on behalf of the King, so the time between 1810 and 1820 is known as the 'Regency'. Nicknamed 'Prinny', the Prince Regent was a charming and good-looking young man, but later in life he became overweight and unhealthy.

Regent Street in London was named after the Prince Regent, later George IV.

He was not always sensible with money: he was extravagant and spent money without thinking carefully about his decisions. He also wasted a lot of money through gambling.

The Prince Regent wanted to make London the most beautiful city in the world so he had much of it rebuilt. He was responsible for the development of Regent's Park, Regent Street and Buckingham Palace.

Despite this great project, most people still thought Prinny was spoilt and greedy. He became King George IV in 1820, and died in 1830. *The Times* wrote: 'There never was an individual less regretted by his fellow-creatures than this deceased king.'

George IV did not have a son, so the crown passed to his brother William IV. Nicknamed 'The Sailor King' due to his time spent in the Royal Navy, William IV had never expected to be king, and did not like it very much. During his coronation ceremony he snatched the crown from a courtier, placed it on his head, and declared, 'the Coronation is over'. The Sailor King died in 1837 with no son or daughter who could succeed him, so the crown passed to his niece, Victoria.

This cartoon shows King George IV as a voluptuary, which means someone who lives for pleasure.

Queen Victoria: 'I will be good'

One day, when she was eleven years old, Victoria was in her schoolroom studying history. She looked at the Royal family tree and noticed that her uncles George and William had no children who could inherit the crown, and for the first time in her life she realised that she was likely to become Queen. The young Victoria started to cry. After she had recovered, she declared: 'I will be good'.

Most people agree that Victoria kept her promise. Her mother and her governess (a lady who taught and looked after her), brought her up to be hard-working and well behaved – nothing like her uncles. She was only eighteen years old and less than five feet tall when she became Queen, but after her first council meeting her ministers said that she acted 'as if she had been doing it all her life'. She was intelligent and confident, and she quickly became friends with the Prime Minister, Lord Melbourne. They had a great friendship, and Melbourne helped her to understand how politics worked.

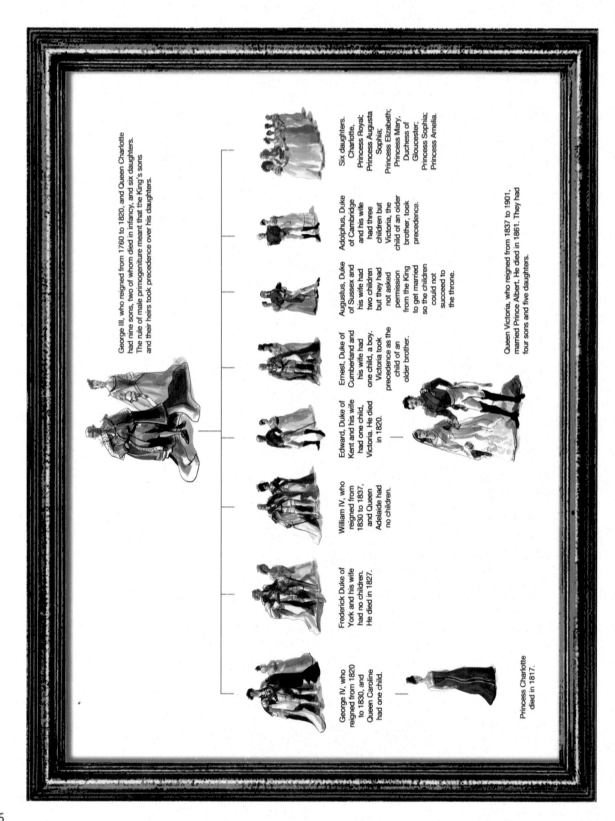

George III, who reigned from 1760 to 1820, and Queen Charlotte had nine sons, two of whom died in infancy, and six daughters. The rule of male primogeniture meant that the King's sons and their heirs took precedence over his daughters.

George IV, who reigned from 1820 to 1830, and Queen Caroline had one child.

Princess Charlotte died in 1817.

Frederick Duke of York and his wife had no children. He died in 1827.

William IV, who reigned from 1830 to 1837, and Queen Adelaide had no children.

Edward, Duke of Kent and his wife had one child, Victoria. He died in 1820.

Ernest, Duke of Cumberland and his wife had one child, a boy. Victoria took precedence as the child of an older brother.

Augustus, Duke of Sussex and his wife had two children but they had not asked permission from the King to get married so the children could not succeed to the throne.

Adolphus, Duke of Cambridge and his wife had three children but Victoria, the child of an older brother, took precedence.

Six daughters. Charlotte, Princess Royal; Princess Augusta Sophia; Princess Elizabeth; Princess Mary, Duchess of Gloucester; Princess Sophia; Princess Amelia.

Queen Victoria, who reigned from 1837 to 1901, married Prince Albert. He died in 1861. They had four sons and five daughters.

Queen Victoria's love of Scotland

In 1852 Queen Victoria and Prince Albert bought a house called Balmoral in the Scottish Highlands and had it rebuilt in a very romantic medieval style. They enjoyed their life in the Highlands and commissioned artists to paint the beautiful scenery and animals. One of the most famous of these paintings is of a stag, called *The Monarch of the Glen*, by Sir Edwin Landseer.

The Monarch of the Glen

Balmoral Castle

The Queen's Piper

Queen Victoria loved to be reminded of her beautiful home in the highlands. She often wore tartan and liked to hear the music of the bagpipes. There has been a close connection between the royal family and Scotland ever since. Even today, the present Queen takes her family to Balmoral every year for a holiday, and, whether she is living in Scotland or London, the Queen's Piper plays the bagpipes under her window every morning at nine o'clock.

Queen Victoria married a German prince, Albert of Saxe-Coburg-Gotha, in 1840. Prince Albert was very important during Queen Victoria's reign, advising her and helping her to make decisions. They were very happy together and had nine children. When Albert died in 1861, Victoria was overcome by grief and it was many years before she took up her royal duties again. Queen Victoria reigned for over sixty years and was very popular in the

Queen Victoria and her family in 1846

later years of her reign. People name the entire period the 'Victorian age' because she seemed to represent a time of great industrial expansion and the growth of a worldwide empire.

What Caused the Industrial Revolution?

For the whole of human history up to 1760, people depended on human muscle, animal muscle and wind to make power. All things that were transported on land were moved by horse or by foot, and all goods, like clothes

Industrial: To do with turning raw materials into other goods in factories.

Revolution: The change of a system.

and furniture, were made by hand. However, the Industrial Revolution saw the invention of engines and machines that would change the world forever. By using the power of fossil fuels, like burning coal to create steam power, the Industrial Revolution started a period of change in technology that we are still living through today. It all started in a few small towns in the north of England.

Cotton

The first product to be made on a large scale by machines was cotton. Cotton grows naturally in tropical regions and was imported from colonial plantations to Britain. Then the fluffy raw cotton was spun into threads, and the threads were woven into textiles. This was a time-consuming process done almost entirely by hand, until a series of inventions led to a huge increase in British cotton production.

The most important of these inventions came from a man named Richard Arkwright. He was one of seven children whose father was a poor tailor who could not afford to send him to school. Arkwright was desperate to make his fortune. In 1769, he invented the water frame, which produced very fine thread and was powered by running water. In 1771 he built a mill next to a river in Cromford, Derbyshire and filled it with water frames.

The river flowing past Cromford Mill powered its machines.

The Cromford Mill employed 1,000 workers. Many claim it was the world's first-ever factory. A factory is a place where large numbers of people come together with raw materials and machinery to *mass produce* something – in this case, cotton thread. Arkwright built more factories in Manchester and Scotland, each mass-producing cotton thread and working twenty-four hours a day. He died the richest commoner in England. (To describe Arkwright as a *commoner* means he was not a member of the aristocracy who had inherited his wealth.)

Before the Industrial Revolution, it took one worker with a spinning wheel 500 hours (can you work out how many days that is?) to spin 1 lb (about half a kilogram) of cotton. In comparison, in a cotton factory, or 'mill', it took one worker three hours to spin 1 lb of cotton. Cotton spinners in their cottages could not make as much cotton as the mills and had to shut down their businesses.

The smoking chimneys of Cottonopolis

Arkwright built Manchester's first cotton mill in 1783. By 1830 there were 99 mills and Manchester was the leading producer of cotton in the world. It was nicknamed 'Cottonopolis'. At first, the cotton threads still had to be woven into textiles by hand with a loom, but in 1830 the power loom was perfected. By 1857 there were around 250,000 power looms in Britain, and 1,650,000 British workers had jobs in the textiles industry.

Steam Engines

In the cotton mills of Manchester, the spinning frames were powered by steam engines. This was the second great invention of the Industrial Revolution. These days, we are used to engines driving our cars, power plants and factories. However, in the 1760s the engine was a completely new idea.

A steam engine uses boiling water and cylinders to create movement. A man from Glasgow named James Watt designed the first successful model. He had his idea in 1763, but struggled to find anyone with enough money to pay for his work until he met a factory owner from Birmingham called Matthew Boulton. Together, Boulton and Watt designed and built their first engine in 1776.

An early steam engine built by Watt and Boulton in 1786

For the first time in human history, coal could be used to provide power – by heating the water which turned into steam. The first use for these engines was to pump water out of mines, but they went on to find many other uses: spinning cotton, grinding grain and powering transport.

Between 1775 and 1800, Boulton and Watt built around 450 steam engines at the Soho Manufactory in Handsworth, Birmingham. It is hard to think of an invention that has had as great an effect upon the world. Whilst showing a writer called James Boswell around the Soho Manufactory in Birmingham, Boulton boasted: 'I sell here, Sir, what all the world desires to have – power.'

> Why was the invention of the steam engine so important in Britain?

Iron and Coal

James Watt's steam engines and Arkwright's spinning frames had to be made from a resilient metal that was easy to mould. They chose iron. Before the Industrial Revolution, a new process for producing enormous amounts of high quality iron was developed by Abraham Darby. He invented the *blast furnace*, where coke (made from coal) was used to

This painting 'Coalbrookdale by Night' shows how the furnaces of the ironworks in the coalmining town of Coalbrookdale lit up the night sky.

smelt iron. (Smelting is a process that produces iron from iron ore.) By 1815, Merthyr Tydfil in Wales had the largest iron works in the world.

In order to feed the steam engines and blast furnaces of the Industrial Revolution, Britain needed a lot of coal. Fortunately, Britain sits on some of the most abundant coalfields in the world. In South Wales, Yorkshire, Northumberland, Durham, Nottinghamshire and Scotland there were enormous supplies buried deep underground, so large coalmines were constructed. In 1770, six million tons of British coal were extracted from the ground. By 1830, this figure had risen to 30 million tons.

Canals

How do you think heavy goods like iron and coal were transported around the country? It was not easy. Goods had to be loaded onto sturdy packhorses and taken across country. This took time and energy, which made the goods expensive. To solve this problem, man-made rivers called canals were built. Canals changed everything. A packhorse can only carry one-eighth of a ton of coal on its back. However, if coal is loaded onto a floating canal barge and pulled by a horse walking alongside it, that horse can transport fifty tons of coal.

> How did canals change how goods were transported across Britain?

The Duke of Bridgewater, a rich landowner who ran a Lancashire coalmine, built Britain's first canal in 1761 to transport his coal to Manchester. By 1815, there were 2,600 miles of canals in England, and 500 miles in Scotland and Ireland. Canals had to be flat, so how could barges travel up and down hills? They had to enter locks, which allowed them to move higher and lower by changing the level of the water. Aqueducts were built to carry the water over valleys, and tunnels were dug to allow it pass through hillsides. Coal, bricks, stones, slate, iron, grain and pottery could now be shipped all over the country at very low cost. This greatly helped the growth of British industry.

This horse is pulling a barge along the canal, just like the packhorses that used to pull boats loaded with iron and coal.

Trains

Canal technology was followed by an even greater invention: the steam train. Inventors realised that if James Watt's steam engine could be placed on top of a wagon and used to power its wheels, the wagon could drive itself forward. Such a vehicle would be called the 'steam locomotive' or 'train'.

Early versions of the locomotive used a lot of coal and often broke down. However, people in Liverpool and Manchester were keen to improve this new technology. In 1829 they held a competition to see who could design the best locomotive. It was won by George Stephenson with his locomotive The Rocket. You can read about George Stephenson and his son Robert on the next page.

You can see The Rocket at the Science Museum in London.

On 27 September 1825, the first ever railway for passengers was opened between Stockton and Darlington. The steam train was called Locomotion No. 1 and was built by George Stephenson's works. It pulled 33 wagons containing coal, flour and 600 passengers and took two hours to travel 12 miles. Because steam trains were still a new technology, horses were still used to pull some wagons, but in September 1830 a railway line was opened that was entirely designed for trains: the Liverpool to Manchester Railway. Stephenson's locomotives carried goods and 1,200 passengers a day between the two cities. The whole world was astounded by this new invention; people were travelling at a speed faster than anyone had ever known.

The opening of the Liverpool to Manchester Railway

Not everyone was happy about the birth of the train, which was nicknamed the 'Iron Horse'. People thought the speed would cause their lungs to collapse and the sound would cause cows' milk to go bad. Despite this, the railways spread across Britain. Between 1820 and 1860, about 10,000 miles of railways were built, so people could travel between many major cities. In 1821, it took 24 hours to travel from London to Birmingham by a horse drawn carriage; in 1845 the same journey took just four hours by train. The Railway Age had begun.

> How did the invention of the steam train change Britain?

George and Robert Stephenson

George Stephenson was born in 1781. His father worked in a colliery (which means coalmine) looking after one of the engines. Young George followed his father into colliery work, and aged 17 he was an engineman himself. However, it was not until he was 18 that he began, in his spare time, to learn to read and write. In 1811 he repaired the pumping engine at High Pit, Killingworth. As a result the colliery owners put him in charge of engines for the surrounding collieries of Killingworth. At this time, mines were very dangerous places to work. Miners carried lamps with candles, which they needed to be able to see what they were doing, but when the flames came into contact with a gas that was known as 'marsh gas' (we call it methane) there were explosions, causing many deaths. Stephenson set himself the task of solving this problem. The flame of the candle could not burn unless it was in contact with oxygen from the air, so it could not be enclosed. Stephenson devised a 'miner's safety lamp' in which air could only reach the flame of the candle through small tubes. It worked! At about the same time Sir Humphry Davy was working on the same problem in London and came up with a similar solution. Sir Humphry Davy was given the credit for the invention and presented with a gift of £2,000 for his work, but Stephenson received only 100 guineas (£105). The people of the North East were so annoyed by this that they collected another £1,000 to give to Stephenson!

You can read about Sir Humphry Davy on page 339.

Because he was interested in engineering, and because he worked in collieries, Stephenson turned his attention to trains, which were then called locomotives. A locomotive is an engine mounted on wheels to run on tracks. Trains were used to transport coal before anyone thought of carrying passengers on them. Stephenson made so many important improvements to these colliery railways that he was appointed as engineer to the Stockton and Darlington Railway – the first one to carry passengers. Although the owners wanted it set up so that horses could pull the wagons as well as trains, Stephenson argued that engines would be much better than horses, and laid strong iron tracks, instead of wooden tracks that had been used before.

He realised the engines had to be made more efficient to be able to pull heavy loads at speed without

Locomotion No. 1 *is now in the North Road Railway Museum in Darlington.*

breaking down, so in 1823 George, with his son Robert and three partners, opened the world's first purpose-built locomotive factory in Newcastle upon Tyne. The company's first engine, *Locomotion No. 1*, was used to pull the very first train on the Stockton and Darlington Railway. The factory went on to export locomotives to developing railways all over the world.

George Stephenson was then appointed as engineer to the Liverpool and Manchester Railway. Once again, the owners of the line were not sure that they wanted locomotives to pull the carriages. They thought

This painting, called Birthplace of the Locomotive, *shows George Stephenson, seated with a miner's safety lamp. Killingworth Colliery and his first steam train, designed for the colliery, can be seen in the background. His son Robert stands to the right of the picture.*

it would be better to have engines fixed beside the tracks, pulling the carriages from one engine to another. Stephenson said that locomotives, or mobile engines, would be better, so the owners announced a competition: anyone who could produce a locomotive to travel at 10 miles per hour, pulling a certain weight, would be given a prize of £500. Stephenson won the competition with his engine called *Rocket* which he had built with his son Robert in their factory in Newcastle. The Liverpool and Manchester Railway opened on 15 September 1830, and this date has been described as the dawn of the railway age. George Stephenson's genius had convinced people that railways were the best way to carry goods and passengers. He had a vision of a railway network that would connect the whole country, so he insisted on what he called his 'standard gauge', which meant that the rails on the track were spaced 4 feet 8½ inches apart. All railway tracks in Britain were then spaced out in this way and other countries did the same thing. Now we can travel at high speed all across Britain on our network of railways. George's son Robert Stephenson became as famous as his father, making great improvements to railways and designing bridges that were longer and stronger than any known before. The Stephensons, father and son, changed the way in which people travelled, which also changed the way in which people lived. Next time you are taking a train, think of their remarkable *Rocket*.

How Did the Industrial Revolution Change Britain?

Goodbye to the Old Ways

In just one generation, the Industrial Revolution changed customs and lifestyles that had survived for centuries. The new inventions put a lot of people out of work because just a few machines were able to do the work of many people.

Before the development of trains, people rode in stagecoaches pulled by horses.

For example, stagecoach drivers were no longer needed. Before 1830, the stagecoach was a popular way to travel throughout Britain. In 1846, the last ever stagecoach journey departed from London. After that, unused stagecoaches could be found abandoned all over the countryside.

Luddites broke the frames of many machines that were taking their jobs.

Some workers rebelled against losing their jobs like this. In Nottinghamshire, skilled workers who wove stockings (like thin socks) and lace were being put out of work by a machine called the stocking frame. In 1811 the workers attacked the new factories and destroyed the machines. They wanted their jobs back and thought destroying the machines would help with this. These bands of workers claimed to be following a leader named General Ned Ludd, so they were named Luddites.

The mythical General Ludd was the Robin Hood of early nineteenth-century England. His armed followers organised themselves like an army and paraded the country with marching drums. They spread northwards to Lancashire and Yorkshire, attacking the textile mills and spinning machines which had destroyed their jobs. In 1812, the Prime Minister, Spencer Perceval, passed a law called the Frame-Breaking Act making the Luddite attacks punishable by death. A force of 12,000 soldiers was sent to the northern counties to stop the protest and the Luddites were either executed or transported to Australia, which was where many convicts were sent at that time.

> Why did people want to attack the new machines and factories?

Industrial Work

Factory work in the early nineteenth century meant long hours, clattering noise, horrible heat and cruel punishments. The writer William Cobbett compared factory workers to slaves, 'compelled to work fourteen hours a day, in a heat of eighty-four degrees, and who are liable to punishment for looking out at a window of the factory!'

Working in a coalmine was not much better. Miners had to crawl through tunnels deep underground with only a lamp for light. These tunnels would sometimes collapse or flood, trapping and drowning those inside. Worst of all, pockets of flammable gas (that can catch fire) could be released and would explode when they came into contact with the flame of a miner's lamp. Often, canaries would be kept in the mines, as they would die of gas poisoning and warn the miners that gas had escaped into the air. The miner's safety lamp was invented in 1815. You can read about it on pages 133 and 340.

Growth of Cities

Many farmers and other workers who lost their jobs due to the Industrial Revolution flocked to towns and cities to work in the newly built factories. In 1851, for the first time ever, more British people lived in towns than in the countryside.

By 1861, Britain's largest cities outside London were all in the industrial midlands and north: Liverpool, Manchester, Birmingham, Leeds and Sheffield. Their populations rose rapidly: in 1750, Manchester was a town of 18,000 people. By 1861, it had grown to 338,000 people. Some towns, such as Middlesbrough, grew out of nothing. It was a farming village of 25 people in 1801, but a town of 19,000 people by 1861. When a nation's towns and cities grow this quickly, we call this *urbanisation*.

The living conditions for industrial workers were very bad. Poor people arriving from the countryside had to cram into cheaply-built houses, sometimes with whole families living in just one room. Houses were built without gardens and were called 'back-to-backs'. Often, back-to-backs had no running water and whole streets would share one water pump and one outdoor toilet.

This cartoon shows the germs lurking in one drop of Thames water

Disease spread very quickly. The killer disease of the early nineteenth century was called cholera. This was a horrible disease to catch: you would suffer severe diarrhoea and vomiting, your skin would turn blue and you would die after a few days. To begin with, people did not understand what caused the disease, which made it very difficult to prevent outbreaks. There were repeated outbreaks around the country until 1854, when a doctor called John Snow discovered that cholera was caused by drinking water contaminated by human waste. Once people understood this, they realised that sewers had to be built to get human waste out of cities and away from the supply of drinking water. The London sewers were built between 1859 and 1875. After that there were no more outbreaks of cholera in London. Sadly, this disease can still be found in countries that have poor sewage systems and many people still die from cholera every year.

> **Why did so many people die from cholera during the Industrial Revolution?**

> **Why do fewer people die from cholera today?**

Children at Work

Poor families moving to industrial towns often had to send their children to work. Small children were made to work as 'scavengers' in cotton mills. Scavengers would crawl underneath the moving machinery, picking up stray bits of cotton. If they were not careful, machine parts caught and cut off fingers and limbs, and loose bits of clothing stuck in the spinning cogs. In the worst cases, children were dragged into the machines and were killed.

Children were taken from orphanages to work in factories almost as slaves. They could be made to work for six days a week, fourteen hours a day, with only oats and milk as food. Any misbehaviour or sleeping on the job would result in punishment – often being beaten with a leather strap by a factory overseer.

Children were at great risk when they were made to crawl underneath machinery.

One of the worst jobs for children was being a chimneysweep's apprentice, or 'climbing boy'. Chimney sweeps would adopt orphans and poor children and put them to work, climbing up chimneys and brushing away the soot. This is the black dust which blocks the inside of a chimney when you burn coal. If you don't get rid of the soot, then when the fire is lit, the room fills with smoke because it can't escape out of the chimney. Sometimes children would become trapped and die of suffocation. If the chimney sweep thought they were not doing the job properly, the climbing boy would be poked with a long spiked pole, or a fire would be lit beneath them. An author called Charles Kingsley wrote a children's story called *The Water Babies* to draw attention to this cruelty.

Social and Industrial Reform

Many people in Britain believed something had to be done about these terrible working conditions. Employers were unlikely to improve conditions themselves, because it would cost them money. Parliament would have to become involved so that all employers had to improve conditions at the same time. However, many politicians and factory owners thought Parliament had no right to get involved in the workings of businesses. They believed in an idea called laissez-faire, which is French for 'let it be'.

Anthony Ashley Cooper, the seventh Earl of Shaftesbury, was an aristocrat and Member of Parliament. He was a Christian and believed it was Parliament's duty to improve working conditions for the poor. In response to his campaigns, the government passed the 1833 Factory Act. It limited the hours that children could work in a factory and stated child labourers had to be provided with two hours of education a day. Parliament passed many more Factory Acts and by 1850 factories could not work women and children past 6 PM, and had to provide workers with an hour's break for meals. Shaftesbury also took on the cause of climbing boys, and in 1875 the Chimney Sweepers Act finally outlawed the practice.

The Workhouses

Due to the Industrial Revolution, more people were losing their jobs to machinery. If you were very poor, paying bills and buying things your family needed would have been very difficult. Instead of living in a house, very poor people had to live in a workhouse. Workhouses were like prisons for people who had no jobs. Inside the workhouses, families would be split up, with different areas for men, women and children. The people in the workhouse had to wear prison-style uniforms and do boring, pointless tasks. They were given bad food

Mealtime for women at the St Pancras workhouse in London

and had to eat in silence. The workhouses were made so terrible in order to encourage people to get jobs and work hard. Life in a workhouse was the very last resort of desperate people. The British poor lived in constant fear of being sent to the workhouse and Charles Dickens wrote the novel *Oliver Twist* to show people how terrible these places were.

What happened to Oliver Twist when he asked for more? You can read about it on page 26 and you can sing 'Food, Glorious Food' along with the workhouse children on page 204.

How were people treated inside the workhouses?

A New Prosperity

The Industrial Revolution may have caused problems in areas where traditional jobs disappeared, but most British people enjoyed big improvements in the way they lived. During the 1850s and 1860s, Britain exported goods across the globe and came to be known as 'the workshop of the world'. At the centre of this trading Empire was London, the world's largest city with a population of over six million people by 1900.

Prince Albert, Queen Victoria's husband, took a great interest in these industrial and technological changes. He decided to stage an international exhibition to showcase the achievements of people from all around the world. It would be known as the Great Exhibition.

You can read a poem about London, written in the 1890s, on page 8.

An enormous new building was needed in London to host the event, and an architect named Joseph Paxton had the inspired idea to make it out of iron and glass. The exhibition centre was built in Hyde Park and looked astonishing: it was 1,848 feet (563 metres) long, 108 feet (33 metres) high, and made out of 300,000 individual panes of glass. The building was so beautiful people named it the 'Crystal Palace'. Inside the Crystal Palace were over 100,000 objects from around the world, including a steam hammer, a folding piano,

The Crystal Palace was so large that it covered several of the trees in Hyde Park, like a huge greenhouse.

an early sort of bicycle called the velocipede and the world's largest diamond. An estimated four million visitors came to see these magnificent exhibits. The Great Exhibition is remembered as one of the most important moments of Queen Victoria's reign. She later wrote of the day she opened it: 'It was the greatest day in our history and the triumph of my beloved Albert.'

Prince Albert is shown holding the catalogue of the Great Exhibition in his statue on the Albert Memorial in Kensington Gardens, near to where the exhibition took place.

How Did Power Move to the People?

Old Corruption

William Hogarth showed the corruption of the political system in his series of paintings Humours of an Election. *Candidates bought food and drink for people in exchange for their votes.*

By 1830, Britain was becoming a modern, industrial nation. However, there had been no big changes in the political system in a very long time. Of the 14 million people living in Britain, only 400,000 (three per cent) had the right to vote to decide who should be in the government. Britain was divided into boroughs and counties, which would vote to send Members of Parliament (MPs) to the House of Commons. If you were allowed to vote, people would often try to bribe you to vote for them, or your employer or landlord might threaten you with bad consequences if you didn't vote for his candidate. Your vote was not secret, so people might force you to vote for them and check that you had done so.

Because the system was so old, the cities that had grown rapidly during the Industrial Revolution often had no MPs. Birmingham, Manchester and Leeds were three of the largest cities in Britain, but they had no one to speak for them in Parliament.

The power in Britain still lay in the hands of the wealthy, land-owning class known as the aristocracy. The people of Britain thought this whole system was in need of change. Some even thought a revolution, like the one in France, was necessary.

Peterloo

In 1819, around 60,000 people gathered in St Peter's Field, Manchester to demand the right to vote. They were there to listen to Henry Hunt, a campaigner who disliked the way the government was set up. Hunt wanted things to change in a big, or radical, way, so he and his supporters were known as 'radicals'. Ten minutes into Hunt's speech, the crowd saw a group of soldiers on horseback charging towards them with their swords drawn. The soldiers had been sent to arrest Hunt,

The massacre of 'Peterloo'

but chose to kill his supporters. Eleven people were left dead and 500 injured. In reference to the heroic Battle of Waterloo, which had taken place four years earlier, the massacre was named 'Peterloo'. Such awful treatment was intended to stop the British people from complaining about voting, but although people were now scared, they still wanted to vote.

> **Why did people fight for the right to vote?**

The 1832 Great Reform Act

As you can tell from his name, Earl Grey was an aristocrat. We learnt about the aristocracy in Year 5. However, Earl Grey thought that to avoid a war or revolution, the British Parliament would have to change how it worked. In 1831, he proposed some changes including one that would allow any man who lived in a property worth over £10 a year in rent to vote. He introduced a Bill into parliament that became known as the Great Reform Bill.

The aristocrats in the House of Lords refused to accept Grey's suggestions, and riots erupted around the country. A mob burnt down Nottingham Castle, which belonged to the Duke of Newcastle, and a crowd of 100,000 people in Birmingham threatened to take weapons and march to London. Eventually the House of Lords gave in. The Great Reform Act was passed in 1832. The Act only increased the electorate (people with the right to vote) to 650,000 people. Nevertheless, it was a great turning point in British history. It started a process that carried on into the next century, giving more and more people the vote. Over these years, England was changing and was becoming a democracy. This word means 'rule by the people'. In the past, England was ruled by kings and other wealthy people, but now more ordinary people could have their say in how their country was run. Today every man and woman over 18 can vote (apart from prisoners, people with severe mental illness and members of the House of Lords).

Important Changes in Voting

- 1838– William Lovett wrote the People's Charter which said that all men should be allowed to vote and that voting should be secret.

- 1867– a new law allowed one million more men to vote.

- 1872– a new law allowed people to vote in secret.

- 1884– a new law allowed all men who owned houses to vote. This meant that for the first time, ordinary people such as farm workers and miners could vote.

- 1918– a new law allowed women over 30 to vote if they owned a house or were married to a man who owned a house.

Why Was Ireland Still Ruled by the British?

England's First Colony

Henry VIII and Queen Elizabeth sent soldiers to conquer Ireland and take the land. For many years, people from England and Scotland were encouraged to move to Ireland. This was called *colonising* and the new landowners came to rule much of the country. The Irish people were often Catholics and the English and Scots who came to settle the land were Protestants. From 1782 Ireland had its own parliament in Dublin, but Catholics and Protestants who did not accept the authority of the Church of Ireland were not allowed to vote until 1793. Even then they could not become MPs.

Some Irish people planned a rebellion. They were led by Wolfe Tone, who was not a Catholic. In 1798, at a time when England was at war with France, he invited Napoleon, the leader of the French military, to send troops to support the fight for Irish independence. There was much bloodshed and the revolution did not succeed. In 1800 the Parliament in Dublin voted for the Act of Union with England, although many people in Ireland did not want this to happen. From 1801 Ireland sent over 100 MPs to the House of Commons in Westminster and 28 peers to the House of Lords so that it could share in the government of the United Kingdom. Many Irish people agreed to the union because they were promised that the laws preventing Catholics from being MPs and holding public office would be removed, but Catholic Emancipation (as it was called) was not granted in England and Ireland until 1829.

Potato Famine

In 1845, Ireland was struck by a disaster. The potato had become a very important part of the Irish diet, but in 1845 a potato disease destroyed the entire crop. The Irish people depended on the potato, so the consequences were very serious: many people starved to death. An Irish artist called James Mahoney wrote of a house he entered in Bridgetown: 'I saw the dying, the living, and the dead lying indiscriminately upon the same floor, without anything between them and the cold earth, save a few miserable rags upon them.' It is estimated that around one million

Many Irish people starved during the potato famine.

Irish people died between 1845 and 1852, and another one million left Ireland for other countries, including America and England.

Although the government organised help for the victims of the famine, and large donations were raised all over the Empire, encouraged by Queen Victoria herself, many Irish people felt that not enough had been done, and were very angry. Some blamed the famine on the heartless Anglo-Irish landlords who owned a lot of land in Ireland, but who didn't live there all the year round as they wanted to spend their time in London.

Home Rule

Many people in Britain and Ireland did not believe that Ireland should be governed from London. They thought it should be given back its own parliament in Dublin. The idea that the Irish should be in charge of their own country is called 'Irish Nationalism'. The argument over how Ireland should be governed continued into the next century when, in 1920, Ireland was divided into two countries: Northern Ireland (which is still part of the United Kingdom) and Southern Ireland (which became a separate country and is now the Republic of Ireland).

How Did Victoria Rule her Empire?

An Empire on Which the Sun Never Set

In Year 5, you learnt how Britain gained an Empire. During the reign of Queen Victoria, it reached the height of its power. The British took control of Sierra Leone in 1808, Malta in 1814, South Africa in 1815, Sri Lanka (which was called Ceylon at that time) in 1815, Bahrain in 1820, Singapore in 1824 and Hong Kong in 1842. The British governed their colonies through people called viceroys and governors, appointed by the Colonial Secretary in London. These officials were encouraged to get involved in the local culture and often learnt the local language. They tried to keep peaceful relations with the local people by giving some powers to them.

For the entire nineteenth century, the British Empire ruled unchallenged as the world superpower. A superpower is a country that is very powerful and can influence other countries. By 1900, British rule stretched over one-quarter of the world's landmass and governed one fifth of the world's people. It was described as 'the empire on which the sun never set', because it was always daylight somewhere in the British Empire.

Learn about time zones and why the sun would never set on the British Empire in Queen Victoria's day on page 71.

The Jewel in the Crown

Ever since the eighteenth century, the British East India Company spread its power throughout India. The Company collected taxes, had its own army and its own courts. Where Indian princes still ruled their territories, they were expected to pay taxes and show support for the East India Company.

During this period, the relationship between the British and the Indians became worse. The British began forcing their own customs and ideas onto the Indian people. Ancient practices such as *suttee* (under which an Indian widow was expected to throw herself onto the funeral pyre of her dead husband) were outlawed, and Indian trade and legal systems were changed to become more British. Christian missionaries travelled to India, attempting to convert the Hindu, Sikh and Muslim population.

Many parts of India were encouraged to grow crops such as tea and tobacco which could be sold to other countries, instead of farming food for the Indian people. When droughts struck, the famines were terrible. The Indians were forced to buy British goods such as cotton textiles and were banned from making their own.

Robert Clive's victory at the Battle of Plassey in 1757 increased the British East India Company's military and economic power in India.

The Indian Mutiny, 1857

The mistrust between British colonial government and many Indian people turned into a rebellion in 1857. This rebellion began amongst the *sepoys*, Indian soldiers who served in the East India Company's army.

The sepoys revolted at Meerut in 1857.

Anger between the sepoys and their British officers had been growing for years, but the last straw came when they were issued with new Enfield rifles. These rifles used bullets wrapped in paper that was rumoured to be greased with pork or beef fat. To load their guns, sepoys had to bite these papers to release the gunpowder. Hindu sepoys refused to do this, as cows are sacred to their religion. Muslim sepoys also refused, because eating pork is against their religion.

An order was given to grease the papers with beeswax or mutton fat, but in May 1857, in a town near Delhi called Meerut, 85 sepoys were arrested and imprisoned for refusing to use their rifles. The following day, 2,000 of their fellow soldiers rioted. They freed the prisoners, killed 66 British people and marched to Delhi. They were joined by three other regiments along the way. Once in Delhi, they announced that the 82-year-old Bahadur Shah II, the nominal Mughal Emperor, was now their ruler. News of the rebellion spread fast and Bengal sepoys mutinied throughout northern and central India. Many Indian princes who disliked the British Empire joined forces with the sepoy rebels.

The cities of Delhi, Lucknow and Cawnpore were taken over by rebels. British soldiers were cut off and held prisoner. Many atrocities took place on both sides. After two long sieges, the British and the majority of Indian soldiers who remained loyal managed to take back Lucknow and Delhi, and the rebellion was largely over by the end of 1857. Indian princes and nobles who took part in the rebellion were executed.

The British Raj

Britain's Empire had very nearly lost control of India, known as the 'jewel in her crown'. The British had been taken by surprise and wanted to make sure such an event never happened again. Their solution was to strengthen their control over India but to relax their control over the Indian people. The East India Company was disbanded and India was ruled directly by a British viceroy. (A viceroy is someone who has the authority to rule on behalf of the king or queen.) In 1876, Queen Victoria was crowned Empress of India.

In return, the British promised to allow, even celebrate, Indian culture. Indian customs and practices were allowed to grow again and Christian missionaries were discouraged from visiting. Indians were given the chance to gain promotion to the higher ranks of the British army. Remarkably, the British were able to rule a nation of 300 million Indians with only 20,000 troops and officials. A new name was given to this era of Indian rule – the British Raj.

During the Raj, attempts were made to improve India's infrastructure and economy. By 1904, 24,000 miles of railway tracks had been laid, much of which is still used today. Major irrigation schemes were developed to get water to areas where crops were growing, and between 1880 and 1900 the amount of irrigated land in India doubled.

The Indian railways built by the British during the Raj are still being used today.

The Scramble for Africa

By the 1870s, attention had turned to the vast and unexplored continent of Africa. Governments of European countries saw it as an untapped source of riches. They all wanted to gain power in the continent, so this time was known as the 'scramble for Africa'.

To start with, Britain focused on the northeast of Africa, around

The new Suez Canal was opened in 1869.

the Suez Canal. This man-made trading route was finished in 1869 and made a shipping route from the Mediterranean to the Indian Ocean, avoiding the expensive and treacherous journey around the Cape of Good Hope in South Africa. In 1882 the British decided to make sure they controlled the canal by invading and occupying Egypt. To make sure they had control of the whole region, Britain occupied Uganda in 1888 and the Sudan in 1889.

Great Explorers: David Livingstone

In the nineteenth century, the continent of Africa was almost unknown to Europeans. Although there had been trade with African countries for centuries, most of the European traders went no further than the ports where they bought their goods. The interior of Africa seemed a strange and unexplored land. David Livingstone, who was born in 1813 in the Scottish town of Blantyre, became one of the most famous European explorers to travel through Africa. He was also a *missionary*, meaning a person who travels to other countries to encourage people to become Christians.

David Livingstone's father was a devout Christian who taught at a Sunday School. He did not want his son to read about science, which he thought could undermine his belief in God. He preferred books on religion but David was more curious than his father. He saved as much of his money as possible so that he could study medicine at Edinburgh University, while also going to religious lectures.

After his studies, he wanted to travel the world. He decided to go to Africa so that he could talk to the people there about his Christian faith. At this time, both European colonists and some African tribes were involved in capturing people in Africa and selling them into slavery. Livingstone thought this was a terrible thing to do to people. He believed that the best way to put a stop to it was to convert more local Africans to Christianity and to help Africans develop trade with the rest of the world.

He set sail for Kuruman, which is now part of South Africa, in December 1840 and arrived in July 1841. He spent several years exploring Africa, including the parts that were a long way from the sea and harder to get to. He discovered several important places, including Lake Ngami, Lake Malawi, Lake Bangweulu, as well as a huge waterfall, Mosi-oa-Tunya, which means 'the waters that thunder'. He renamed this Victoria Falls in honour of Queen Victoria in 1855. It is now on the border of the countries of Zambia and Zimbabwe.

He made maps of the places he visited, and was interested in discovering the lakes and rivers that would allow people to travel through Africa. He also wanted to find the source of the Nile, the longest river in the world, that flows through much of North Africa, into Egypt and then out into the Mediterranean Sea. He searched for it from 1866 until the time of his death in 1873, but he never found it. It turned out that he was searching too far south in what is now Tanzania. The real source of the Nile is further north in what is now Burundi.

While exploring, David Livingstone would spend long periods with no contact at all with his family and friends outside Africa. People would not know whether he was alive or dead. Once, when he had not been heard from for a long time, an American newspaper called the *New York Herald* sent a journalist, Henry Morton Stanley, to track him down. Stanley found him in October 1871 at a town called Ujiji by Lake Tanganyika, today in the country of Tanzania. Even though he had never met him before, he knew it must be Livingstone since he was the only other European who could be in such a distant land. So he greeted him by saying 'Dr Livingstone, I presume?'

Livingstone's maps were very useful to people who were trying to learn more about Africa, and he helped to persuade the British government to set up colonies by saying that there were great opportunities to make money from trade. He did everything he could to fight against slavery and he is still remembered in Africa where two towns are named after him: Livingstone, in Zambia beside the Victoria Falls, and Blantyre in Malawi, named after the place of his birth.

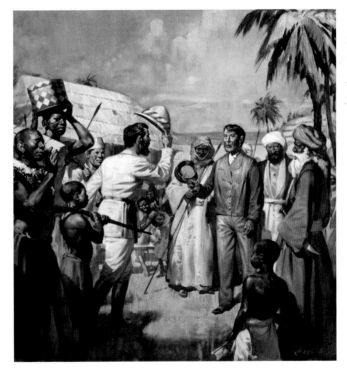

'Dr Livingstone, I presume?'

The Boer War

The most important person in the British Empire's African conquests was Cecil Rhodes. Rhodes was ill as a child, so was sent to live with his brother in South Africa when he was 17. He made lots of money buying and selling diamonds and wanted the British to gain more control of Africa. One colony in southern Africa was called Rhodesia after Cecil Rhodes.

In South Africa there were two independent states named Transvaal and the Orange Free State. Boer farmers, who were descended from Dutchmen who settled in South Africa before the British, lived there. The Boers led quiet lives in the countryside, until in 1871 Johannes Nicholaas de Beer discovered diamonds on his farm. In 1886, gold was discovered in the Transvaal. The Boer states were set to become fabulously rich and the British did not want a rival to their power.

This cartoon shows Cecil Rhodes's plans for a telegraph line from Cape Town in South Africa to Cairo, Egypt, which he announced in 1892.

A war between the British and the Boer farmers began in 1899. The Boers were a formidable enemy. As farmers, they were expert horsemen and marksmen, and knew how to use the land to their advantage. They fought in small groups of mounted 'commandos', swiftly ambushing the slow British soldiers. The war dragged on for two years, and Lord Kitchener, the commander of the British army, was determined to end this embarrassing conflict. He ordered the British army to destroy livestock, farms and crops, and imprison Boer civilians in a dreadful new invention – the concentration camp.

In all, 46 concentration camps were built. Bad conditions and a lack of food meant disease spread quickly, and an estimated 28,000 Boers and 20,000 black Africans died. The British eventually won, but at a high moral price. Many people in Britain and the rest of the world were disgusted at the terrible things that had been done.

> **Why did the British feel threatened by the Boers?**

A Global Power

For most of the nineteenth century, the British Empire was so powerful that there were no large global wars. British politicians often claimed that they had created Pax Britannica (British peace). They could also point to other benefits the British Empire gave to the countries under its control. The British introduced a legal system that protected people and their property, making it possible to develop new industries. They introduced laws to give people secure possession of their land, so that it could be farmed and developed. They introduced banks, which are necessary for economic growth. The British built railways, established new industries and expanded the amount of land that was irrigated and could be farmed. British sports such as rugby, cricket and association football took hold in the colonies, and are today enjoyed the world over.

Some people felt that the British had no right to be running their countries and they rebelled. Sometimes they were cruelly punished as a result. Eventually, so many people in Britain came to feel that nations should govern themselves that the Empire was dismantled. Many of the countries that used to be part of the Empire are now members of the Commonwealth of Nations, headed by the Queen. The Commonwealth is a voluntary association which allows the leaders of countries to meet as equals and talk about the things that concern them.

What Was Life Like By 1900?

If you were to travel back in time to Britain in 1900, you would recognise lots of things. After 1875, all newly built housing had running water drains linking to sewers. Gaslight had been invented and now lit many city streets, making it safe to travel at night. Altogether, life had become more comfortable. Thanks to the development of medicines, and the understanding of germs, people were living longer.

This lamplighter is lighting a gaslamp. Can you find any old gaslamps on the streets of your town?

153

This Rolls-Royce from 1905 was one of the early motorcars in Britain.

Trains covered the entire country. The sound of horses' hooves could still be heard around towns and cities, but there was much excitement about a new invention called the motorcar. The Bank Holidays Act of 1871, together with improvements in transport, meant that holidays were established as a normal part of life, with seaside towns such as Blackpool, Southend and Brighton developing. Even going abroad for holidays was possible, thanks to a travel agency started in 1841 by a Derbyshire businessman called Thomas Cook.

In 1870, parliament voted to provide a free education for every British child between the ages of 5 and 13. In the 30 years that followed, 2,500 Victorian schools were built. Many of the buildings are still primary schools today. Most people in the country could now read, and this led to the creation of newspapers: the *Daily News* (founded in 1846), the *Daily Mail* (founded in 1896) and the *Daily Express* (founded in 1900). The spread of the railways meant that papers could be read in every part of the country on the same day as the trains could deliver them overnight.

For proud Victorian homeowners, shopping was now very popular. Oxford Street in London and New Street in Birmingham were fashionable locations to go shopping. Department stores had grown up, where people could buy different things in the different departments of one big shop, without having to go from shop to shop. The first *chains* of shops were appearing: Boots the chemist and Marks and Spencer were already spreading across Britain.

Music hall was something Victorian people enjoyed. They would go to enormous theatres to enjoy songs, comedy and entertainment. The stars of the music hall were as famous as the film stars of today. Another popular kind of entertainment in Victorian times was association football. In 1901, Tottenham Hotspur played Sheffield United in the FA cup final in front of a crowd of 110,000 people. (They drew 2-2, but Tottenham won the replay.)

Perhaps the greatest crowd of Victorian London gathered in 1897, to celebrate Queen Victoria's Diamond Jubilee (meaning that she had reigned for 60 years). A grand procession of military bands, clattering horses and uniformed soldiers marched through London. Representatives of the entire Empire were there, including Nigerian tribesmen, Hong Kong police, Indian lancers and head-hunters from Borneo. All of this was captured on an exciting new invention – the moving camera – and the film could be shown on machines called cinematographs all around the country. At the centre of the procession, no more than five feet tall, was the 78-year-old Queen Victoria. When she had become Queen 60 years previously, no one could have imagined what an extraordinary amount of change Britain was soon to pass through. When she died four years later, on 22 January 1901, there was a feeling that a great era in the history of the nation had drawn to a close.

Crowds lined the streets to see Queen Victoria during the procession for her Diamond Jubilee.

Suggested Resources

Geography

Countries Around the World: Wales by Mary Colson (Raintree) 2012

Understanding World Maps by Jack Gillett (Wayland) 2012

Using Maps by Jack and Meg Gillett (Wayland) 2011

Polar Regions by Charlotte Guillain (Raintree) 2014

Starting Geography: Maps by Sally Hewitt (Franklin Watts) 2009

Countries Around the World: Canada by Michael Hurley, Raintree, 2013

What's Where in the World by R. Houston (Dorling Kindersley) 2013

USA in Our World by Lisa Klobuchar (Franklin Watts) 2012

Rainforests by Chris Oxlade (Raintree) 2014

Mapping (Investigate Geography) by Louise Spilsbury (Heinemann) 2009

Into the Unknown: How Explorers Found Their Way by Land, Sea and Air by Stewart Ross (Walker) 2011

Arctic and Antarctic (Eye Witness) by Barbara Taylor (Dorling Kindersley) 2012

Countries Around the World: Scotland by Melanie Waldron (Raintree) 2012

History

The Usborne History of Britain by Ruth Brocklehurst (Usborne) 2008

The Victorians by Ruth Brocklehurst (Usborne) 2013

History Year by Year by Peter Chrisp et al. (Dorling Kindersley) 2013

The Industrial Revolution by Clive Gifford (Wayland) 2013

Britannia: 100 Great Stories From British History by Geraldine McCaughrean (Orion Children's) 2004

Our Island Story by H.E. Marshall (Civitas/Galore Park) 1905; 2005

Victorian Industry by Neil Tonge (Franklin Watts) 2009

13 Buildings Children Should Know by Annette Roeder (Prestel) 2009

Films & DVDs

Beau Brummell, directed by Curtis Bernhardt, 1954. Follows the relationships between George III, George IV and Beau Brummell

Gone With the Wind, directed by George Cukor, 1939, PG. Various DVD editions. The classic film of the American Civil War, based on Margaret Mitchell's novel.

The Madness of King George, directed by Nicholas Hytner (Channel 4) 2007, PG

Sixty Glorious Years, directed by Herbert Wilcox (DD Video) 1938; 2001, U

Victoria the Great, directed by Herbert Wilcox (Optimum Home Entertainment) 1937; 2011, U

The Young Victoria, directed by Jean-Marc Vallée (Momentum Pictures) 2009, PG

Online

Find out more about the Boulton and Watt steam engine, including an animation, at www.sciencemuseum.org.uk/on-line/energyhall/section4.asp

Places to Visit

Buckingham Palace in London. The official residence of the monarch since Queen Victoria ascended the throne, it contains the ballroom built for her that was the largest room in London at the time. Open to the public during the summer months. http://www.royal.gov.uk/theroyalresidences/buckinghampalace/buckinghampalace.aspx

Didcot Railway Centre in Didcot, Oxfordshire http://www.didcotrailwaycentre.org.uk/

Geffrye Museum in London (domestic interiors covering 400 years) http://www.geffrye-museum.org.uk/

The Discovery Museum in Newcastle upon Tyne www.twmuseums.org.uk/discovery

Edinburgh Castle, where Mary Queen of Scots gave birth to James VI of Scotland and I of England www.edinburghcastle.gov.uk

Hadrian's Wall – Days Out, English Heritage http://www.english-heritage.org.uk/daysout/hadrianswall/

Ironbridge Gorge Museums in Telford preserve and interpret the remains of the Industrial Revolution in the six square miles of the Ironbridge Gorge. www.ironbridge.org.uk

The International Centre for Life is a science village in Newcastle upon Tyne www.life.org.uk

Kensington Palace in London. See the room in which Queen Victoria held her first Privy Council meeting, the dress she wore and her wedding dress. http://www.hrp.org.uk/KensingtonPalace/

National Railway Museum in York and Shildon, Co Durham http://www.nrm.org.uk/

The Science Museum in London http://www.sciencemuseum.org.uk/

Palace of Holyroodhouse in Edinburgh, the official residence of the Queen in Scotland www.royalcollection.org.uk

Rhondda Heritage Park celebrates the mining heritage of South Wales www.rhonddaheritagepark.com

Ryhope Engines Museum Sunderland www.ryhopeengines.org.uk

Stephenson Railway Museum in North Shields www.twmuseums.org.uk/stephenson

The Victoria and Albert Museum in London. Built using the profits from the Great Exhibition of 1851, the Museum contains some of the original exhibits. http://www.vam.ac.uk/page/g/great-exhibition/

Visual Arts

Introduction

Reading about art in a book like this one with your child is an important way to increase their knowledge and understanding of great art and artists, but it cannot replace the experience – and pleasure – of physically engaging with art. For the Year 6 child, this means seeing the wonderful surfaces, the sizes and the details of paintings (or sculptures, prints and drawings) in a gallery, museum, church, town hall or stately home; then it means going home afterwards and exploring art materials on the kitchen table and trying out the techniques, styles and colours you both liked. You don't need special or expensive materials to experience the pleasure of art at home; simply tracing over a gallery postcard or reproduction, then colouring your tracing, or cutting it and collaging it into a new creation, would be a rewarding, creative and educational art experience. To explore art further still, we suggest you dip into some of the books mentioned at the end of this chapter, and that you make use of the free family creative events which many galleries and museums offer at weekends and during school holidays.

The Renaissance

The Rebirth of the Arts

The Renaissance, which lasted from about 1400 to 1550, was a time when people began to look at the world in a different way. *Renaissance* is a French word meaning rebirth, so what was being reborn? People began to read and think about the civilisations of ancient Greece and Rome, and what had made them great. They looked at the works of art created by the people of these ancient cultures, and wondered if they could use some of the ideas. It was an exciting time, when the Middle Ages came to an end and new ideas were being discussed everywhere.

It started in Italy, where many classical buildings and works of art from long ago could still be seen and studied. These inspired people throughout Europe to build, sculpt and paint. One of the reasons that Renaissance artists admired Greek and Roman sculpture was because it focused on the human body. The Greeks and Romans had decorated their buildings and public spaces with freestanding sculptures that you can walk around, studying them from every angle, so the artists of the Renaissance decided to do the same. The sculptor Donatello, who lived from 1386 to 1466, cast the first free-standing bronze statue of a man on horseback since Roman times. Renaissance artists were ambitious; they used the latest scientific discoveries to create their beautiful paintings and sculptures.

Donatello's friend the architect Filippo Brunelleschi, who lived from 1377 to 1446, studied and measured ancient buildings, as well as reading books written by Roman authors like Vitruvius. Classical buildings were simple and harmonious because they were based on mathematical ratios or proportions. You might be wondering what maths has got to do with building, but in fact architects use maths all the time. It is very important to make sure things are measured properly and architects must get their sums right. What would happen if one wall were to be made shorter than another, or if the roof were too heavy for the walls? But maths is also about the relationship of one thing to another. The equals sign means that whatever is on one side of the sign has the same value as what is on the other side, as in 2 + 2 = 4. Equations in algebra all

This equestrian statue by Donatello is called Gattamelata. Equestrian means 'on horseback'.

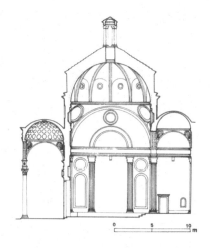

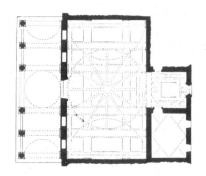

When Brunelleschi drew the plan of this chapel, he sliced the building in half so that you can see the inside, then he drew it from above. How many geometrical shapes can you see in Brunelleschi's design?

depend upon one side of the equation balancing the other. Geometry is all about shapes, and the basic geometrical shapes, like squares and circles, cubes, spheres and hemispheres, were thought to be a pleasure to look at because they were *harmonious.*

What do you think of when you hear the word *harmony*? Do you think of beautiful music, in which different notes blend together to make a lovely sound? This is the sort of harmony we read about on page 191. Or perhaps you think of your family and friends: when people get on well, they are said to have a harmonious relationship. Harmony means getting along, being in tune, working or moving together. In that sense, there is harmony in the universe. As we learnt in Year 4, the planets all orbit around the sun. They never bump into each other, because each planet stays in its own orbit. The ancient Greek philosopher Pythagoras even thought that the planets emit their own sounds, like a hum that we cannot hear. He called it the *music of the spheres.*

Brunelleschi asked himself why some buildings look beautiful and others don't. He decided that, because there is harmony in the universe, we like the things that we make to look harmonious too. For Brunelleschi, that meant that the classical buildings he so loved must be built according to laws of mathematical proportions: he thought that if we could understand these proportions, then everything we made would be beautiful. He wanted to build a dome on the cathedral in Florence, as a dome expressed this idea of universal harmony. It's hard to look at just one part of a dome. Because of its shape, your eye moves along the curves, taking in how every part relates to every other part. Brunelleschi knew that the ancient Romans had perfected the dome, so he travelled to Rome to study ancient buildings. The dome became a popular part of Renaissance architecture. Whereas medieval churches have spires, pointing up to heaven, Renaissance churches and other buildings often have domes, to make us think of things joining together in harmony. Brunelleschi's dome soon became a symbol of Florence, telling people that Florence welcomed new ideas.

The dome of Florence Cathedral

The Renaissance in Italy

The Renaissance began in Italy but new ideas quickly travelled north, to Flanders and Germany, as Italian merchants traded with people all over Europe. They sometimes sent their art and their ideas with the goods they were selling! From 1450, the printed book helped to spread these new ideas.

We learnt about printed books in Year 5.

Italy was not one country in those days; it was made up of city states ruled by powerful families like the Medici in Florence and the Gonzaga in Mantua. These ruling families were proud and ambitious; they wanted their city to be the best. So they employed architects and artists to create beautiful buildings, sculptures and paintings. Trade, especially with the New World (which we now call America), brought great wealth which allowed the Medici and the Gonzaga to spend money on the arts. But Rome would become the most important centre for the arts, because it was the centre of the Roman Catholic Church, and the Popes wanted to use all their power and resources to promote the teachings and influence of the Church.

In the Middle Ages, or Medieval period, painters and sculptors decorated churches and cathedrals. Art was in the service of the Catholic Church; artists were expected to paint scenes from the Bible, especially the life of Christ. Christian beliefs had to be explained through pictures as most people could not read. Artists did not choose what they would paint; such important decisions were made by scholars and priests who studied the Bible. In the Renaissance, art was still in the service of the Church, but the ruling families and powerful guilds associated with important crafts and trades also wanted to pay for works of art. The Medici decorated their palaces with sculptures and paintings; they wanted to show they were intelligent as well as rich and powerful.

At that time there were groups of people who practised the same craft or trade. These groups were called *guilds*. The guilds also wanted to show how rich and powerful they were by paying artists to create painted altarpieces and sculptures. Florence's craft and trade guilds decorated their chapel, known as the *Orsanmichele*, with their patron saints. The three richest guilds chose to have figures made of bronze, which cost approximately ten times more than those carved from stone. Each trade hoped to show they were better than the others by asking artists to make original, groundbreaking, sculptures for public display on Florence's most important street. The armour-makers guild hired Donatello, one of the most daring sculptors of his generation. His sculpture of *St George* (1417),

St George *by Donatello*

the warrior-saint, shows a man preparing himself for action, just before he fights the dragon; he appears so life-like it looks as though the statue could move at any moment. His face has individual features, so he looks like a real young man. His eyes are alert, although his expression is thoughtful; he knows he might die in the battle. The idea of showing what a man was thinking through a statue was new; this was a hero people could believe in. People were excited by the fact that statues could now be made to look so real.

A New Perspective

Medieval art, seen in churches and cathedrals, was not expected to show the real world. Its mission was to encourage people to think about the next world – life after death. Art was used to teach people about the life of Christ and to show them how to live good lives. But Renaissance artists wanted to bring the Bible to life by making their paintings realistic. They wanted you to look at a painting as though it were a window onto the real world. The problem was how to create this illusion or sense of depth on the flat surface of the canvas or wall.

By studying mathematics and optics (the way the eye sees things) they solved the problem. First, they noticed that things look bigger when they are close, while things look smaller as they move away.

Buildings could be slanted, shown diagonally, to make it appear they stretch into the distance. In 1413 a mathematical idea called *linear perspective* was demonstrated by Filippo Brunelleschi. He showed people that if a person stands between two parallel lines that stretch into the distance the lines look as though they get closer and closer until they seem to come together at a point on the horizon called the *vanishing point*. Have you ever looked down a railway track? Does it look like it is getting narrower and narrower until it vanishes? This is what Brunelleschi showed people. Artists realised they could show things on a flat surface that looked like they had depth.

The Florentine painter Masaccio may have asked Brunelleschi for help with his painting *The Trinity, with the Virgin and Saint John and donors* (1427). The barrel vault, divided into squares, is drawn in perspective; the squares get smaller and are foreshortened so that you seem to be looking into a hole in the wall. Your eye is tricked; when you stand in front of the painting you seem to be part of it, as the two 'donors', the man and woman who paid for the painting, appear to be kneeling outside this imaginary chapel. They appear to be in your space. These two donors are very natural; you might imagine them standing up and walking away after saying their prayers. Below the donors you can see a tomb containing a skeleton. Once again, it is so realistic, you could almost believe it is in your space, but all of these things are painted onto the flat wall of the church using perspective.

Piero della Francesca demonstrated his knowledge of linear perspective in *The Flagellation of Christ* (1455-60); he drew a linear grid on the floor, seen as the lines of the pavement, on which he placed his figures.

The Trinity *by Masaccio*

Activity 1: Perspective

Have you ever drawn a picture and thought the things in the picture look a funny size? Renaissance artists wanted to make their paintings look realistic, so they thought a lot about the size of the things they were painting.

We have found out that artists noticed things look bigger when they are close by, but they look smaller when they are further away. Look at the picture of the railway track on the opposite page. On a plain piece of paper, draw some diagonal lines that join at a vanishing point, just like the railway tracks do. Now think about the size of a tree near the vanishing point. What size would it

Rudyard Kipling used perspective when he drew this picture of The Cat That Walked By Himself. *It looks as if the cat has a very long way to walk!*

need to be? Now draw another tree slightly further along the track. The tree would need to be drawn slightly bigger. Keep going until you have a line of trees along the track. The tree nearest the edge of the page, at the front of the picture, should be the largest.

Now look at your drawing. Have you created perspective? You could now try to draw a train hurtling down the track towards you. Think how big the train should be in relation to the trees. The closer the train is to you, the larger it will have to be to look right.

The Flagellation of Christ *by Piero della Francesca*

This meant he could draw the figures correctly; they are the right size for their position in the picture. The meaning of the painting remains a mystery. In the background we see Christ suffering; he is being beaten by his enemies. (Flagellation means beating.) Perhaps the men in the foreground are thinking about Christ's sacrifice. The man with the beard looks like a portrait of a living person; he may be a famous Renaissance philosopher.

Renaissance artists wanted to capture real likenesses, or portraits, to make their works realistic. Flemish artist Jan van Eyck's *The Arnolfini Portrait* or *Arnolfini Wedding* (1434) is considered ground-breaking as it shows us the corner of an actual room with people who really lived, a painting of everyday life. The artist has become an eye witness, recording a promise of marriage in a painting. The objects in the picture add more information to the story: the dog is a symbol of faithfulness and the fruit on the table symbolises the couple's desire to be fruitful and have children. The lady's dress, which is bunched up, also shows that she hopes to have children. The artist used an oil-based pigment to create the rich glowing colours. It was Northern artists who learnt how to mix pigments with oils made out of plant seeds. Northern artists were just as bold and

The Arnolfini Wedding *by Jan van Eyck*

Journey of the Magi to Bethlehem
by Benozzo Gozzoli

inventive as those in Italy. By laying one colour over another they could create a wide range of shades. Spot all the different shades of brown: the fur of the dog, the wooden floor and the man's robe. The glowing surface also mimics natural light; see how the sunlight falls realistically through the window, illuminating the bride. The reflection of the window glows in the mirror on the wall. Jan van Eyck hoped to fool you into thinking you are part of the scene, a witness to this promise of marriage.

Even when painting a biblical scene, the artist could tell the story in a modern setting. Benozzo Gozzoli was asked to paint the *Journey of the Magi to Bethlehem* in the chapel of the Palazzo Medici Riccardi in Florence (1459-61) but he actually recorded a procession of important people who were living at the time, following the Magi – the three wise men – into Florence. Members of the Medici family and their courtiers have been identified; the artist even included himself. He is one of the men wearing red hats, and he has written his name on the hat.

This painting is a *fresco*; the paint is applied to wet plaster and the two materials fuse together. This allowed whole rooms to be painted. Andrea Mantegna's frescoes for the *Camera degli Sposi* or Bridal Chamber (1465-75) in the Ducal Palace, Mantua,

Mantegna has painted the sky on the walls of this room and on the ceiling. Can you see the cherubs looking down?

create a magical illusion, as if the room looks out over the countryside. Your eye is fooled into thinking the ceiling opens to the sky; faces look down on you. You might even fear someone falling on your head!

The Harmony of the Body

Earlier in this chapter, we looked at the way in which ideas about harmony and mathematical proportions affected the sort of buildings people designed. Renaissance artists also used mathematics to draw the perfect human body. By studying famous Greek and Roman sculptures, the Renaissance artist learnt to base his ideal body on harmonious proportions. Beauty was to be found in balance or symmetry. The balanced human body was now a symbol of the order of the universe. As God had created man, according to the Bible, the body of a man must be perfectly made. The Italian artist Leonardo da Vinci, who lived from 1452 to1519, illustrated these ideas in his drawing *Vitruvian Man* (also known as *The Proportions of Man*). The two most perfect geometric forms are the square and the circle; Leonardo shows how these forms relate to the human body. If the man

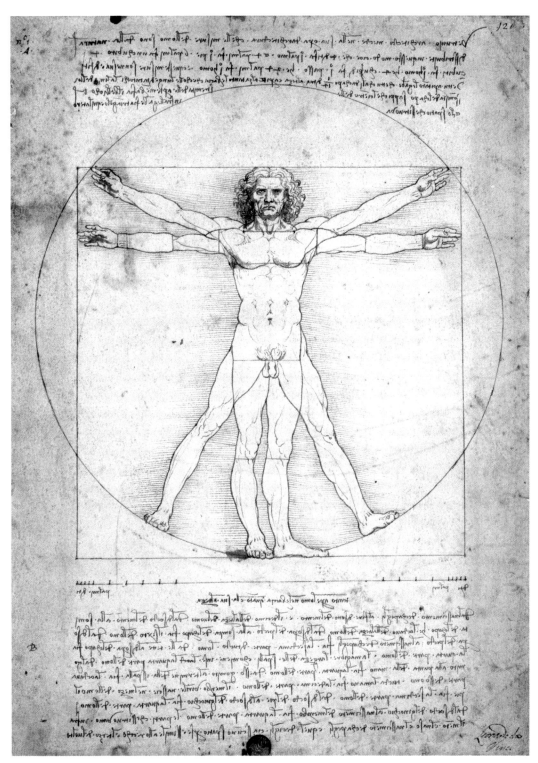

Vitruvian Man *by Leonardo da Vinci*

stretches out his arms and legs in the shape of an X his fingers and toes touch the circle. If he closes his legs and spreads his arms to make a T his fingers and toes touch the square. The man's navel is at the centre of the circle. The human body was divided into portions. These portions relate to each other in a ratio: the ideal body is eight times as high as the head or the same length as the outspread arms. Both bodies and faces have to be balanced to be beautiful. Artists also used the Golden Section or Golden Ratio, a mathematical equation based on proportions, to plan harmonious buildings. In Leonardo's time, art and science worked together, with mathematics providing the basis for art.

The Nude

In the medieval period, it was not considered right to show the naked human body in art, but Renaissance artists thought the naked body was beautiful and heroic. They studied classical sculptures to learn how to create the perfect naked body, which was now called a 'nude'. Sandro Botticelli painted *The Birth of Venus* (1486) for the Medici family; it may have been a wedding present. The story is taken from Greek mythology: Venus, the goddess of love and beauty, was miraculously born from the sea. Botticelli shows the goddess coming to the shore on a seashell. She is being blown by a 'zephyr' or wind in this imaginary scene.

The Birth of Venus *by Botticelli*

Michelangelo Buonarroti created one of the most famous Renaissance nudes, the statue of *David* (1501-04). Like Donatello's *St George*, we see a man preparing for action; the Bible tells a story of David, a shepherd boy who led the Israelites to victory by killing the giant Goliath with a slingshot. His sling is draped over his left shoulder. The muscles in his neck show the tension in his body. Yet although David may be nervous, he is also determined. He stares bravely toward his towering enemy. However, unlike Donatello's *St George*, Michelangelo's *David* is depicted nude, like the heroes of ancient Greece. Michelangelo shows that he knew about the human body. He carved each part of *David's* body realistically – even the veins in his hand. *David* has an athletic physique: he is a super-human man rather than the slender boy we are told of in the Bible. The statue is twice life-size and it sums up the ambitious spirit of the Renaissance – a spirit as daring as that shown by David facing Goliath.

Michelangelo's David.

Michelangelo also painted a very famous nude. He was asked by Pope Julius to paint biblical scenes on the ceiling of the Sistine Chapel (1508-12) in the Vatican; the ceiling was so large that it took him four years to paint. It must have been gruelling and dangerous work, as the ceiling is around sixty feet above the floor. The frescoes begin with the *Days of Creation* and end with *The Last Judgement*, the beginning and the end of the world. The paintings are considered to be the crowning achievement of the Renaissance.

The most famous scene shows *The Creation of Adam*, the first man. Adam leans on one elbow, his outstretched arm reaching towards God. His strong body is still weak and limp as God has only just created him. Adam does not yet have the strength to push himself up from the ground; notice his arm resting on his bent knee. Michelangelo painted a God who is as powerful as Adam is weak. His hair and clothing stream in the wind as he rushes through the heavens stretching out his hand towards Adam. As soon as God's finger touches Adam's, the man's body will be flooded with life. Michelangelo focuses all our attention on the fingers by placing them at the centre of the composition against an empty background. The image is very dramatic but the meaning is clear and easy to understand; God created Man.

The Creation of Adam *by Michelangelo*

Renaissance Men

Architect, sculptor, painter and poet, Michelangelo was a 'Renaissance man', meaning that he was interested in many things, and was good at them all. Leonardo da Vinci is the most famous Renaissance Man, being an artist, mathematician, scientist, student of human anatomy, botanist, engineer and inventor, although he is best known as a painter. Some consider him to be the most talented person ever to have lived; he was a genius. He drew designs for machines that were hundreds of years ahead of their time including a submarine and a flying machine! He painted the most famous picture in the world: the *Mona Lisa* (1503-06). This portrait of a woman (we are not even sure who she is) has fascinated us for centuries. Her smile is described as 'enigmatic', meaning we are not sure why she is smiling. Some see it as a happy smile, while others feel she is sad. Some people believe she understands the mysteries of the universe and has deep knowledge or wisdom. Yet the *Mona Lisa* remains very puzzling. The strange landscape in the background adds to this mystery; the jagged mountains are frightening. Why is she posed against this background? We don't know, just as we can't solve the mystery of her smile.

Leonardo was very famous; today we would call him a celebrity. He is said to have died in the arms of Francis I, the King of France. After his death, Francis declared there had never been another man who knew as much as Leonardo and that he was a very great philosopher. In the Middle Ages an artist was just a craftsman, like a carpenter or a blacksmith. However, Michelangelo and Leonardo could think as well as paint; they were well educated, self-assured and proud of their talent. As important people, they could talk to and even argue with noblemen and popes. One day Pope Julius II asked Michelangelo when he would finish painting the Sistine Chapel ceiling and he snapped back: 'When I can, Holy Father.' The Pope was equally fond of the work of the painter Raphael,

Mona Lisa *by Leonardo da Vinci*

who lived from 1483 to 1520. Leonardo, Michelangelo and Raphael form a *trinity* (meaning a group of three) of great masters who mark the high point of the Renaissance.

Raphael's famous *The School of Athens* in the Vatican, which was painted between 1509 and 1511, shows us that painters were now very learned as well as very skilled. The fresco includes many important Greek philosophers, men known for their wisdom. Renaissance thinkers also wanted to understand the world; they too had a thirst for knowledge. In the centre, Plato and Aristotle appear to be discussing an important point; Plato, who is pointing upwards, is said to be a likeness of Leonardo. Michelangelo was the model for the seated figure leaning on his elbow deep in thought. *The School of Athens* is said to represent the classical spirit of the Renaissance.

Can you spot Leonardo da Vinci and Michelangelo in Raphael's The School of Athens?

The German painter, engraver, printmaker, mathematician and philosopher Albrecht Dürer, who lived from 1471 to 1528, was also confident of his ability and talent; his *Self-portrait* shows us a confident gentleman, fashionably and expensively dressed with carefully curled hair. He could be a high born and well educated aristocrat rather than an artist. He looks directly at the viewer, as if challenging us to question his high opinion of himself. He demands our respect, holding a social position he believed an artist of his ability was entitled to. The artist was now a gentleman rather than a tradesman, an important man in society.

Albrecht Dürer's Self-portait

Activity 2: Shading

Renaissance artists wanted to make their work realistic. As we read on page 166, Flemish artist Jan van Eyck painted a scene from everyday life called *The Arnolfini Wedding*. The artist's choice of oil-based pigment creates rich and glowing colours in the painting. Can you see the different shades of brown that van Eyck has used? The floor is brown, the dog is a different brown and the man's coat is a darker brown. This was achieved by laying one colour over another, using a special oil paint made from plant seeds.

To create shades of colours, artists often add black to the colour they are using. Try this for yourself. Mix a colour that you would like to use and paint a little onto a page. Now add a small amount of black paint. Be very careful – if you add too much, the colour will change very quickly. You should now have a darker shade of your original colour. Paint a little next to your first colour. Keep repeating this process until you have several shades of your colour, getting darker each time. You

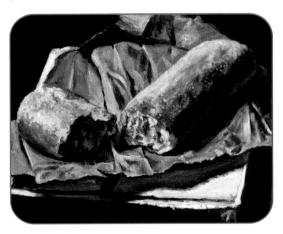

will see you have created many different shades of the colour you chose. Can you use some of your shades in a painting? If you make the colour of whatever you are painting get darker as it gets further from the light, it will make the object look three-dimensional, like the broken loaf of bread and the brown wrapping paper in this painting.

Victorian Art

People in Victorian Britain knew that they were living through a period of great changes. As we read on page 128, the industrial revolution changed the way in which people lived and worked. It created great wealth, but living conditions for some of the people who worked in the mines and factories were very bad. Many people moved from the countryside to the new industrial cities, where hundreds of thousands of people lived very close to one another, but without really knowing the other people they were living among.

Many people wanted to improve the conditions of life for poor people. We read on page 140 about the Earl of Shaftesbury's Factory Acts and on page 90 about the 'model village' that William Lever built for his workers in the Sunlight Soap factory. However, some thinkers and artists felt that the industrial revolution had made life so much worse than it was before that they wanted to turn the clock back to what they saw as a simpler, kinder way of life. In particular, they looked back to the Middle Ages.

An architect called Augustus Welby Pugin produced a book called *Contrasts*, in which he drew pictures of an imaginary town in 1440 and in 1840. He made the medieval town look attractive and welcoming, but he made the town of his own day look ugly. Compare the two pictures on the right. What differences do you notice? In 1440, the skyline is dominated by church spires; in 1840 by smoking chimneys. Can you see the large octagonal prison in the Victorian town? Some of the churches and chapels have been demolished, rebuilt or allowed to fall into ruin. Which scene would you prefer to look at? Pugin believed that, in the Middle Ages, poor people and sick people were better looked after by monks and nuns in religious hospitals.

An imaginary town in 1440...

...and 1840 by Augustus Welby Pugin

The style of architecture that was popular in the Middle Ages is called Gothic. Buildings built in the Gothic style often have pointed arches, lots of stone carving and tall spires on churches. Do any buildings in your area have any of these features? As the Gothic style became popular, people called this trend the Gothic Revival. The word 'revival' shows that the style was coming back into fashion. The people who liked the Gothic style became known as *Gothic Revivalists*. Pugin, and other leaders of the Gothic Revival, argued that the Gothic style could be used for modern buildings, not just churches. In 1834 the Houses of Parliament burnt down and there was a debate about what style they should be rebuilt in. People who admired the glories of ancient Rome said that they should be built in the classical style, like a Roman building with columns and a symmetrical layout, because many people saw Britain as the new Rome. However the Gothic Revivalists said that Gothic architecture was more than just another style: it represented the Christian faith, because the Middle Ages had been a time of great religious faith in Britain. They therefore argued that a Christian nation should have its parliament building in the style of what they called Christian architecture.

The Gothic Revivalists won the argument, and the Houses of Parliament were designed in a Gothic style by an architect called Charles Barry. However, Barry used Pugin to design all of the decoration, inside and out. Almost everything you can see in the Houses of Parliament was designed by Pugin in the Gothic style: not only the stone work but the furniture, wallpaper, stained glass, floor tiles and even the door handles!

The Houses of Parliament were designed, inside and out, in the Gothic style.

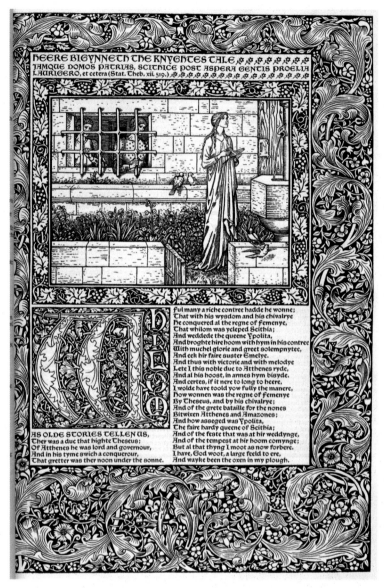

A page from William Morris's edition of The Canterbury Tales

Another artist who was influenced by the Middle Ages was William Morris. Morris believed that working-class people had been better treated in the days before the industrial revolution, so he designed wallpaper, tiles, furniture, fabrics, books and other things that were made by hand instead of by machines to remind people of what he regarded as a better way to organise society. He published a very elaborate edition of *The Canterbury Tales* by Geoffrey Chaucer which was produced on a printing press but was meant to look like a medieval illuminated manuscript. William Caxton, who set up the first printing press in England in the fifteenth century, had chosen *The Canterbury Tales* as his first book. William Morris wanted to get back to Caxton's way of printing books by hand, instead of using machines

William Morris was one of a group of artists who became interested in the stories of King Arthur and the Knights of the Round Table. They believed that these stories reflected values like nobility, courage and selflessness, which they contrasted with the greed and selfishness that they thought people in their own society were showing.

We saw John William Waterhouse's painting of *The Lady of Shalott* in Year 5, and you can look at Aubrey Beardsley's illustrations for *Le Morte d'Arthur* beginning on page 29.

Edward Burne-Jones was an artist who painted and designed many scenes showing the lives and adventures of King Arthur, Guinevere, Lancelot and the other knights. His painting *The Last Sleep of Arthur in Avalon*, begun in 1891, shows King Arthur's final resting place. After dying in battle, Arthur's body was taken to the Isle of Avalon by Morgan Le Fay, the enchantress, and other noble ladies, to heal his wounds. The ladies are painted with elongated bodies that make them look like the statues in medieval cathedrals. Some legends say Arthur may one day awaken and come to the aid of his kingdom. Many believed, like Burne-Jones, that Arthur's death brought the Golden Age of Chivalry to an end.

The Last Sleep of Arthur in Avalon

Activity 3: Why were some buildings built in an old-fashioned style?

Walk around the town or city in which you live, or around the nearest town or city if you don't live in one, and look at the buildings. You will notice that some of them are very modern, built of materials like steel and glass, while some are built in an old-fashioned style. We have looked at two styles of building in this chapter: Renaissance or classical buildings that have round arches, columns and triangular pediments on top of the columns; and Gothic buildings that have pointed arches and lots of decorative carving. Renaissance churches often have domes; Gothic churches have spires. Renaissance buildings are symmetrical; Gothic buildings are not – they are *asymmetrical*.

We learnt about symmetry in Year 3.

There may be some buildings that were really built in the Middle Ages, but you will certainly find more buildings that were built later, perhaps in the nineteenth century, to look like medieval buildings.

Choose one building and write about why you think it was built in an old-fashioned style. Perhaps you could photograph it or draw it, and then write labels to show which bits of it are typical of the style that was chosen.

Here are some of the buildings that you will find in most towns or cities:

- Town hall
- council offices
- railway station
- church
- office block
- shops

Make a table of them and say which style you think is best for each building: Renaissance, Gothic or modern. You could even suggest a different style altogether. For example, some old cinemas and other buildings were designed in the style of ancient Egypt, like this house in Penzance.

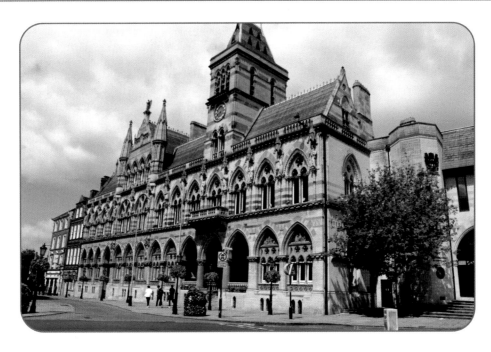

Which style did the architect use for Northampton Town Hall, on the top? And which for Birmingham Town Hall, on the bottom? What do you think the architect of each building was trying to suggest?

Suggested Resources

Leonardo Da Vinci: Discover the world of Leonardo through his apprentice's diary by Steve Augarde (Kingfisher) 2011

The Story of the World's Greatest Paintings by Charlie Ayres (Thames and Hudson) 2010

The Story of Painting by Abigail Wheatley (Usborne) 2013

Where to Find the Works of Art in this Chapter

Tommaso Masaccio, *The Trinity*, 1427-1428 (Santa Maria Novella) Florence, Italy

Piero della Francesca, *The Flagellation of Christ*, 1463-1464 (Galleria Nazionale delle Marche) Urbino, Italy

Jan van Eyck, *The Arnolfini Wedding*, 1434 (The National Gallery) London, UK

Benozzo Gozzoli, *The Journey of the Magi to Bethlehem*, 1460 (Palazzo Medici-Riccardi) Florence, Italy

Leonardo da Vinci, *Vitruvian Man*, 1492 (Galleria dell' Accademia) Venice, Italy

Sandro Botticelli, *The Birth of Venus*, 1485 (Galleria degli Uffizi) Florence, Italy

Michelangelo Buonarroti, *David*, 1501-04 (Galleria dell' Accademia) Florence, Italy

Michelangelo Buonarroti, *The Creation of Adam* (Sistine Chapel Ceiling), 1511-12 (Vatican Museums and Galleries) Vatican City

Leonardo da Vinci, *Mona Lisa*, 1503-6 (Louvre) Paris, France

Raphael (Raffaello Sanzio da Urbino), *The School of Athens*, 1510-1511 (Vatican Museums and Galleries), Vatican City

Albrecht Dürer, *Self Portrait with Gloves*, 1498 (Prado) Madrid, Spain

Augustus Welby Pugin, 'a Catholic town in 1440' and 'a town in 1840', *Contrasts: Or, A Parallel between the Noble Edifices of the Middle Ages and Corresponding Buildings of the Present Day*, 1836 (Cambridge University Press, 2013)

William Morris, *Works of Geoffrey Chaucer*, 1896, illustrations by Edward Burne-Jones (The British Library) London, UK

Sir Edward Coley Burne-Jones, *The last sleep of Arthur in Avalon*, 1881-98 (Museo de Arte de Ponce), Puerto Rico

Music

Introduction

This chapter introduces some vocabulary, symbols and concepts that will help children to understand and appreciate music. It builds on what students should already know about musical notation and introduces spirituals. It also profiles a few composers and prints the lyrics to some popular songs.

The value of this chapter will be greatly enhanced if children are able to listen to the classical selections described. You will find a list of good recordings of all the pieces mentioned here at the end of the chapter.

In music, as in art, students benefit from learning by doing. Singing, playing instruments, following musical notation and dancing all sharpen a child's sense of how music works. We encourage you to share good music with children by playing and/or singing some of the songs presented here, attending concerts, listening to the radio and playing recordings.

The Elements of Music

What All Music Has in Common

What kinds of music do you like to sing and listen to? Do you like classical music played by an orchestra? Church music sung by a choir? Rock music played with electric guitars? These kinds of music can sound very different, but they all have something in common. They can all be written down in a special language called *musical notation* so that others will be able to play the music, too.

Looking at musical notes on a page and singing or playing them is called *reading music*. Once you learn the language of music, you can look at the symbols written down in a piece of music and tell whether to play your instrument loudly or softly and whether to sing high or low.

High Notes and Low Notes

Here's a simple example of musical notation. It shows the notes and words for a song you probably already know.

Music is read from left to right and top to bottom, just like printed English. When musicians write music, they organise the notes on a stave made up of five lines and four spaces. When a note is written low on the stave, it has a *low pitch*. When it is written high on the stave, it has a *high pitch*. Can you see how the first two notes of 'E-I-E-I-O' are played and sung at a higher pitch than the next two? The last letter in the sequence – 'O' – is played at an even lower pitch.

Short Notes and Long Notes

Pitch isn't the only thing you need to know to sing or play a note. It's also important to know how long to hold the note. When composers write music, they use different musical symbols to tell you how long a note should sound. A semibreve tells you to hold the note for as long as four crotchets, a minim for two crotchets, a quaver for half a crotchet, and a semiquaver for a quarter of a crotchet.

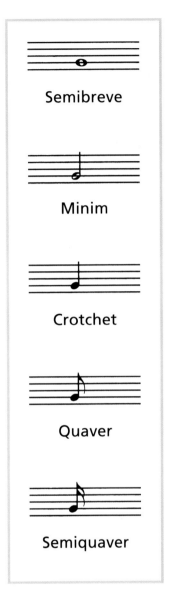

Semibreve

Minim

Crotchet

Quaver

Semiquaver

Notice how the single quaver note shown to the left has a single flag. When two or more quavers are written side by side, they are connected by a bar called a *beam*, like this:

A single semiquaver has two flags; grouped semiquavers have two beams, like this:

Look back at the music for 'Old MacDonald'. As you sing the first line, can you feel how you hold the note for 'farm' longer than the earlier notes? 'Farm' gets a minim, whereas the earlier words and syllables get crotchets. Sing the line 'Here a chick, there a chick, everywhere a chick, chick'. Do you notice how you don't stay very long on most of the words in that phrase? When you sing those words, you're singing clusters of quavers mixed in with a few crotchets.

Dotted and Tied Notes

If a composer wants to make a note last longer than a minim but not as long as a semibreve, putting a little black dot to the right of the note will do the job. That dot tells the performers to hold the note half as long again. See how the last minim in 'Old MacDonald' is dotted? It's not uncommon for the last note of a song to be held a little longer.

Another special symbol can be used to show that a note should be held for a long time. A composer uses a *tie*, or a curved line that links two notes at the same pitch together, to tell the musician to continue to hold the first note through the time of the second. How many tied notes do you see in the sample below?

185

Time for a Rest

Rests tell musicians when to be silent. The shapes or position of the various rests tell how long the silence should last. In $\frac{4}{4}$ time, a semibreve rest means silence for a whole bar, a minim rest for two crotchet beats, a crotchet rest for one beat, and a quaver rest for half a crotchet. Note that a semibreve rest lasts as long as a semibreve, a minim rest as long as a minim, etc. The box at the right shows the symbols for rests of different lengths. Can you find any rests in the music for 'Old MacDonald'?

Bars and Bar Lines

Look once more at the music for 'Old MacDonald'. Do you see the vertical (up-and-down) lines that separate the notes into groups? These lines are called bar lines. They divide the music into *bars*. How many bars are shown for 'Old MacDonald'?

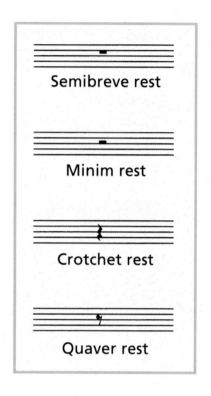

Semibreve rest

Minim rest

Crotchet rest

Quaver rest

Composers use a single bar line to mark the end of a bar and a double bar line to mark the end of a section or a whole piece.

Repeats

Composers use *repeat* signs to tell musicians to go back and play or sing a section again. The section to be repeated is marked with a begin-repeat sign and an end-repeat sign. The begin-repeat sign is a double bar line with two dots to the right; the end-repeat sign is a double bar line with two dots to the left. When the musicians get to the end-repeat sign, they go back to the begin-repeat sign.

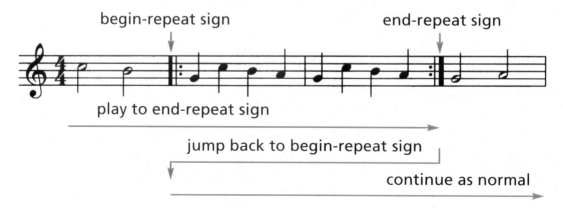

begin-repeat sign

end-repeat sign

play to end-repeat sign

jump back to begin-repeat sign

continue as normal

Time Signature

Do you see the two stacked numbers at the beginning of the music for 'Old MacDonald' – the ones that look like a fraction without a line? Those numbers are called the time signature. The top number in the time signature tells how many beats are in each bar of a piece of music and the bottom number tells what kind of note represents one beat.

For 'Old MacDonald', the time signature is $\frac{4}{4}$. The 4 on top means that there are four beats per bar, and the 4 on the bottom means that each beat is a crotchet.

You can see that the first bar of 'Old MacDonald' is made up of four crotchets, each of which is held for one beat. The second bar is a little different. It contains only three notes, but the one that goes with the word 'farm' is held twice as long – for two beats. So this bar still lasts just as long as four crotchets. Look at the eleventh bar – the one beginning 'Here a chick'. In this bar, there are six notes, but since quavers last only half as long as crotchets, the bar is still only as long as four crotchets would be.

When the time signature is $\frac{4}{4}$, we say the song is written in 'four-four time'. Many popular songs are written in $\frac{4}{4}$ time, which is also called 'common time' and is sometimes indicated with a large C. But you will also see songs written in $\frac{2}{4}$, $\frac{3}{4}$, and $\frac{6}{8}$ time. Here's an example of a song you probably already know that can be written in $\frac{6}{8}$ time. The six quavers in a bar are divided into two groups of three. You can see clusters of six quavers in the bars that go with 'merrily, merrily'. Count slowly 'one, two, one, two', or quickly 'one two three, four five six, one two three, four five six'.

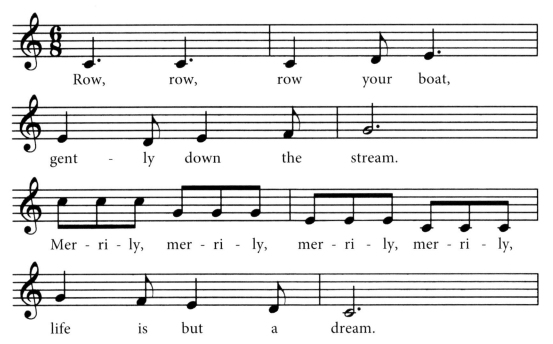

187

The Treble Clef

You've learnt that composers represent sounds by placing musical notes on a stave. The higher a note is on the stave, the higher its pitch. The various notes are named after the first seven letters of the alphabet: A, B, C, D, E, F, G. Each line and each space on the stave corresponds with one of these letters.

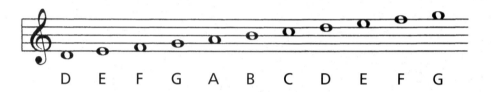

Notice that the letters repeat themselves as they go from low to high. The lowest note shown is D. Then, as the notes go up, we get E, F, and G. But there is no H. Instead, the series starts again with A.

How can you remember which positions on the stave correspond with which letters? Notice that the letters that are located on the lines, from bottom to top, are E, G, B, D, F. You can remember these letters by memorising the following sentence: 'Every good boy deserves favour'.

Another way to remember which positions on the stave stand for which letters is to look at the *treble clef*. The treble clef is a curly symbol located at the beginning of a piece of written music. The treble clef is also called a 'G clef', because the innermost circle of the clef circles around the line that stands for G – the second line on the stave. If you remember this, you can work out all the other notes above and below G.

The lowest note shown on the diagram above is D. What would happen if the composer wanted to write a note one lower than D? He or she would just draw a short line segment below the stave and place the note on the line segment. This particular note actually has a special name. It is called 'middle C', because the key that sounds this note is located in the middle of a piano keyboard.

Middle C

From Sheet Music to Sound

The notes in a piece of music can be played on a keyboard. If you don't have a piano or electronic keyboard at home, you can pretend to play notes on the keyboard on the next page.

On a piano keyboard, every white key has a letter name that matches one of the notes on the stave.

If you wanted to play the first two bars of 'Old MacDonald' on this section of a piano keyboard, you would press the G key three times, then the D key, then the E key twice, and finally the D key again – and you would hold that last D twice as long as the previous notes because it's a minim, while the others are crotchets. You would read all of this information from the printed sheet music and translate it into finger motions on the keyboard. At first it might take you a long time to translate the notes on the sheet music into finger motions on the keyboard, but if you practise, you will get better. With lots of practice, the process can become automatic.

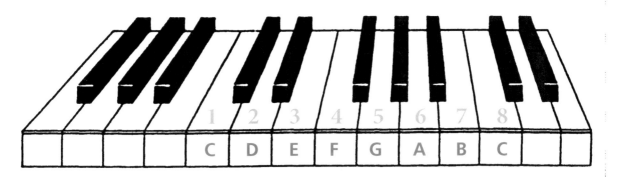

Sharps and Flats

We've talked about the white keys on the keyboard. But what about the black keys? The black keys get their names from the white keys on either side. Find the G note on the keyboard. The black key to the left of G is called G-*flat*, or G ♭. G-flat is a little bit lower in pitch than G. The black key to the right is called G-*sharp*, or G#. G-sharp is a little bit higher in pitch than G.

A black key can have two names. It can be called a flat of the note to its right or a sharp of the note to its left. No matter what it is called, it sounds the same on the keyboard. F-sharp is the same key as G-flat.

Italian for Composers

Sometimes just writing down the notes is not enough; sometimes the composer wants to give the performers more specific instructions about how to play the notes. For example, composers write the word *crescendo* [kresh-EN-doh] when they want the musicians gradually to get louder, and *diminuendo* [di-min-yoo-EN-doh] when they want them to get quieter, bit by bit. Both words are Italian. Many composers from all over the world write their musical directions in Italian. This is a tradition that goes back to the 1600s, when Italian opera was very popular throughout Europe.

Composers can create tension and excitement in their music by increasing and decreasing the volume. A good example of this is Beethoven's Fifth Symphony, discussed later in this chapter. Beethoven was a master at changing speeds and creating drama and excitement in his works.

Other Italian words and abbreviations tell musicians how soft or loud they should play the music. Here's a list of terms, arranged from softest to loudest:

pp = pianissimo	[pee-ah-NISS-ee-moe]	(very soft)
p = piano	[pee-AH-noh]	(soft)
mp = mezzo piano	[MET-zo pee-AH-noh]	(moderately soft)
mf = mezzo forte	[MET-zo FOR-tay]	(moderately loud)
f = forte	[FOR-tay]	(loud)
ff = fortissimo	[for-TISS-ee-moe]	(very loud)

Composers use other Italian words to tell how fast or slow a piece should be played. *Accelerando* [axe-ell-er-AN-doh] means 'speeding up', while *ritardando* [REE-tar-DAN-do] means 'slowing down'.

Legato [leg-AR-toe] means that the notes should be played smoothly, without gaps in between. The symbol for legato is a curved line connecting two or more notes. *Staccato* [stack-AH-toe] means the notes should be separated.

The Italian words *Da capo al fine* [dar-CAP-oh al FEE-nay] give instructions to go back to the beginning of the piece and repeat until the word *fine*. *Da capo* means 'from the top' and *al fine* means 'to the end'.

Rhythm

Have you ever heard music that makes you want to dance or march across the room? The rhythm in the music is what makes you feel that way. Most music is written in steady beats with the accent falling on the first beat, which is also called the downbeat. Have you ever seen and heard a marching band? Imagine someone calling out a steady beat for them: 'ONE two ONE two ONE two'. The beat of a march is strong, steady and predictable.

In most music, the beat stays steady, like the ticking of a clock. Sometimes, however, the composer introduces syncopation. In syncopation, the accent moves from the strong beat to the weak beat. The change is like a hiccup. It takes us by surprise and gets

We learnt about syncopation in Year 5.

our attention. If you've ever heard jazz music, you've heard syncopated music.

Verse and Refrain

To make songs fun to sing, composers often write songs with several verses, each of which is followed by a *refrain*, or chorus. The verses are all different, but the refrain or chorus is the same throughout the song. When you sing in a crowd, you might notice that most voices come in stronger when they sing the refrain. (It's the part everybody remembers!) When the word *refrain*, or *chorus*, appears at the end of a verse, it means to sing the refrain or chorus again.

In the songs given later in this chapter, you can see examples of verse and refrain. Both 'Blaydon Races' (which is a funny song) and 'Swing Low, Sweet Chariot' (which is a serious song) have choruses that are sung between each of the verses.

Harmony

Some songs seem meant for just one voice: it might be a song about someone you love or a song you've made up that's just for you. But other songs benefit from many voices.

If you sing a song about peace or about marching to war, it will send a powerful message if lots of voices sing it together.

Blending voices and sounds can have a powerful effect. When you sing or play two notes at the same time and they have a pleasing sound, you have played *harmony*. If you have a keyboard handy, find C on the keyboard, and then find E, which is two white keys to the right of C. Play C and E together and listen to the sounds blend. You just played a *chord*. A chord makes a richer, fuller sound than one note could make on its own. A chord is the basis of harmony.

Try playing other notes together. How does it sound when you play two white keys that are side by side? How does it sound when you play two white keys that are separated by one key? Two? Three? You will find that some combinations harmonise better than others.

Listening and Understanding

Polyphonic Music

During the Middle Ages, most music was created for the church. When people sang together in church, they all sang the same melody, and they usually sang *a cappella*, which means they sang without any instruments to accompany them. Indeed, the phrase *a cappella* is an Italian phrase that means 'in the chapel style'. Since instruments were not allowed in many churches and chapels, singing *a cappella* meant singing in the church-approved manner.

Choir 'The Sixteen' singing polyphony by Renaissance composers

During the Renaissance, *polyphonic music* became popular. *Polyphony* is a Greek word meaning 'many voices'. Polyphonic music is what you get when, instead of everyone singing the same notes, different voices sing different melodies or words at the same time. When different notes are sung by different voices at the same time, they blend together and *harmonise*.

Canons and Rounds

One kind of polyphonic music is called a *canon*. In a canon, one voice begins singing a melody. After the first few notes, another voice joins in, singing the same melody but maybe at a higher or lower pitch. All the voices sing their parts all the way to the end. The voices mingle and harmonise in a way that can be hauntingly beautiful.

Another kind of polyphonic music is called a *round*. A round is a song that travels around in circles. In rounds, everyone sings the same melody and the same words, but they start at different times. When the first person finishes the first line of the song, the next person joins in. As the various persons sing, their voices overlap and harmonise.

One of the simplest and most beautiful rounds is very old. It's a religious song called 'Dona Nobis Pacem' and it was written during the Renaissance. This round has only three Latin words – the title is the whole song! *Dona* means 'donate' or 'give', *nobis* means 'to us', and *pacem* means 'peace'. [Doh-nah no-beece pah-chem]. 'Give us peace'.

Another very old round comes from a manuscript in the British Museum that was probably written by one of the monks in Reading Abbey in the thirteenth century. In those days, people spoke English in a different way, which we call Middle English, and the round is called 'Sumer is icumen in'. In modern English, it translates as:

Summer is a'coming in,

Loudly sing cuckoo!

Grows the seed and blooms the mead

And greens the wood anew.

Sing cuckoo!

As each singer reaches 'in', at the end of the first line, the next person starts to sing. This round can last forever! Rounds are still popular today. 'Frère Jacques', which we sang in Year 2, and 'London's Burning', which we sang in Year 4, can both be sung as rounds.

Lute Music

In the 1500s, almost every musician had a lute, a wooden stringed instrument shaped like a half pear with a long neck. People plucked it in a way similar to playing a guitar. But the lute was more delicate, with a sweeter, softer sound. It was perfect for love songs sung by one voice. Have you ever heard the song 'Greensleeves'? (You might know the melody even if you've never heard the words.) 'Greensleeves' was originally a lute song. It was popular in England during the time of Queen Elizabeth I and is mentioned in Shakespeare's plays. It is a lovely tune, but sad. It tells about a man who has loved a woman and given her lots of pretty things, but she no longer cares for him. The first verse explains the situation:

Alas, my love, you do me wrong,
To cast me off discourteously.
For I have loved you well and long,
Delighting in your company.

Then comes the chorus, or refrain:

Greensleeves was all my joy,
Greensleeves was my delight,
Greensleeves was my heart of gold,
And who but my lady Greensleeves.

Then another verse:

Your vows you've broken, like my heart,
Oh, why did you so enrapture me?
Now I remain in a world apart,
But my heart remains in captivity.

John Dowland

We don't know who wrote 'Greensleeves', but we do know that John Dowland was responsible for many other smash hits of Renaissance lute music. Indeed, Dowland was probably the greatest composer of lute music who ever lived. He was born in England in 1563 and his songs were popular throughout Europe. His biggest hit was 'Lachrimae', which means 'tears' in Latin.

Dowland based much of his music on two kinds of dance music: a lively dance called a *galliard* [GALLY-ard] and a slow, sombre dance called a *pavan* [pav-ann]. Most of his music was sad and beautiful at the same time.

Mendelssohn's Midsummer Night

The German composer Felix Mendelssohn (1809-1847) lived many years after the Renaissance, but he drew inspiration from one of Shakespeare's plays. When Mendelssohn was only seventeen years old, he wrote an overture, or musical introduction, to Shakespeare's comedy *A Midsummer Night's Dream*. The overture tells the story of Shakespeare's play, a funny story about lovers who spend the night in a wood, where fairies play tricks on them.

The music begins with four chords played by woodwind. The mysterious sound leads us into the world of Oberon and Titania, the king and queen of the fairies. Violins introduce the first melody of the overture. Fairies scurry in and out with the light and distinct staccato notes played by violins.

There is a grand theme for the king and queen and a tender one for lovers. About three minutes in, you start hearing rude, heavy noises from the horns. These represent the working men who are trying to put on a play. Then, when the strings play three notes up, three notes back down (the same noise that some lorries make when reversing), you hear the sound of a braying ass.

Felix Mendelssohn

That is a short high note and a long low one from violins and clarinets.

Years after Mendelssohn wrote the overture, the King of Prussia wanted Shakespeare's play to be performed at Berlin's royal theatre. Mendelssohn wrote a dozen new pieces to follow the overture he had written many years earlier. One of the new pieces was a *scherzo*. *Scherzo* is the Italian word for 'joke'. A *scherzo* is usually a lively, fun piece. Mendelssohn's *scherzo* captures an argument between Oberon and Titania.

Bottom the weaver is given an ass's head by the mischievous faries in A Midsummer Night's Dream

The most famous of the later pieces is the 'Wedding March', written for the scene at the end of the comedy in which Duke Theseus marries Hippolyta, Queen of the Amazons. The two pairs of young lovers get married at the same time. Queen Victoria's eldest daughter, also called Victoria, liked this piece so much she decided to have it played at her own wedding when she married Prince Frederick of Prussia. Ever since, brides have requested it as the recessional, or exit music, for their weddings. You have probably heard it without realising that you were listening to music written for *A Midsummer Night's Dream*!

Beethoven: A Stormy Life Set to Music

Ludwig van Beethoven [LUD-vig von BAY-toe-ven], one of the world's greatest composers, was born in Germany in 1770. As soon as he showed promise as a musician, his father forced him to practise constantly. He soon became an accomplished musician.

With the help of an Austrian prince, Beethoven moved to Vienna to study music. He even met Mozart, the great Austrian composer, who was fourteen years older. After hearing Beethoven play, Mozart said: 'Someday he will give the world something to talk about.'

Beethoven earned his living as a concert pianist. He performed for royalty and well-to-do people, but he always demanded to be treated as an equal. Once, when a nobleman talked while Beethoven played the piano, the musician jumped up and shouted: 'For such pigs I do not play!'

Ludwig van Beethoven

In his late twenties, just as Beethoven began to succeed as both a concert pianist and composer, he realised he was going deaf. He became angry and bitter that the one thing more important to him than anything else – the pleasure he gained from listening to music – was slipping away. In time he went completely deaf – so deaf that he could not give piano concerts or conduct an orchestra. He could communicate only by writing in a little notebook he carried. People wrote notes and he scribbled a response. Beethoven was so miserable he once said that only music kept him alive. Beethoven took long walks through the countryside surrounding Vienna, imagining music inside his head, waving his arms in time to it and muttering sounds. Every now and then, he'd stop to jot down music in his notebook. People thought he was mad.

Beethoven wrote many kinds of music, but his Fifth Symphony is probably the best known symphony in the world. The first four notes – three quick Gs and a long E-flat – sound like a knock on the door. Beethoven repeats this four-note *motto* over and over again throughout the first part, or movement, of the work. Then he gives us different variations on the theme. That means he changes it in little ways so that it stays interesting. The second movement has a warm and gentle melody. The third movement is a *scherzo*. Its lively theme begins with strings and wind instruments. The four-note knock at the door comes in again, this time played on a single note by horns. After a middle section of scurrying quavers, starting low and working up through the orchestra, the *scherzo* theme comes back, hushed and mysterious. Then a rapid *crescendo* leads straight into the dramatic last movement.

The fourth movement is warm and bright, like the sun breaking through clouds. When you think it might be ready to finish, it goes quiet and the strings start playing the four-note rhythm from the *scherzo*. It winds up towards the finish, getting louder and faster, timpani rolling and piccolos swooping up to their highest notes, until they all play the last chord many, many times to let you know that the music has arrived home.

Beethoven added instruments to the orchestra for a bigger sound: the contrabassoon to reach the deepest notes, the piccolo to reach the highest ones, and three trombones. Listen to the symphony and see if you can hear loud and soft, bright and dark, fast and slow in the music.

Ralph Vaughan Williams and Folk Music

A lot of great music has been written for people who were rich and powerful: kings and queens, aristocrats and leaders of the church. However, there is also a long tradition of ordinary people creating music that reflects their own lives. It is called folk music, and for a long time no one paid much attention to it. Eventually, people realised that folk music is an important part of any country's musical tradition. Scholars began to travel to country areas, asking people to sing traditional songs to them. These would then be written down, published and performed, just like other types of music. We have come across some of them in previous books: we sang 'What Shall We Do With the Drunken Sailor?' in Year 2, 'On Ilkley Moor Baht 'At' in Year 4 and 'Loch Lomond' in Year 5.

Ralph Vaughan Williams (1872-1958) was one of the greatest English composers, and he did a lot to draw attention to the important tradition of folk music. His father was a vicar who died when Ralph was only two. His mother came from the Wedgwood family, famous for their china-making factories. His great-uncle was Charles Darwin, the famous naturalist whom we read about in Year 5. The family went to live with relatives at Leith Hill Place, in Surrey. At school, like many composers before him, he learnt to play the viola but his family preferred him to play the organ. It was more useful in church where it could help people to sing hymns. After leaving school, he studied music and history at Cambridge and had further music lessons in London from several teachers, some of whom were also well-known composers.

After all that study and practice, Vaughan Williams knew everything about how to write big, impressive music. He wrote symphonies, operas, ballets and music for films, as well as music to be sung by large choirs. At the same time, he was careful to remember that big music is built up from small elements. Vaughan Williams

This statue of Ralph Vaughan Williams stands outside the Dorking Halls where the Leith Hill Festival takes place.

travelled around England and Scotland collecting folk songs and carols. Wherever he visited, he asked about the local singers, invited them to sing for him and wrote the songs down.

Do you remember 'Loch Lomond', that we sang in Year 5? He wrote a version for a singer and men's choir. How about 'Greensleeves'? He added many lines of harmony so that it could be sung by a large chorus.

When he was asked to produce a hymn book, called the *English Hymnal*, for the Church of England, Vaughan Williams wrote a few new tunes of his own. The most famous is called 'Down Ampney', after the village where his father was vicar. He found some hymns that had been sung for hundreds of years, originally in Latin but now translated into English. Others were taken from German collections, like the tunes made popular by J. S. Bach. However he also used some of the folk tunes in his collection. He fitted many poems to tunes he had heard sung when touring English villages and provided them with accompaniments to be played on the organ.

Vaughan Williams loved the sound of people singing. The cathedral choirs of Gloucester, Worcester and Hereford joined together to perform large musical works at the Three Choirs Festival. He wrote music for them, but he also started a festival of his own in Surrey, called the Leith Hill Festival, which still takes place. Local choirs compete to win banners. If you visit the festival in Dorking, you can see a statue of the composer outside the concert hall, with his hands raised as if conducting a large orchestra and chorus.

Spirituals

Sorrow Songs

In the History section of this book, we read about the terrible suffering of slaves who were forced to work on plantations in the West Indies and the Southern states of the USA. For these slaves, music was a source of consolation in their difficult lives, and also a way to express their hopes for the future.

Many slaves became Christians and learnt traditional hymns. They blended their way of singing with the Christian hymns to make songs called *spirituals*. They were sometimes called 'sorrow songs' because they were filled with sadness and pain.

Spirituals weren't just about being sad, though. They also helped people to cope with their suffering and sadness. Many songs included a message of hope about the future. The spiritual 'Wayfaring Stranger' says that this world is a world of woe, but it also says that things will be better in the life after death promised by Christianity:

I'm just a poor wayfaring stranger
A-travelin' through this land of woe.
But there's no sickness, toil, nor danger
In that bright world to which I go.

Many spirituals make a comparison between the African-American slaves and the ancient Hebrews. The Old Testament tells the story of the Hebrew people and how they toiled in slavery in Egypt until their leader, Moses, led them out of Egypt, across the Jordan River, and into the 'Promised Land' of Canaan. The African-Americans found themselves in a similar situation, enslaved but hoping they might someday reach a Promised Land where they could be free. So the slaves began to use words and phrases from the Old Testament to describe their own lives.

In some spirituals, going to the Promised Land seems to mean going to heaven, and crossing the Jordan seems to mean dying. In other songs, the Promised Land seems to refer to free territory in the North, and crossing Jordan seems to refer to crossing a river from a slave state to a free state, like the Ohio River. Either way, crossing Jordan and entering the Promised Land were intended to refer to something better than the slaves' present state.

When slave owners heard their slaves singing spirituals, they thought they were about events in the Bible that had taken place many years before. However, the slaves who sang the songs had their minds on the future and on freedom.

These former slaves in the state of Virginia made recordings of their spirituals so that they would be remembered.

Swing Low Sweet Chariot

You can find a Welsh rugby song on page 77.

This famous spiritual was written by Wallis Willis, a freed slave. It is the anthem of the English rugby team.

[chorus]

Swing low, sweet chariot
Coming for to carry me home,
Swing low, sweet chariot,
Coming for to carry me home.

I looked over Jordan, and what did I see
Coming for to carry me home?
A band of angels coming after me,
Coming for to carry me home.

[repeat chorus]

Sometimes I'm up, and sometimes I'm down,
(Coming for to carry me home)
But still my soul feels heavenly bound.
(Coming for to carry me home)

[repeat chorus]

The brightest day that I can say,
(Coming for to carry me home)
When Jesus washed my sins away.
(Coming for to carry me home)

[repeat chorus]

If I get there before you do,
(Coming for to carry me home)
I'll cut a hole and pull you through.
(Coming for to carry me home)

[repeat chorus]

If you get there before I do,
(Coming for to carry me home)
Tell all my friends I'm coming too.
(Coming for to carry me home)

[repeat chorus]

Folk Songs

Widecombe Fair

This folk song from Devon is all about a fair that takes place every year in the tiny village of Widecombe-in-the-Moor on Dartmoor. The phrase 'Uncle Tom Cobley and all' has come to mean absolutely anyone and everyone!

Tom Pearce, Tom Pearce, lend me your grey mare
(All along, down along, out along lea)
For I want for to go to Widecombe Fair,

[chorus]

With Bill Brewer, Jan Stewer, Peter Gurney,
Peter Davy, Dan'l Whiddon, Harry Hawke,
Old Uncle Tom Cobley and all,
Old Uncle Tom Cobley and all.

> On page 63 we learnt another way of describing anyone and everyone.

And when shall I see again my
grey mare?
(All along, down along, out along lea)
By Friday soon, or Saturday noon,

[repeat chorus]

So they harnessed and bridled the old
grey mare
(All along, down along, out along lea)
And off they drove to Widecombe fair,

[repeat chorus]

Then Friday came, and Saturday noon
(All along, down along, out along lea)
But Tom Pearce's old mare hath not
trotted home,

[repeat chorus]

So Tom Pearce he got up to the top o'
the hill
(All along, down along, out along lea)
And he seed his old mare down a-
making her will,

[repeat chorus]

So Tom Pearce's old mare, her took sick
and died
(All along, down along, out along lea)
And Tom he sat down on a stone, and
he cried

[repeat chorus]

But this isn't the end o' this shocking affair
(All along, down along, out along lea)
Nor, though they be dead, of the
horrid career
Of Bill Brewer…

[repeat chorus]

When the wind whistles cold on the
moor of the night
(All along, down along, out along lea)
Tom Pearce's old mare doth appear
ghastly white,

[repeat chorus]

And all the long night be heard skirling
and groans
(All along, down along, out along lea)
From Tom Pearce's old mare in her
rattling bones,

[repeat chorus]

The Blaydon Races by George Ridley

Blaydon is a small town in Gateshead. Can you find Gateshead on the map on page 93?
This song uses the 'Geordie' dialect of the North-East of England. Like other dialect songs,
such as 'On Ilkley Moor Baht 'At', you can usually work out what the words mean if you
sound them out loud. Here's a hint: 'Whi stole the cuddy?' means 'Who stole the horse?' and
'hyem' means home.

Aa went to Blaydon Races,
'Twas on the ninth of June,
Eighteen hundred and sixty-two,
on a summer's afternoon;
We took the bus from Balmbras
and she was heavy laden,
Away we went along Collingwood Street,
that's on the road to Blaydon.

[chorus]

Oh me lads, you should've seen us gannin',
passing the folks along the road
just as they were stannin',
Aal the lads and lasses there,
aal wi' smilin' faces,
Gannin' along the Scotswood Road
te see the Blaydon Races.

We flew past Armstrong's factory
and up by the 'Robin Adair',
Gannin' ower the railway bridge
the bus wheel flew off there.
The lasses lost their crinolenes
and the veils that hide their faces.
Aa got two black eyes and a broken nose
gannin' te Blaydon Races.

[repeat chorus]

Now when we got the wheel back on
away we went again,
But them that had their noses broke,
they went back ower hyem;
Some went to the dispensary
and some to Doctor Gibbses,
And some to the Infirmary
to mend their broken ribses.

[repeat chorus]

Now when we got te Paradise
there were bonny games begun;
There were four and twenty on the bus
and how we danced and sung;
They called on me to sing a song
and aa sung 'em 'Paddy Fagan',
Aa danced a jig and aa swung me twig
the day we went to Blaydon.

[repeat chorus]

The rain it poured doon all the day
and made the ground quite muddy,
Coffee Johnny had a white hat on –
they were shoutin' 'Whi stole the cuddy?'
There were spice stalls and monkey shows
and owld wives selling ciders,
And a chap on a ha'penny roundaboot
saying 'noo me lads for riders'.

[repeat chorus]

More Songs to Sing

Food Glorious Food by Lionel Bart

This song was written for Oliver!, *Lionel Bart's musical version of* Oliver Twist *by Charles Dickens. You can read about what happened when Oliver Twist asked for more on page 26.*

Is it worth the waiting for?

If we live 'til eighty four

All we ever get is gru...el!

Ev'ry day we say our prayer –

Will they change the bill of fare?

Still we get the same old gru...el!

There's not a crust, not a crumb can we find,

Can we beg, can we borrow, or cadge,

But there's nothing to stop us from getting a thrill

When we all close our eyes and imag...ine

Food, glorious food!

Hot sausage and mustard!

While we're in the mood –

Cold jelly and custard!

Pease pudding and saveloys!

What next is the question?

Rich gentlemen have it, boys –

In-di-gestion!

Food, glorious food!

We're anxious to try it.

Three banquets a day –

Our favourite diet!

Just picture a great big steak –
Fried, roasted or stewed.
Oh, food,
Wonderful food,
Marvellous food,
Glorious food.

Food, glorious food!
Don't care what it looks like –
Burned! Underdone! Crude!
Don't care what the cook's like.
Just thinking of growing fat –
Our senses go reeling
One moment of knowing that
Full-up feeling!

Food, glorious food!
What wouldn't we give for
That extra bit more –
That's all that we live for.
Why should we be fated to
Do nothing but brood
On food,
Magical food,
Wonderful food,
Marvellous food,
Fabulous food,
Beautiful food,
Glorious food!

The Mountains of Mourne by Percy French (1896)

The potato famine that we read about on page 145 forced many Irish people to emigrate, which means to go and live in another country. Many Irish men worked as labourers in the construction industry in England, building roads and railways. The singer in this song has been told that the labourers digging up the road are actually digging for gold. He is homesick for the beauty of his homeland, and contrasts the artificial fashions of the day with the simple beauty of the Irish landscape and his Irish love.

Oh, Mary, this London's a wonderful sight,
With people all working by day and by night.
Sure they don't sow potatoes, nor barley, nor wheat,
But there's gangs of them digging for gold in the street.
At least when I asked them that's what I was told,
So I just took a hand at this digging for gold,
But for all that I found there I might as well be
Where the Mountains of Mourne sweep down to the sea.

I believe that when writing a wish you expressed
As to know how fine ladies in London were dressed,
Well if you'll believe me, when asked to a ball,
They don't wear no top to their dresses at all,
Oh I've seen them meself and you could not in truth,
Say that if they were bound for a ball or a bath.
Don't be starting such fashions, now, Mary Macree,
Where the Mountains of Mourne sweep down to the sea.

I've seen England's king from the top of a bus
And I've never known him, but he means to know us.
And tho' by the Saxon we once were oppressed,
Still I cheered, God forgive me, I cheered with the rest.
And now that he's visited Erin's green shore
We'll be much better friends than we've been heretofore
When we've got all we want, we're as quiet as can be
Where the mountains of Mourne sweep down to the sea.

You remember young Peter O'Loughlin, of course,
Well, now he is here at the head of the force.
I met him today, I was crossing the Strand,
And he stopped the whole street with a wave of his hand.
And there we stood talkin' of days that are gone,
While the whole population of London looked on.
But for all these great powers he's wishful like me,
To be back where the dark Mourne sweeps down to the sea.

There's beautiful girls here, oh never you mind,

With beautiful shapes nature never designed,

And lovely complexions all roses and cream,

But let me remark with regard to the same:

That if of those roses you venture to sip,

The colours might all come away on your lip,

So I'll wait for the wild rose that's waiting for me

In the place where the dark Mourne sweeps down to the sea.

Lean On Me

by Bill Withers

Sometimes in our lives

We all have pain, we all have sorrow

But if we are wise

We know that there's always tomorrow

Lean on me when you're not strong

And I'll be your friend, I'll help you carry on

For it won't be long

'Til I'm gonna need somebody to lean on

Please, swallow your pride

If I have things you need to borrow

For no one can fill those of your needs

That you won't let show

You just call on me, brother, when you need a hand

We all need somebody to lean on

I just might have a problem that you'll understand

We all need somebody to lean on

Lean on me when you're not strong

And I'll be your friend, I'll help you carry on

For it won't be long

'Til I'm gonna need somebody to lean on

You just call on me, sister, when you need a hand

We all need somebody to lean on

I just might have a problem that you'll understand

We all need somebody to lean on

If there is a load

You have to bear that you can't carry

I'm right up the road, I'll share your load

If you just call me

Suggested Resources

Radio

Discovering Music, BBC Radio 3 series (90 – 92 FM or digital radio and online at www.bbc.co.uk/programmes/b012r8c2)

Charlotte Green's Great Composers, Classic FM series, Sundays 3 – 5 PM

Building a Library, BBC Radio 3 series (90 – 92 FM or digital radio and online at www.bbc.co.uk/podcasts/series/bal)

Audio Recordings

Civitas Sancti Tui by Byrd, performed by the King's Singers, from *1605: Treason and Dischord* (Signum Classics) 2005

Sellinger's Round by Byrd, performed by Patrick Ayrton, from *William Byrd, Keyboard Works* (Globe) 2013

Lachrimae Pavan by Dowland, performed by Nigel North (lute), from *Dowland's Tears* (Naxos) 2006

Greensleeves, performed by Julianne Baird (soprano) and Ronn McFarlane (lute), from *Greensleeves, a Collection of English Lute Songs* (Dorian) 1989

Symphonies No. 5 and 7 by Beethoven, performed by the Vienna Philharmonic Orchestra, conducted by Carlos Kleiber (Deutsche Grammophon) 1995

Piano Sonata No.8 (Pathétique) by Beethoven, performed by Alfred Brendel, from *Beethoven: Favourite Piano Sonatas* (Decca) 1994

A Midsummer Night's Dream by Mendelssohn, performed by Dame Judi Dench and the Boston Symphony Orchestra, conducted by Seiji Ozawa (Deutsche Grammophon) 2000

Fantasia on a Theme of Thomas Tallis by Vaughan Williams, performed by the Sinfonia of London, conducted by Sir John Barbirolli, from *The Essential Vaughan Williams* (EMI) 2008

Greensleeves by Vaughan Williams, performed by Greg Tassell (tenor) and the Esterhàzy Singers, from *Jewels in the Crown* (Priory) 2010

The Blaydon Races, performed by the Black Dyke Mills Band, from *Traditionally British* (Chandos) 1999

Books About Music

Young People's Guide to Classical Music by Helen Bauer (Amadeus Press) 2009

First Discovery: Beethoven by Yann Walcker (ABRSM) 2001

Children's Book of Music: an introduction to the world's most amazing music and its creators by various authors (Dorling Kindersley) 2010

Songbooks

The Six Nations Rugby Songbook, S Harris (editor) (Y Lolfa) 2010

150 Rounds by Edward Bolkovac and Judith Johnson (Boosey and Hawkes) 1996

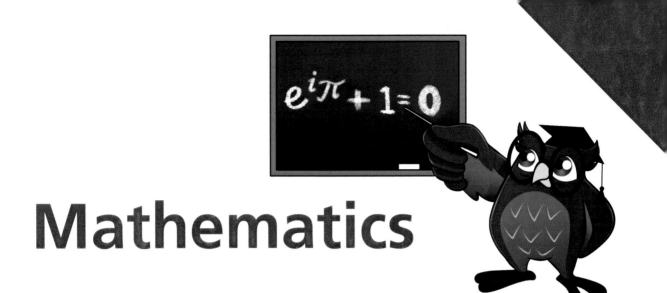

$$e^{i\pi} + 1 = 0$$

Mathematics

Introduction

This chapter sets out essential maths topics for Year 6, including number sense, ratios, percentages, fractions, decimals, multiplication, long division, measurement, geometry, probability and statistics, and a tiny bit of pre-algebra.

Success in learning maths comes through practice: not mindless, repetitive practice but thoughtful practice, with a variety of problems. While it is important to work towards the development of 'higher-order' problem-solving skills, such skills depend on a sound grasp of basic facts and an automatic mastery of fundamental operations. Since practice is the secret to mastery, practice is a prerequisite for more advanced problem-solving.

Some well-meaning people fear that practice in mathematics – memorising arithmetic facts or doing timed worksheets, for example – constitutes joyless, soul-killing drudgery for pupils. Nothing could be further from the truth. It is not practice but anxiety that kills the joy in mathematics. And one way of overcoming anxiety is by practising until the procedures become so easy and automatic that anxiety evaporates.

One effective way to practise is to have children talk out loud while doing problems, explaining computational steps along the way. In this way, the child's mental process becomes visible to you, and you can correct misunderstandings as they happen.

The brief outline presented here does not constitute a complete maths programme, since it does not include as many practice problems as a child ought to do while learning this material. To learn maths thoroughly, children need to be shown these concepts and then encouraged to practise, practise, and practise. Practice is especially important with the algorithms, or procedures, relating to arithmetic and computation, such as multiplication and long division. We therefore urge that parents and teachers elect a maths programme that allows plenty of opportunities to practise.

The best maths programmes incorporate the principle of incremental review: once a concept or skill is introduced, it is practised again and again through exercises of gradually increasing difficulty (including story problems). One result of this approach is that a child's arithmetic skills become automatic. Only when children achieve automatic command of basic facts are they prepared to tackle more challenging problems. Maths learning programmes that offer both incremental review and varied opportunities for problem solving achieve the best results.

Numbers and Number Sense

Billions

One year not long ago, the United Kingdom sold goods to the rest of the world worth £124,182,000,000. That's one hundred and twenty-four billion, one hundred and eighty-two million pounds!

You should already know about thousands and millions. Billions may be new to you. A billion is the same as a thousand million. A billion is a very large number. If you counted out one number a second, it would take you more than thirty years to count to one billion.

In our number system, groups of three digits are separated by commas. The commas are optional but they make it easier to read a number. Each group contains three columns: a hundreds column, a tens column and a ones column. Sometimes these columns are called places.

billions			millions			thousands			ones		
hundreds	tens	ones	hundreds	tens	ones	hundreds	tens	ones	hundreds	tens	ones
1	2	4	1	8	2	0	0	0	0	0	0

Practise writing and reading large numbers. How would you write four hundred and eleven billion? How would you read 32,401,175,013?

Place Value and Expanded Form

You should be able to identify the place and value of specific digits in numbers. In **31**,457,018,000 the bold 3 is in the ten billions place. Its value is 30,000,000,000. The bold 8 is in the thousands place. Its value is 8,000. What is the value of the bold 4?

Sometimes it can be useful to write a number in expanded form. This helps you see the value of each digit in the number. Here's what the number 32,401,075,013 looks like in expanded form: 30,000,000,000 + 2,000,000,000 + 400,000,000 + 1,000,000 + 70,000 + 5,000 + 10 + 3.

How would you write 567,892,324,567 in expanded form?

Comparing Large Numbers

Remember that < means 'is less than', > means 'is greater than' and = means 'is equal to'. Which symbols would you use to describe the relationships between these numbers?

567,456,321,010	99,345,934,999
39,999,999,999	42,345,000,000
7,890,000,000	489,000,000

Positive and Negative Numbers

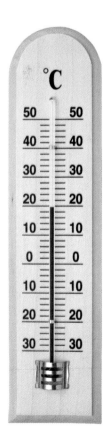

Whole numbers, as opposed to mixed numbers or fractions, are called integers. (The word integer means 'whole'.) The positive integers are the numbers ⁺1, ⁺2 , ⁺3... The negative integers are the numbers ⁻1, ⁻2, ⁻3... A complete collection, or set, of all the integers would include the positive integers, the negative integers and zero.

In Year 4 we learnt that, on a Celsius thermometer, 0° (zero degrees) is the temperature at which water freezes. A common room temperature is ⁺20° and ⁻10° is the outdoor temperature of a very cold winter day.

The number ⁺20, or 20, is a positive number. You read it as 'positive 20', or just '20'. The number ⁻10 is a negative number. You read it as 'minus 10'.

You can write positive numbers with or without a ⁺ sign: ⁺3 = 3 ('positive three equals three'). You must always write a ⁻ (minus) sign with a negative number.

We can show positive and negative numbers on a number line.

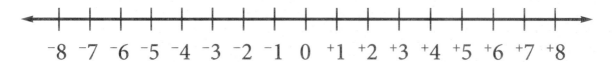

Numbers to the left of 0 on the number line are negative. Numbers to the right of 0 are positive. The number 0 is neither positive nor negative.

Two numbers that are the same distance from zero but in opposite directions are called opposites.

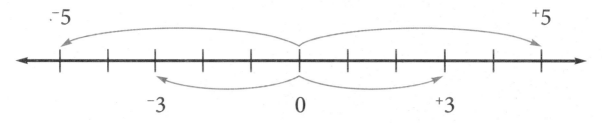

The numbers ⁻3 and ⁺3 are opposites. To find the opposite of a number, simply change its sign: the opposite of ⁻5 is ⁺5; the opposite of ⁺10 is ⁻10.

Zero is its own opposite: ⁺0 = ⁻0 = 0.

Integers

We often use integers in everyday life. The six chairs around a table furnish an example of the positive integer ⁺6; the three spoons missing from the cutlery set is an example of the negative integer ⁻3. Seven points for a converted try in rugby union is an example of the positive integer ⁺7; conceding ten goals more than you score in a football league is an example of the negative integer ⁻10. To mark a contour line showing the sea floor 25 metres below sea level, we can use the negative integer ⁻25; to mark a contour line 240 metres above sea level on a mountain, we can use the positive integer ⁺240. For the summit, we can round the height to the nearest integer, which could be ⁺382.

Comparing Integers

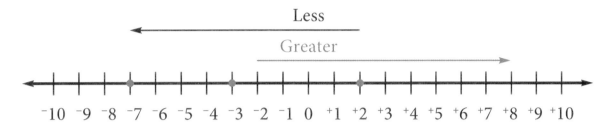

An integer on the number line is greater than those to its left and less than those to its right. $^-7 < {}^-3 < 2$. In general remember the following rules:

- A positive integer is always greater than a negative integer $(1 > {}^-100)$
- The farther to the left a negative integer is from zero, the less its value is $(^-1 > {}^-100)$.

Adding Integers

You can show the sum of two integers by using arrows on a number line. You already know how to find the sum of $^+5 + {}^+3$. Starting at 0, first move 5 units to the right and then 3 units to the right. Therefore, $^+5 + {}^+3 = {}^+8$. (Remember, positive integers are most often written without positive signs: $5 + 3 = 8$.)

Now find the sum of $^-5 + {}^-3$. Starting at 0, first move 5 units to the left, and then 3 more units to the left.

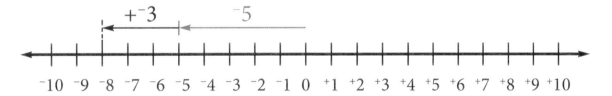

Therefore, $^-5 + {}^-3 = {}^-8$. You can add two negative integers the same way you add two positive integers, but because you are moving in the opposite direction, the sum is negative.

Here are two rules for adding integers:

- The sum of two positive integers is positive.
- The sum of two negative integers is negative.

We have seen how to add integers that have the same sign. Now let's practise using arrows on a number line to see what happens when you add integers with opposite signs.

To find the sum of $^-9 + {}^+5$, start at 0. First move left nine units and then move right 5 units.

$$^-9 + {}^+5 = {}^-4.$$

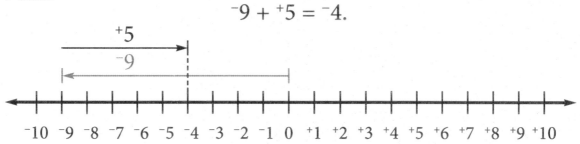

Now find the sum of their opposites. Starting at 0, first move right 9 units and then move left 5 units. $9 + {}^-5 = 4$. When you add a negative number, it is the same as subtracting, so you could think of this problem as $9 - 5 = 4$.

$$9 + {}^-5$$

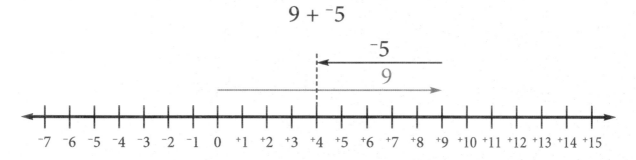

Draw your own number lines to show the sum of $^+5 + {}^-8$ and $^-5 + {}^+8$. See if you can invent your own rules to explain what happens when you add integers with opposite signs. Explain your rules, using examples, to a friend or a parent. Make sure you can find sums such as $^-64 + 41$ or $^+18 + {}^-67$.

Notice that $^-6 + {}^+6 = 0$ and $3 + {}^-3 = 0$. The sum of an *integer* and its *opposite is always zero.*

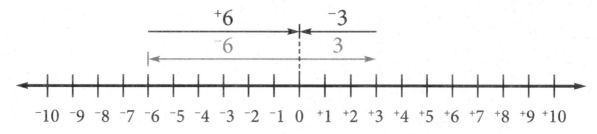

Subtracting Integers

Remember that if 9 − 6 = 3, then 6 + 3 = 9. We can also say that the *difference* of 9 and 6 is the number you have to add to 6 to get 9. We can define subtraction with integers the same way. The difference of two integers $a − b$ is the number you have to add to b to get a.

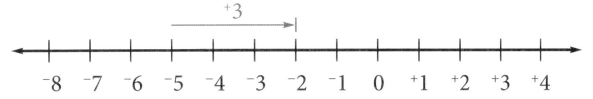

Consider ⁻2 − ⁻5. The difference (⁻2 − ⁻5) is the number you have to add to ⁻5 to get ⁻2. To get from ⁻5 to ⁻2, you add ⁺3. So ⁻2 − ⁻5 = ⁺3. Notice what happens when, instead of subtracting ⁻5, you add its opposite. ⁻2 + ⁺5 = ⁺3.

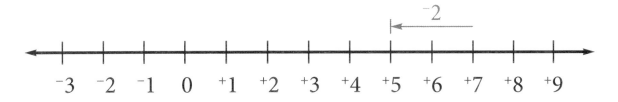

Now try ⁺5 − ⁺7. The difference (⁺5 − ⁺7) equals the number you have to add to ⁺7 to get ⁺5. ⁺5 − ⁺7 = ⁻2. Now instead of subtracting ⁺7, add its opposite. ⁺5 + −7 = ⁻2. This example shows a general rule that will always work to subtract an integer:

To subtract an integer, add its opposite.

Rounding

We have practised rounding in Years 3 and 4. You know that, to round a number to a certain place, you look at the digit to the right of that place and see whether you should round up or down.

Sometimes rounding a number to a certain place involves changing digits to the left of that place. Round 49,857 to the nearest thousand. 49,857 is between which two thousands? It is between 49 thousand and 50 thousand. The digit to the right of the thousands place is 8. So you round 49,857 up to 50,000.

A good way to practise rounding (especially in problems like the last one) is to write a double inequality first, showing which two round numbers the number is between. To round 2,947,024 to the nearest hundred thousand, you can set it up this way:

$$2,900,000 < 2,947,024 < 3,000,000$$

2,947,024 rounded to the nearest hundred thousand is 2,900,000.

Squares and Square Roots

When you multiply a number by itself, you square the number. Since $2 \times 2 = 4$, 2 squared is 4. In Year 5, we looked at pictures showing how 9, 16 and 25 are square numbers. A shorthand way of writing two squared is 2^2. It is useful to know the squares of the numbers from 1 to 12:

$1^2 = 1$	$4^2 = 16$	$7^2 = 49$	$10^2 = 100$
$2^2 = 4$	$5^2 = 25$	$8^2 = 64$	$11^2 = 121$
$3^2 = 9$	$6^2 = 36$	$9^2 = 81$	$12^2 = 144$

The relationships above can also be expressed using the term *square root*. We say that the square root of 144 is 12, or, using the symbol for square root, $\sqrt{144} = 12$. That means that $12 \times 12 = 144$. What is $\sqrt{64}$? $\sqrt{36}$?

You have already seen how a perfect square can be arranged in a pattern. There are other patterns in square numbers. You have learnt the squares to 12^2. By multiplying, work out the squares to 20^2. First, write the answers in two rows of ten:

$1^2=$	$2^2=$	$3^2=$	$4^2=$	$5^2=$	$6^2=$	$7^2=$	$8^2=$	$9^2=$	$10^2=$
$11^2=$	$12^2=$	$13^2=$	$14^2=$	$15^2=$	$16^2=$	$17^2=$	$18^2=$	$19^2=$	$20^2=$

Do you notice a pattern in the last digits?

For another pattern, work out the difference between each perfect square and the one before it.

$$2^2 - 1^2 = 4 - 1 = 3$$
$$3^2 - 2^2 = 9 - 4 = 5$$

Keep going for a few more. When you have spotted the pattern, you can work out the difference without having to calculate the subtraction. For perfect squares, it will always work.

Now write the answers in a zigzag changing direction every five answers, like this:

$1^2=$ $2^2=$ $3^2=$ $4^2=$

→ $5^2=$

$9^2=$ $8^2=$ $7^2=$ $6^2=$

$10^2=$ ←

$11^2=$ $12^2=$ $13^2=$ $14^2=$

→ $15^2=$

$19^2=$ $18^2=$ $17^2=$ $16^2=$

$20^2=$ ←

Do you see any pattern in the last digits this time? What do you think 0^2 will be? What will be the last digit of 21^2?

If you want a clue about the differences between each perfect square and the one before, trying making a list of the first 10 odd numbers.

Exponents

When we write 2^2 or 5^2 we are using exponents. An *exponent* is a small, raised or *superscript* number that shows how many times a number is used as a factor in multiplication.

For example, 3^4 means the number three is used as a factor four times: $3 \times 3 \times 3 \times 3$. You read 3^4 as 'three raised to the fourth power'. The number that is being used as a factor is called the *base*. In 3^4, 3 is the base and 4 is the exponent.

You have learnt in Year 5 that when a number has an exponent of 2, we usually read it as 'squared'. 5^2 is usually read as 'five squared', though it is also correct to say 'five raised to the second power'. When a number is raised to the 3rd power, we usually read it as 'cubed'. So 4^3 is read as 'four cubed' (or 'four raised to the third power').

$$4^3 = 4 \times 4 \times 4 = 64$$

2^5 is read as 'two raised to the fifth power'.

$$2^5 = 2 \times 2 \times 2 \times 2 \times 2 = 32$$

Powers of Ten

The exponents or *powers* of ten are very important in working with place value because the decimal system is based on powers of ten.

> What do you think 10^0 is? The answer feels strange but it is a 1 and no zeros. Ten raised to the power zero equals 1.

$10^1 = 10$

$10^2 = 10 \times 10 = 100$

$10^3 = 10 \times 10 \times 10 = 1,000$

$10^4 = 10 \times 10 \times 10 \times 10 = 10,000$

$10^5 = 10 \times 10 \times 10 \times 10 \times 10 = 100,000$

$10^6 = 10 \times 10 \times 10 \times 10 \times 10 \times 10 = 1,000,000$

Notice that 10^1 equals 10. A number raised to the first power is usually simply written as the number itself.

The number of zeros in each of the numbers 10, 100, 1,000, 10,000… tells you what power of ten it is. Since 10,000 has 4 zeros, it is 10^4. Furthermore, the exponent in a power of 10 tells you the number of zeros the number has when it is multiplied out. 10^9 has 9 zeros. 10^9 equals 1,000,000,000 or 1 billion.

Sets

A *set* is a collection of things. The things in a set are called its *members*. You list the members of a set inside braces like these: {}. For example, here is a set of the first six odd numbers: {1, 3, 5, 7, 9, 11}. Sets can contain things besides numbers. For instance, here is the set of different letters used in the word 'taramasalata': {t, a, r, m, s, l}. How would you record the set of even numbers between 21 and 29?

Prime Numbers

Imagine that you are part of a class of 23 students. One day the teacher asks you to divide into equal groups. You try to divide into 2 equal groups but find you can't do it because 23 is not evenly divisible by 2. One group is always larger than the other. Then you try to split into 3 equal groups, but that doesn't work either. And neither does 4 or 5, or any of the other numbers you try. That's because 23 is a *prime number*.

A prime number is a number that cannot be divided evenly by any other number except itself and the number 1. The number 23 is prime because it can't be divided evenly by any numbers except 1 and 23. The number 4, on the other hand, is not prime because it can be divided evenly by 1 and itself (4) but also 2. Numbers that are not 1 and not prime are called *composite* numbers. A composite number is a number that can be built up by multiplying smaller numbers, called *factors*, together. You can make the number 4 by multiplying 2 × 2. You can make the number 6 by multiplying 2 × 3. So neither of these numbers is a prime number. But what about 7?

More than 2,000 years ago, the Greek mathematician Eratosthenes came up with a clever way of seeing which numbers are prime. You can use his method, too. First, make a grid of all the numbers from 2 to 100 in rows of ten, like this:

2	3	4	5	6	7	8	9	10	
11	12	13	14	15	16	17	18	19	20
21	22	23	24	25	26	27	28	29	30,

etc.

You want to cross out all the composite numbers, leaving only the prime numbers. First circle the number 2. It is a prime number, evenly divisible only by 2 and 1. Then cross out all the multiples of 2. Each of these numbers is divisible by 2 and therefore not prime.

Next, find the smallest number that has not been crossed out: 3. This number is prime, so circle it. Cross out all the multiples of 3 that have not already been crossed out. Continue by circling the smallest remaining number and crossing out its multiples. The circled numbers are the prime numbers. If you did everything right, there should be 25 prime numbers circled.

Prime Factors

Any composite number can be broken down into several prime factors. For instance, the number 6 can be broken down into the factors 3 and 2. When these prime factors are multiplied together, they give the composite number 6. In the same way, the number 16 can be broken down into 4×4. But 4 itself can be broken down into 2×2. So if we want to break 16 down to its prime factors, we need to do it like this:

$$16 = 2 \times 2 \times 2 \times 2$$

This can be expressed as an exponent:

$$16 = 2^4$$

Can you break the number 32 down into prime factors, expressed as exponents? How about 27?

Greatest Common Factor

Sometimes it is useful to find the largest factor that two numbers have in common.

The factors of 12 are 1, 2, 3, 4, 6 and 12.

The factors of 16 are 1, 2, 4, 8 and 16.

Which factors do they have in common? The common factors of 12 and 16 are 1, 2 and 4. The *greatest common factor* (GCF) of 12 and 16 is 4 since that is the largest number that is a common factor.

What are the common factors of 24 and 60? What is their greatest common factor?

Many mathematicians prefer the term *divisor* instead of factor, so you may also see the abbreviation GCD (greatest common divisor).

Least Common Multiple

Sometimes it is useful to find common multiples. Suppose you were asked to find the smallest number that is a multiple of both 2 and 3.

Multiples of 2 include 2, 4, 6, 8, 10, 12, etc.

Multiples of 3 include 3, 6, 9, 12, 15 and so on.

Which of these multiples of 3 are also multiples of 2? 6 and 12 are both common multiples, but 6 is the smallest. We say that 6 is the *least common multiple* (LCM) of 2 and 3.

Computation

Properties of Addition

There are certain rules, or properties, that are always true of addition.

1) *Commutative Property of Addition*

   Addends can be added in any order without changing the sum.

   $5 + 3 = 8$ and $3 + 5 = 8$, so $5 + 3 = 3 + 5$

2) *Associative Property of Addition*

   Addends can be grouped in any way without changing the sum.

   $(2 + 6) + 3 = 11$ and $2 + (6 + 3) = 11$, so $(2 + 6) + 3 = 2 + (6 + 3)$

Variables

When a letter stands for a number it is called a *variable*. For example, instead of writing

   $6 + ? = 8$, we can write $6 + x = 8$. In this equation, $x = 2$.

We can also write $x + 4 = 10$. In the second equation, $x = 6$. We call a letter like x a *variable* because it can vary, or change; it can stand for different numbers. Finding what number the variable in an equation stands for is called *solving* the equation.

Inverse Operations and Equations

Remember that addition and subtraction are *inverse*, or opposite, operations. That is why you can write a related subtraction fact from an addition fact, or a related addition fact from a subtraction fact.

$$8 + 7 = 15$$

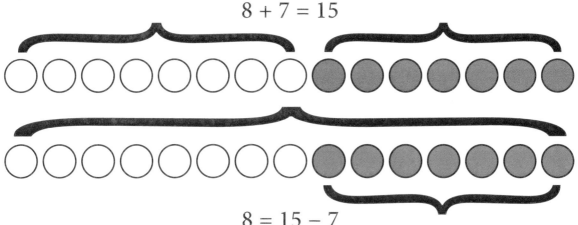

$$8 = 15 - 7$$

$8 + 7 = 15$ and $8 = 15 - 7$ are two different ways of writing the same problem. You can use addition and subtraction as inverse operations to solve equations. To solve the equation $n + 43 = 74$, rewrite it as a subtraction problem. Subtract 43 from 74.

$$n + 43 = 74$$
$$n = 74 - 43$$
$$n = 31$$

To solve the equation $a - 6 = 8$, rewrite it as an addition problem. Add 6 to 8:

$$a - 6 = 8$$
$$a = 8 + 6$$
$$a = 14$$

Properties of Multiplication

Like addition, multiplication is commutative and associative.

1) *Commutative Property of Multiplication*

   Factors can be multiplied in any order without changing the product.

   $8 \times 6 = 48$ and $6 \times 8 = 48$, so $8 \times 6 = 6 \times 8$

2) *Associative Property of Multiplication*

   Factors can be grouped in any way without changing the product.

   $(4 \times 5) \times 2 = 40$ and $4 \times (5 \times 2) = 40$, so $(4 \times 5) \times 2 = 4 \times (5 \times 2)$

   Another property of multiplication involves addition as well.

3) *Distributive Property of Multiplication over Addition*

When a sum is multiplied by a number, for example $5 \times (3 + 7)$,

- you can multiply each addend by the number, and then add the products:

  $5 \times (3 + 7) = (5 \times 3) + (5 \times 7) = 15 + 35 = 50$

- Or you can add, then multiply:

  $5 \times (3 + 7) = 5 \times 10 = 50$

You have the same result either way. So the distributive property tells us that:

$5 \times (3 + 7) = (5 \times 3) + (5 \times 7)$

Learn the names of these three properties and be able to write equations showing what each one means. Also practise using the distributive property to write the answers to problems in two different ways. For example, you could find what $(12 \times 6) + (13 \times 6)$ equals in two ways:

$$(12 \times 6) + (13 \times 6) = 72 + 78 = 150$$
$$(12 \times 6) + (13 \times 6) = (12 + 13) \times 6 = 25 \times 6 = 150$$

You can use the properties of multiplication to solve problems. For instance, suppose you need to calculate 3×27. You could use the distributive property to divide this multiplication problem into two easier problems, like this:

$$3 \times 27 = (3 \times 20) + (3 \times 7)$$
$$= 60 + 21$$
$$= 81$$

Multiplication and Division as Inverse Operations

Like addition and subtraction, multiplication and division are inverse, or opposite, operations. $6 \times 4 = 24$ and $6 = 24 \div 4$ are two different ways of writing the same problem.

You can use multiplication and division as inverse operations to solve equations. To solve the equation $a \times 12 = 192$, rewrite it as a division problem. Divide 192 by 12:

$$a \times 12 = 192$$
$$a \quad = 192 \div 12$$
$$a \quad = 16$$

To solve the equation $n \div 13 = 12$, rewrite it as a multiplication problem. Multiply 12 by 13:

$$n \div 13 = 12$$
$$n \quad = 12 \times 13$$
$$n \quad = 156$$

Multiplying Large Factors

You multiply by a number in the thousands using the same methods you have learnt already:

$$
\begin{array}{r}
5{,}627 \\
\times \quad 4{,}338 \\
\hline
45{,}016 \\
168{,}810 \\
1{,}688{,}100 \\
22{,}508{,}000 \\
\hline
24{,}409{,}926
\end{array}
\qquad
\begin{array}{l}
\rightarrow \quad 8 \times 5{,}627 \\
\rightarrow \quad 30 \times 5{,}627 \\
\rightarrow \quad 300 \times 5{,}627 \\
\rightarrow \quad 4{,}000 \times 5{,}627
\end{array}
$$

First you multiply $8 \times 5{,}627$, then $30 \times 5{,}627$, then $300 \times 5{,}627$ and finally $4{,}000 \times 5{,}627$. Then you add these four subtotals to find the product. Remember that before you multiply by the digit in the tens place, you first write a zero in the product. Before multiplying the digit in the hundreds place, you write 2 zeros, and before multiplying the digit in the thousands place, you write 3 zeros in the product. Using these same methods, you can multiply even larger numbers.

Estimating a Product

Sometimes you don't need to know the exact product. In such cases you can estimate. For instance, suppose you wanted to know about what $3{,}979 \times 509$ equals. You could round 3,979 to 4,000 and 509 to 500. Then multiply: $4{,}000 \times 500 = 2{,}000{,}000$.

Division and Divisibility

You can write a division problem in three ways. 28 divided by 7 can be written in these three ways, which all mean the same thing:

$$
28 \div 7 \qquad\qquad 7\overline{)28} \qquad\qquad \frac{28}{7}
$$

We say that a number is *divisible* by another number if it can be divided by that number without leaving a remainder. For example, 30 is divisible by 2, because $30 \div 2 = 15$. Thirty is not divisible by 7, because $30 \div 7$ leaves a remainder of 2.

To find out if one number is divisible by another, you can always divide and see if there is a remainder. There are also rules that let you determine, without dividing, whether a number is divisible by certain numbers.

Here are some tests for divisibility.

Testing the last digit works for 2, 5 and 10. This is called the last-digit test. A whole number is divisible:

- By 2, if it has an even number (0, 2, 4, 6 or 8) in the ones place

- By 5, if it has a 0 or 5 in the ones place

- By 10, if it has a 0 in the ones place

Testing the sum of the digits works for 3 and 9:

- By 3, if the sum of its digits is divisible by 3

- By 9, if the sum of its digits is divisible by 9

Short Division

When the divisor is a one-digit number, you can use a shorter form of division, known as short division. Divide, multiply and subtract in your head. Write the remainder, if there is one, in front of the next place, then continue dividing. For example, to divide 6,258 by 8, you go through the following steps:

A) Divide the 62 hundreds.

Think: 8 into 62 goes 7 times.

62 – 56 = 6. Write the 6 hundreds in small handwriting next to the 5 tens, making 65 tens.

$$\begin{array}{r} 7 \\ 8\,\overline{)\,6\,,\,2^6 5\,8} \end{array}$$

B) Divide the 65 tens.

Think: 8 into 65 goes 8 times.

65 – 64 = 1. Write the 1 ten next to the 8 ones, making 18.

$$\begin{array}{r} 7\,8 \\ 8\,\overline{)\,6\,,\,2^6 5^1 8} \end{array}$$

C) Divide the 18 ones.

$$7\ 8\ 2\ \text{R2}$$
$$8\ )\ \overline{6\ ,\ 2^6 5^1 8}$$

Practise using short division to do division problems with one-digit divisors.

Long Division

When you are dividing by a two-digit divisor, you can use long division. Before you begin to divide, always work out first how many digits the quotient will have.

Find the quotient of 8,150 divided by 26.

First ask: can I divide 26 into 8? No, there are not enough thousands to divide. How about 26 into 81? Yes, there are enough hundreds to divide. The first digit of the quotient goes in the hundreds place. The quotient will have three digits.

As you do the long division, round the divisor to the nearest ten and make an estimate of what each digit in the quotient will be. Sometimes your estimate will be too high or too low; then you have to adjust the quotient. Here are the steps:

A) Divide the hundreds. Round 26 to 30.

Think: $30\overline{)81}$ so, since $2 \times 30 = 60$ try 2.

$$
\begin{array}{r}
2 \\
26\overline{)8,150} \\
-5\ 2 \\
\hline
2\ 9
\end{array}
$$

Check: is 29 < 26? No.

B) Increase the quotient by 1, so try 3.

$$
\begin{array}{r}
3 \\
26\overline{)8,150} \\
-7\ 8 \\
\hline
3
\end{array}
$$

Check: is 3 < 26? Yes.

Now the quotient is correct.

C) Bring down the 5 tens and divide the tens.

Think: $30\overline{)35}$ or $26\overline{)35}$. Try 1.

$$
\begin{array}{r}
31 \\
26\overline{)8,150} \\
-7\ 8 \\
\hline
35 \\
-26 \\
\hline
9
\end{array}
$$

Check: is 9 < 26? Yes. The quotient is correct.

D) Bring down zero ones and divide the ones.

Think: $30\overline{)90}$. Try 3.

$$
\begin{array}{r}
313\ R12 \\
26\overline{)8,150} \\
-7\ 8 \\
\hline
35 \\
-26 \\
\hline
90 \\
-78 \\
\hline
12
\end{array}
$$

Check: is 12 < 26? Yes.
The quotient is correct; the remainder is 12.

At each step in the division, check to make sure the remainder is less than the divisor. You were dividing by 26 in the last problem. What is the largest remainder you could have had? 25. Why?

You can check division problems by multiplying the divisor and the quotient, and adding the remainder. ▶

You can write your answer in the same form as the check, a multiplication and an addition, followed by an inequality. ▼

$$8,150 = (26 \times 313) + 12 \qquad 12 < 26$$

$$
\begin{array}{r}
313 \\
\times\ 26 \\
\hline
1,878 \\
6,260 \\
\hline
8,138 \\
+\ 12 \\
\hline
8,150\ ✔
\end{array}
$$

You can also do a quick mental check of your answer by estimating the quotient. To estimate the quotient of

$26)\overline{8,150}$, round the divisor to the greatest place value. Then round the dividend to a number that makes it easy to divide. Round 26 to 30. Then round 8,150 to 9,000. You could round to 8,000, but you cannot divide 8,000 by 30 easily. You can divide 9,000 by 30 easily:

$$\begin{array}{r} 300 \\ 30)\overline{9,000} \end{array} \qquad \qquad 26)\overline{8,150} \text{ is about } 300 \; ✔$$

More Two-Digit Divisors

Let's try that again. Find the quotient of 227,194 divided by 74. First, work out how many digits the quotient will have. Can you divide 74 into 2? No, there are not enough hundred thousands to divide. How about 74 into 22? No, there are not enough ten thousands to divide. How about 74 into 227? Yes, there are enough thousands to divide. The first digit of the quotient goes in the thousands place. The quotient will have 4 digits. Here are the steps for long division.

A) Divide 227 thousands.

$$\begin{array}{r} 3 \\ 74)\overline{227,194} \\ -222 \\ \hline 5 \end{array}$$

Think: 5 < 74 ✔

B) Bring down the 1 hundred.

You cannot divide 51 hundreds by 74.

Write 0 in the hundreds place.

$$\begin{array}{r} 3,0 \\ 74)\overline{227,194} \\ -222 \\ \hline 5,1 \end{array}$$

C) Bring down the 9 tens.

Divide 519 tens.

Think: $70\overline{)519}$

$$
\begin{array}{r}
3{,}07 \\
74\overline{)227{,}194} \\
-222 \\
\hline
5{,}19 \\
-5{,}18 \\
\hline
1
\end{array}
$$

$1 < 4$ ✔

D) Bring down the 4 ones.

You cannot divide 14 ones by 74.

Write 0 in the ones place.

$$
\begin{array}{r}
3{,}070 \ \text{R}14 \\
74\overline{)227{,}194} \\
-222 \\
\hline
5{,}19 \\
-5{,}18 \\
\hline
14
\end{array}
$$

$14 < 74$ ✔

$$
\begin{array}{r}
3{,}070 \\
\times\ 74 \\
\hline
12{,}280 \\
214{,}900 \\
\hline
227{,}180 \\
+\ 14 \\
\hline
227{,}194
\end{array}
$$
✔ $227{,}194 = (74 \times 3{,}070) + 14$ $14 < 74$

Three-Digit Divisors

Practise doing long division problems with three-digit divisors. First decide how many digits the quotient will have; then round the divisor to the nearest hundred to estimate each digit of the quotient.

Divide 163,220 by 321.

A. Think: $321\overline{)163}$?

No, not enough thousands to divide.

Try $321\overline{)1,632}$

Yes, there are enough hundreds to divide. The quotient will have three digits.

B) Divide 1,630 hundreds.

Think: $300\overline{)1,630}$ ⟶ Try 5.

$$
\begin{array}{r}
5 \\
321\overline{)163,220} \\
-160,5 \\
\hline
2,72
\end{array}
$$

You can't divide 272 tens by 321. Write 0 in the tens place. Then divide 2,720 ones.

Think: $300\overline{)2,720}$ ⟶ Try 9.

$$
\begin{array}{r}
509 \\
321\overline{)163,220} \\
-160,5 \\
\hline
2,720 \\
-2,889
\end{array}
$$

2,889 is greater than 2,720, so the quotient 9 is too great. Try 8.

$$
\begin{array}{r}
508 \\
321\overline{)163,220} \\
-160,5 \\
\hline
2,720 \\
-2,568 \\
\hline
152
\end{array}
$$

$152 < 321$

$$
\begin{array}{r}
508 \\
\times\ 321 \\
\hline
508 \\
10,160 \\
152,400 \\
\hline
163,068 \\
+\ 152 \\
\hline
163,220 \ ✔
\end{array}
$$

In this problem, because $300\overline{)2,720}$ is just barely 9, and you rounded 321 *down* to 300, you might have guessed that 9 was too large a quotient. When making your estimated quotients, always think about whether you rounded the divisor up or down. The more you do long division, the better you will get at estimating quotients.

Decimals, Fractions and Mixed Numbers

Decimals

When you want to indicate a part of an integer, you can use a fraction or you can use a decimal. For example, one way to write five and a half is to use a fraction: 5½. Another way is to use a decimal point: 5.5

The first place to the right of the decimal point is the tenths place; the second place is the hundredths place; the third place is the thousandths place. The fourth place to the right of the decimal point is the ten-thousandths place.

ones	**.**	*tenths*	*hundredths*	*thousandths*	*ten-thousandths*
0	.	5	6	7	2

Places to the right of the decimal point are called decimal places. When a number has four decimal places, you read the decimal places in ten-thousandths. 0.5672 is read: 'five thousand, six hundred and seventy-two ten-thousandths'. People often read decimals in a shorter way. You can read 0.5672 as 'point five six seven two'. You can read 18.289 as 'eighteen and two hundred and eighty-nine thousandths' or 'eighteen point two eight nine'.

Learn to give the value of a digit in a decimal in digits or in words. In 0.6928, the value of the 6 is 0.6 or six tenths; the value of the nine is 0.09 or nine hundredths; the value of the 2 is 0.002 or two thousandths; the value of the 8 is 0.0008 or eight ten-thousandths. You could write this decimal in expanded form, like this:

$$0.6 + 0.09 + 0.002 + 0.0008$$

Decimals on a Number Line

You can show decimals that come between other decimals on a number line.

This number line shows nine numbers with two decimal places between 2.3 and 2.4.

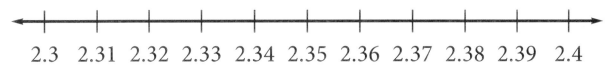

2.3 2.31 2.32 2.33 2.34 2.35 2.36 2.37 2.38 2.39 2.4

You can also show decimals with patterns. Complete this pattern:

4.73, 4.731, ___ , ___ , ___ , ___ , ___ , ___ , ___ , ___ , 4.74

With this pattern in mind, think about how many numbers with three decimal places you can write between 2.33 and 2.34. You can write nine. Could you write other decimals between those decimals?

Comparing Decimals

You can add zeros after the last place of a decimal without changing the value. To compare 13.62 and 13.625, you can write 13.62 as 13.620, so that both numbers have the same number of decimal places.

$$13.620$$
$$13.625$$

Start with the greatest place value, the tens place. All the places are the same from the tens place to the hundredths place. However, 5 thousandths is greater than 0 thousandths, so 13.625 > 13.620 and 13.625 > 13.62.

Decimal Sums and Differences

Remember that addition is commutative. So you can check a decimal sum by adding the decimals in a different order. If you found this decimal sum by adding downwards, check by adding upwards.

$$
\begin{array}{r}
9.607 \\
3.23 \\
+ 18.76 \\
\hline
31.597 \checkmark
\end{array}
$$

Remember that addition and subtraction are opposite, or inverse, operations. Add to check each difference of decimals.

To check this subtraction:

$$
\begin{array}{r}
95.27 \\
-82.96 \\
\hline
12.31
\end{array}
$$

Do this addition:

$$
\begin{array}{r}
12.31 \\
+82.96 \\
\hline
95.27
\end{array}
$$

You can also make a quick check to see if a decimal sum or difference is about right by estimating. To estimate a decimal sum or difference, round each number to its greatest place value and then add or subtract.

To estimate		Round to greatest place value.	
	9.607		10
	3.23		3
	+ 18.76		+ 20
			33

To estimate		Round to greatest place value.	
	95.27		100
	−82.96		−80
			20

One of the things your estimate can tell you is how many digits to expect before the decimal point.

We often estimate by rounding all the numbers to the same place value. Suppose you wanted to know the approximate difference of 95.27 and 82.96 in whole numbers. You would round each number to the nearest whole number and then subtract.

		Round to the nearest whole number.	
	95.27		95
	−82.96		−83
			12

Notice that this estimate of 12 is much closer to the actual difference (12.31) than the estimate you got by rounding each number to its greatest place value.

Multiplying Decimals

Multiplying with different units can help you learn how to multiply a decimal and a whole number. If a small packet of biscuits costs 69p, how much do 9 packets cost?

You can multiply 69p by 9, or you can write 69p with a pound sign and a decimal point and multiply.

$$\begin{array}{r} 69p \\ \times\ 9 \\ \hline 621p \end{array}$$

$$\begin{array}{r} £0.69 \\ \times\ 9 \\ \hline £6.21 \end{array}$$ – two decimal places

£0.69 – two decimal places

£6.21 – two decimal places

621p = £6.21. You get the same product either way you multiply.

Notice that there are the same number of decimal places in the product (£6.21) as in the decimal factor (£0.69). Whenever you multiply a decimal by a whole number, the product will have the same number of decimal places as the decimal factor. Sometimes the last place will be zero. When we talk about money, we always have only two decimal places.

Multiplying Decimals by 10, 100 and 1,000

When you multiply any decimal number by 10, you hold the decimal point steady and move the digits one place to the left. You make the place value of each digit ten times as large.

$$10 \times 2.345 = 23.45 \qquad 0.026 \times 10 = 0.26$$

Notice that when you are multiplying a whole number like 6 by 10, moving the digits one place to the left is the same as adding one zero.

$$10 \times 6.0 = 60 \qquad 10 \times 6 = 60$$

When you multiply a number by 100, you hold the decimal point steady and move the digits two places to the left. You make the place value of each digit 100 times as large.

$$100 \times 2.345 = 234.5 \qquad 0.026 \times 100 = 2.6$$

When you multiply a number by 1,000, you hold the decimal point steady and move the digits three places to the left. You make the place value of each digit 1,000 times as large.

$$1000 \times 2.345 = 2345 \qquad 0.026 \times 1000 = 26$$

Practise multiplying decimal numbers by 10, 100, and 1000, comparing the decimal point and the digits in each problem. Also practise doing problems like these, in which you must think what the multiplication has been.

$$\underline{\hspace{2cm}} \times 43.82 = 438.2$$

$$\underline{\hspace{2cm}} \times 0.008 = 8$$

$$100 \times \underline{\hspace{2cm}} = 32.56$$

Estimating Decimal Products

You can estimate the product of a decimal and a whole number by rounding each factor to its greatest place value and multiplying. You can use this estimate to check how many digits and decimal places there should be in the product.

Estimate to check: Round and multiply.

$$
\begin{array}{r}
7.63 \\
\times\ 12 \\
\hline
15.26 \\
76.30 \\
\hline
91.56
\end{array}
\qquad\qquad
\begin{array}{r}
8 \\
\times\ 10 \\
\hline
80
\end{array}
$$

You have rounded one figure down, so your accurate answer should be a bit higher than 80. Was it? Multiplying by a whole number, you keep all the decimal places but remember that the last digit may be a zero.

Multiplying a Decimal by a Decimal

When you multiply a decimal by a decimal, you should think all the time about where to put the digits in the product.

Look at this example: $45.6 \times 12.3 = \underline{\qquad}$

$$
\begin{array}{r}
45.6 \\
\times\ 12.3 \\
\hline
91.2
\end{array}
$$

If you round 45.6 up to 50 and 12.3 down to 10, you know that the product will be close to 500. Just this once, let's work in a funny order. We will start with the ones, because we know how to multiply decimals by whole numbers.

$$
\begin{array}{r}
45.6 \\
\times\ 12.3 \\
\hline
91.2 \\
456
\end{array}
$$

Moving to the tens, we are working with the place to the left of the ones, so the product goes one place to the left.

Now think. The tens were one place to the left. We wrote the product one place to the left. The tenths are one place to the right, so where does the product go? Well done if you answered one place to the right.

$$\begin{array}{r} 45.6 \\ \times\ \ 12.3 \\ \hline 91.2 \\ 456 \\ +\ \ 13.68 \\ \hline 560.88 \end{array}$$

The rule is that the product has the same number of decimal places as the number of decimal places in the factors added together.

Usually we start multiplying with the smallest digit. When you start writing in the products, move the digits one place to the right for each decimal place. We can check our example by multiplying with the factors reversed. We should get the same answer.

$$\begin{array}{r} 12.3 \\ \times\ 45.6 \\ \hline \end{array}$$

With one decimal place in each factor, there will be two decimal places in the product, because 1 + 1 = 2.

$$\begin{array}{r} 12.3 \\ \times\ \ 45.6 \\ \hline 7.38 \\ 61.5 \\ +\ 492 \\ \hline 560.88 \end{array}$$

7.38 ⟵	12.3 × 0.6	2 decimal places
61.5 ⟵	12.3 × 5	1 decimal place
+ 492 ⟵	12.3 × 40	0 decimal places

Tens and hundreds are like negative numbers of decimal places. Did you notice that 12.3 (one decimal place) × 40 (minus one decimal place) = 492 (zero decimal places)?

Here are two more examples. Start by working out the full number of decimal places, then work from right to left as usual.

$$\begin{array}{rl} 49.6 & \text{1 decimal place} \\ \times\ \ \ \ 3.8 & +\ \text{1 decimal place} \\ \hline 39.68 & \\ +\ 148.8 & \\ \hline 188.48 & \text{2 decimal places} \end{array}$$

$$\begin{array}{rl} 3.867 & \text{3 decimal places} \\ \times\ \ \ \ 8.2 & +\ \text{1 decimal place} \\ \hline 0.7734 & \\ +\ 30.936 & \\ \hline 31.7094 & \text{4 decimal places} \end{array}$$

Remember that if the factors end with a 5, the smallest decimal place may be a zero.

$$
\begin{array}{rl}
15.125 & \text{3 decimal places} \\
\times \quad 1.6 & \text{+ 1 decimal place} \\
\hline
9.0750 & \\
+ \ 15.125 & \\
\hline
24.2000 & \text{4 decimal places}
\end{array}
$$

Sometimes when you multiply two small decimals, you need to add zeros to the product so that it has the right place value.

There should be 4 decimal places in the product, so you write three zeros to the left of 6 and then the decimal point.

$$
\begin{array}{rl}
0.03 & \text{2 decimal places} \\
\times \ 0.02 & \text{+ 2 decimal places} \\
\hline
0.0006 & \text{4 decimal places}
\end{array}
$$

Checking Decimal Products

You can check decimal products by changing the order of the factors. Remember that multiplication is commutative.

To check:
$$
\begin{array}{r}
49.6 \\
\times \quad 3.8 \\
\hline
39.68 \\
+ \ 148.8 \\
\hline
188.48
\end{array}
$$

Multiply:
$$
\begin{array}{r}
3.8 \\
\times \ 49.6 \\
\hline
2.28 \\
34.2 \\
+ \ 152 \\
\hline
188.48
\end{array}
$$

Practise multiplying decimals by whole numbers and decimals by decimals. Remember to work out the decimal places first. Check each product by changing the order of the factors.

Decimal Division

You divide decimals by whole numbers the same way you divide whole numbers by whole numbers. You put the decimal point in the quotient above the decimal point in the dividend.

$$\begin{array}{r}3.14\\6\overline{)18.84}\\-18\\\hline0.8\\-0.6\\\hline.24\\-.24\\\hline0\end{array}$$

You can estimate the quotient by rounding the dividend to a number that is easy to divide.

$$\begin{array}{r}3\\6\overline{)18}\end{array}\;\checkmark$$

The quotient is about 3, which is close to 3.14. So you know that you have put the digits in the right places.

Sometimes you need to put zeros in the quotient so that it has the right place value.

$$\begin{array}{r}0.03\\32\overline{)0.96}\\-0.96\\\hline0\end{array}$$

You can't divide 9 tenths by 32 ($32\overline{)0.9}$ doesn't work because 32 > 9); you can divide 96 hundredths by 32 ($32\overline{)0.96}$). Write a zero in the tenths place to show that the quotient is 3 *hundredths*.

Writing Zeros in the Dividend

When you divide a decimal, you do not usually write a remainder. You continue to divide, adding zeros after the last place of the decimal.

Divide 505.8 by 12. Since 505.8 = 505.80 = 505.800, you can add as many zeros after the last place of the dividend as you need to, in order to complete the division.

1. Divide 50 tens, 25 ones, and 18 tenths. ▶

$$\begin{array}{r}42.1\\12\overline{)505.8}\\-48\\\hline25\\-24\\\hline1.8\\-1.2\\\hline.6\end{array}$$

$$\begin{array}{r} 42.15 \\ 12\overline{)505.80} \\ -48 \\ \hline 25 \\ -24 \\ \hline 1.8 \\ -1.2 \\ \hline .60 \\ -.60 \\ \hline 0 \end{array}$$

◀ **2.** You are left with 6 tenths (0.6). Add a nought (a zero) to the dividend and divide 60 hundredths (0.60).

When you get a remainder of zero, the division is complete. When the remainder is zero, it is easy to check the division of a decimal. Multiply the quotient by the divisor to check. ▶

$$\begin{array}{r} 42.15 \\ \times\ 12 \\ \hline 84.30 \\ 421.50 \\ \hline 505.80\ \checkmark \end{array}$$

Dividing Whole Numbers Without Remainders

$$\begin{array}{r} 21 \\ 16\overline{)340} \\ -32 \\ \hline 20 \\ -16 \\ \hline 4 \end{array}$$

◀ Instead of writing a remainder, you can continue to divide whole numbers in the same way. Divide 340 by 16.

Remember that $340 = 340.0 = 340.00$ ▶ Add noughts and continue to divide 40 tenths, then 80 hundredths.

Check: ▶

$$\begin{array}{r} 21.25 \\ \times\ 16 \\ \hline 127.50 \\ 212.50 \\ \hline 340.00\ \checkmark \end{array}$$

$$\begin{array}{r} 21.25 \\ 16\overline{)340.00} \\ -32 \\ \hline 20 \\ -16 \\ \hline 4.0 \\ -3.2 \\ \hline .80 \\ -.80 \\ \hline 0 \end{array}$$

Dividing by 10, 100 and 1,000

When you divide a number by 10, you keep the decimal point in the same place and move the digits one place to the right. You make the place value of each digit ten times smaller.

$$693.8 \div 10 = 69.38 \qquad 5.4 \div 10 = 0.54$$

When you divide a number by 1,000, you keep the decimal point in the same place and move the digits three places to the right. You make the place value of each digit 1,000 times smaller.

$$693.8 \div 1,000 = 0.6938 \qquad 5.4 \div 1,000 = 0.0054$$

Practise multiplying and dividing decimals by 10, 100 and 1,000 until you can change the place values easily.

Also practise thinking what the divisor or dividend must have been in problems like these:

$$26.2 \quad \div \quad \underline{\hspace{2cm}} \quad = \quad 2.62$$

$$\underline{\hspace{2cm}} \quad \div \quad 100 \quad = \quad 0.084$$

$$670 \quad \div \quad \underline{\hspace{2cm}} \quad = \quad 0.67$$

Rounding Decimal Quotients

```
        12.39
   23)285.00
      -23
      ----
       55
      -46
      ----
       9.0
      -6.9
      ----
       2.10
      -2.07
      -----
          3
```

Even when you continue to add zeros to the dividend, not all divisions finish exactly. In these division problems, you can round the quotient to a certain place. Sometimes you also round the quotient in problems where the division works out exactly. To round a quotient, divide to one place *beyond* the place to which you are rounding.

◀ Find the quotient of 285 divided by 23, to the nearest tenth. Since you are asked for the nearest tenth, divide until you get a quotient with hundredths, and then round.

12.39 rounds to 12.4. The quotient of 285 ÷ 23 to the nearest tenth is 12.4.

If you had been asked for a quotient to the nearest hundredth, you would have continued to divide until you had a quotient with thousandths. ▶

12.391 rounds to 12.39.

```
        12.391
   23)285.000
      -23
      ----
       55
      -46
      ----
       9.0
      -6.9
      ----
       2.10
      -2.07
      -----
         30
        -23
        ----
          7
```

The quotient of 285 ÷ 23 to the nearest hundredth is 12.39

Often you round quotients because you want to give an answer to the nearest whole unit. Suppose that 4 litres of oil weigh 2,850 grams. How much does 1 litre of oil weigh, to the nearest gram?

Divide to the tenths of a gram and then round.

$$71\,2.\,5$$
$$4\overline{)\,285^{1}0.^{2}0}$$

712.5 rounds to 713. To the nearest gram, 1 litre of oil weighs 713 g.

Inexact Division

Practise dividing decimals and whole numbers by whole numbers a lot. Finish divisions that are exact by continuing to divide. When the division is not exact, divide to a certain place value. Always check each division by multiplying the quotient by the divisor. With whole numbers you may still need to add on a remainder. With decimals, if the answer is not exact there will still be a small difference that you have not divided. Add this back on too and you should be back to your original dividend.

Equivalent Fractions

In Year 5 we looked at *equivalent fractions* which name the same amount. When you multiply or divide the numerator and the denominator of a fraction by the same number, you name an equivalent fraction.

Here are some examples.

$$\frac{1 \times 4}{2 \times 4} = \frac{4}{8} \qquad \frac{1}{2} = \frac{4}{8}$$

$$\frac{18 \div 6}{30 \div 6} = \frac{3}{5} \qquad \frac{18}{30} = \frac{3}{5}$$

Practise solving equations like these, so that the fractions are equivalent.

$$\frac{5}{10} = \frac{n}{20}$$ Think: $$\overset{\times 2}{\underset{\div 2}{\frac{5}{10} = \frac{10}{20}}}$$ so $n = 10$

$$\frac{18}{24} = \frac{6}{n}$$ Think: $$\overset{\div 3}{\underset{\times 3}{\frac{18}{24} = \frac{6}{8}}}$$ so $n = 8$

Lowest Terms

A fraction is in *lowest terms* when its numerator and denominator have no common factor greater than 1. You can write an equivalent fraction in lowest terms by dividing both the numerator and denominator of a fraction by their greatest common factor (GCF).

Put $^{12}\!/_{16}$ in lowest terms. The GCF of 12 and 16 is 4.

$$\frac{12 \div 4}{16 \div 4} = \frac{3}{4}$$ ¾ is in lowest terms.

The numerator and denominator are called the *terms* of a fraction. Putting a fraction in lowest terms is also called putting it in *simplest form*. Because you divide to put a fraction in lowest terms, people often say you *reduce* a fraction to lowest terms.

Comparing Fractions

You can compare two fractions that have the same denominator by comparing the numerator.

$$\frac{4}{5} > \frac{3}{5}$$ because $4 > 3$

To compare fractions with different denominators, you first give them a common denominator – you make their denominator the same. Once their denominators are the same, you can compare them easily. To give fractions a common denominator, first find the lowest common multiple (LCM) of the two denominators; then write the fractions as equivalent fractions that have this LCM for a denominator.

For example, to compare ⅔ and ⅗ first find the LCM of the denominators 3 and 5. The LCM is 15. Write both ⅔ and ⅗ equivalent fractions with a denominator of 15.

$$\frac{2 \times 5}{3 \times 5} = \frac{10}{15} \qquad\qquad \frac{3 \times 3}{5 \times 3} = \frac{9}{15}$$

Now compare the fractions. Since ¹⁰⁄₁₅ > ⁹⁄₁₅ , you know that ⅔ > ⅗ .

You can find many common denominators for fractions. Any common multiple of the denominator can be used as a common denominator for fractions. For example, you can also write ⅔ and ⅗ with a common denominator of 30, since 30 is a common multiple of 3 and 5.

When you use the LCM to find a common denominator of fractions, you find their *lowest* common denominator (LCD). Learn to compare fractions by writing them with their LCD.

Comparing Fractions on a Number Line

Seeing fractions on a number line can help you to compare them. Here are number lines divided into twelfths, sixths, quarters, thirds, and halves.

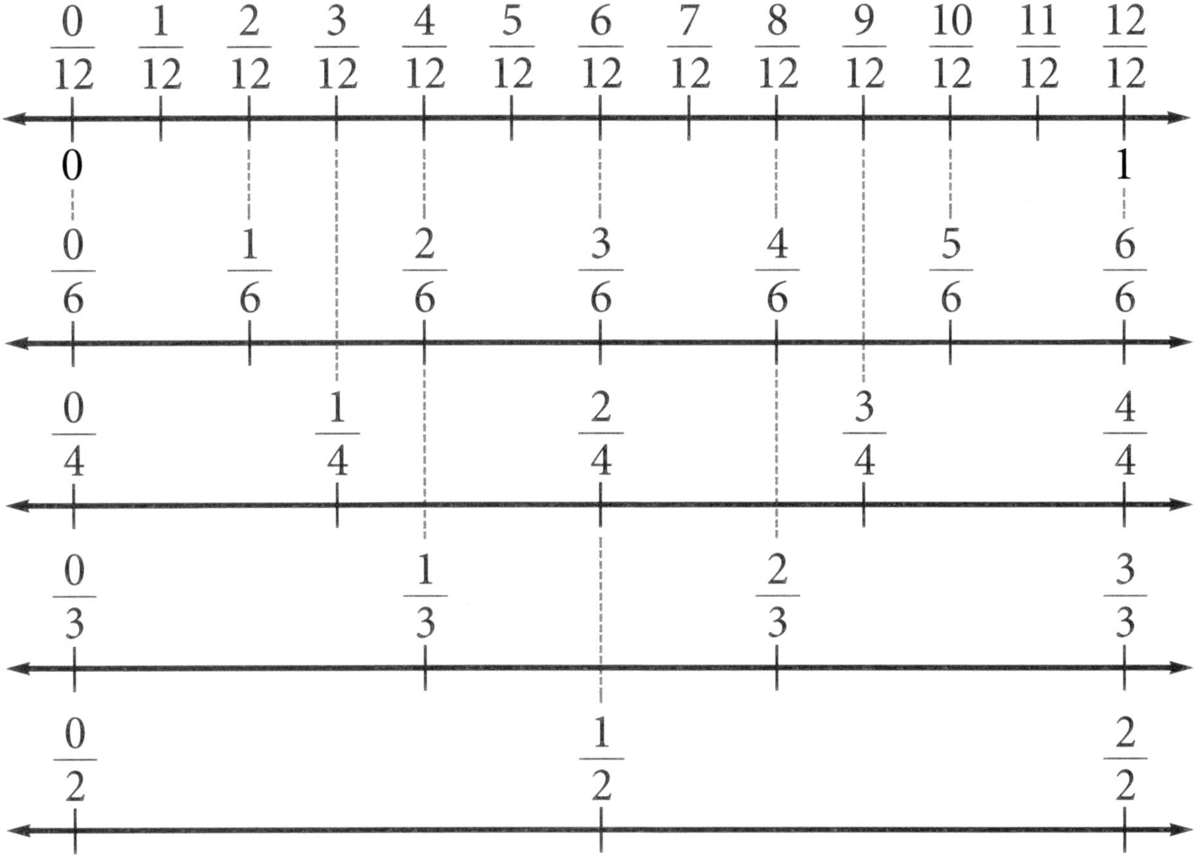

You can see from these number lines that ⅔ < ¾ and that ³⁄₆ = ½. Practise drawing a number line divided into twelfths in which you also write each fraction in lowest terms.

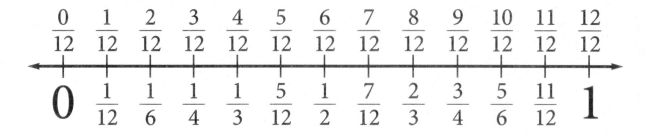

Also practice drawing number lines, divided into eighths or sixteenths. These number lines will help you to get a good mental sense of which fractions are greater, which are less, and which are equivalent.

Notice that a fraction in which the numerator is very small compared to the denominator is close to zero. For example, ¹⁄₁₂ is close to zero. When the numerator is about half of the denominator, the fraction is about ½. ⁵⁄₁₂ and ⁷⁄₁₂ are both close to ½.

When the difference between the numerator and the denominator is small compared to their size, the fraction is close to 1. ¹¹⁄₁₂ is close to 1. Practise estimating whether fractions are close to 0, ½ or 1.

Adding Fractions

You add fractions with the same denominator by adding the numerator. You write each sum in lowest terms.

$$\frac{2}{3} + \frac{2}{3} = \frac{4}{3} = 1\frac{1}{3}$$

$$\frac{3}{16} + \frac{5}{16} = \frac{8}{16} = \frac{1}{2}$$

To add fractions with different denominators, you must first write them with a common denominator. Then you can add. You cannot add numerators when their denominators are different, because you would be adding parts of different sizes.

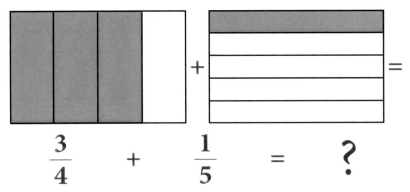

$$\frac{3}{4} \quad + \quad \frac{1}{5} \quad = \quad ?$$

You cannot add these fractions yet because their denominators are different. To add, first write ¾ and ⅕ as equivalent fractions with a common denominator. Use the LCM of 4 and 5 to find the LCD. The LCD of ¾ and ⅕ is 20.

$$\frac{3 \times 5}{4 \times 5} = \frac{15}{20} \qquad\qquad \frac{1 \times 4}{5 \times 4} = \frac{4}{20}$$

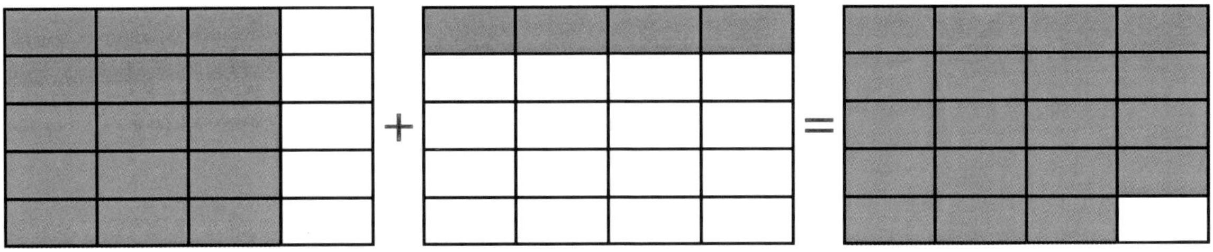

$$\frac{3}{4} \quad + \quad \frac{1}{5} \quad = \quad \frac{15}{20} \quad + \quad \frac{4}{20} \quad = \quad \frac{19}{20}$$

Always write a fraction sum as a mixed number or fraction in lowest terms.

The LCD of ⁴⁄₇ and ²⁄₂₁ is 21.

$$\frac{4}{7} \quad + \quad \frac{2}{21} \quad = \quad \frac{12}{21} \quad + \quad \frac{2}{21} \quad = \quad \frac{14}{21} \quad = \quad \frac{2}{3}$$

Sometimes you have to find the LCD of three or more fractions to add them. The LCD of ⅚, ⅓ and ⅝ is 24.

$$\frac{5}{6} \quad + \quad \frac{1}{3} \quad + \quad \frac{5}{8} \quad = \quad \frac{20}{24} \quad + \quad \frac{8}{24} \quad + \quad \frac{15}{24} \quad = \quad \frac{43}{24} \quad = \quad 1\frac{19}{24}$$

Practise adding two or more fractions with different denominators lots of times until it seems easy.

Subtracting Fractions

You subtract fractions with the same denominator by subtracting the numerator. You write each difference in lowest terms.

$$\frac{7}{8} - \frac{3}{8} = \frac{1}{2}$$

To subtract fractions with different denominators, you must first write them with a common denominator. You cannot subtract parts that are of a different size. For example, you cannot take ¼ from ⅗ until you make the parts in the two fractions the same size. To find ⅗ – ¼, write ¼ and ⅗ with their LCD and then subtract. The LCD of ⅗ and ¼ is 20.

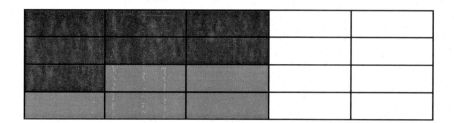

$$\frac{3}{5} - \frac{1}{4} = \frac{3 \times 4}{5 \times 4} - \frac{1 \times 5}{4 \times 5} = \frac{12 - 5}{20} = \frac{7}{20}$$

Now try ⅚ – 4/9. The LCD of ⅚ and 4/9 is 18.

$$\frac{5}{6} = \frac{15}{18} \qquad \frac{4}{9} = \frac{8}{18} \qquad \frac{15 - 8}{18} = \frac{7}{18}$$

You can use any common denominator when you add or subtract fractions with different denominators, but using the LCD as the common denominator will make your work quicker and easier. Practise subtracting fractions with different denominators until you feel like a pro.

Mixed Numbers and Fractions

A mixed number contains an integer and a fraction. 2½ is an example. You sometimes want to round mixed numbers to the nearest whole number. If the fractional part of a mixed number is less than one half, round the mixed number down. If the fractional part is one half or greater, round the mixed number up. A fraction equals one half if its numerator is half its denominator.

Round to the nearest whole number:

$6\dfrac{2}{7}$ 2 is less than half of 7, so $\dfrac{2}{7} < \dfrac{1}{2}$ $6\frac{2}{7}$ rounds down to 6.

$7\dfrac{11}{19}$ 11 is more than half of 19, so $\dfrac{11}{19} > \dfrac{1}{2}$ $7\frac{11}{19}$ rounds up to 8.

$5\dfrac{7}{14}$ 7 is half of 14, so $\dfrac{7}{14} = \dfrac{1}{2}$ $5\frac{7}{14}$ rounds up to 6.

Decimals, Mixed Numbers and Fractions

You should know how to write decimals as fractions or mixed numbers. Here are two examples.

$$0.067 = \frac{67}{1000} \qquad 8.24 = 8\frac{24}{100} = 8\frac{6}{25}$$

You can also write fractions as decimals. There are two ways you can do this. You can write a fraction as an equivalent fraction with a denominator of 10 or 100 or 1,000. Then write this equivalent fraction as a decimal. For example, to write ⅖ as a decimal, convert it to an equivalent fraction with a denominator of 10.

$$\frac{2}{5} = \frac{2 \times 2}{5 \times 2} = \frac{4}{10} = 0.4$$

Another example:

$$\frac{17}{25} = \frac{68}{100} = 0.68$$

You can use this method only when the denominator is a power of 10, like 100 or 1,000, etc.

You can also remember that the fraction bar is the same as the division sign. To write ⅛ as a decimal, do the division problem 8)1 until the division finishes.

$$
\begin{array}{r}
0.125 \\
8\overline{)1.000} \\
-8 \\
\hline
20 \\
-16 \\
\hline
40 \\
-40 \\
\hline
0
\end{array}
$$

So ⅛ = 0.125

Check:
$$
\begin{array}{r}
0.125 \\
\times 8 \\
\hline
1.000 \checkmark
\end{array}
$$

Recurring Decimals

For many fractions, this division goes on and on, and the quotient just repeats. You cannot write all the decimal places for these fractions but you can spot the pattern. These are called *recurring decimals*.

Write ⅓ as a decimal to the nearest hundredth.

$$
\begin{array}{r}
0.333 \\
3\overline{)1.000} \\
-9 \\
\hline
10 \\
-9 \\
\hline
10 \\
-9 \\
\hline
1
\end{array}
$$

Check:
$$
\begin{array}{r}
0.333 \\
\times 3 \\
\hline
0.999 \\
+ 0.001 \\
\hline
1.000 \checkmark
\end{array}
$$

0.333 rounds to 0.33

⅓ to the nearest hundredth is 0.33

Notice that this division will continue to give a 3 in each decimal place, as long as you divide. When you discover a pattern like this, you can find the next digit or digits in the quotient without dividing.

To write a mixed number as a decimal, change the fractional part to a decimal. The whole number part remains unchanged.

Write 4⁴/₁₁ as a decimal to the nearest thousandth. The whole number 4 remains unchanged.

$$
\begin{array}{r}
0.3636 \\
11\overline{)4.0000} \\
-\ 3.3 \\
\hline
70 \\
-\ 66 \\
\hline
40 \\
-\ 33 \\
\hline
70 \\
-\ 66 \\
\hline
4
\end{array}
$$

Notice the pattern.

If you were to continue to divide, can you predict what the next two digits of the quotient would be?

0.3636 rounds to 0.364. To the nearest thousandth, 4⁴/₁₁ is 4.364. Practise writing fractions and mixed numbers as decimals.

Adding Mixed Numbers

To add mixed numbers with the same denominator, first add the fractional parts and then add the whole number parts.

Add the mixed numbers

$$12\frac{1}{7} + 5\frac{3}{7}$$

First add the fractions

$$\frac{1}{7} + \frac{3}{7} = \frac{4}{7}$$

Then add the whole numbers

$$12 + 5 = 17$$

Lastly, put them together

$$17 + \frac{4}{7} = 17\frac{4}{7}$$

When the denominators of the fractional parts are different, write the fractions with their LCD and then add. Sometimes you will get an improper fraction in the sum. Always *convert*, or change, your answer to a mixed number in lowest terms.

The LCD of ⅔, ½, and ⅙ is 6.

Add:

$$2\frac{2}{3} + 3\frac{1}{2} + 6\frac{1}{6} = \qquad 2\frac{4}{6} + 3\frac{3}{6} + 6\frac{1}{6}$$

$$\frac{4}{6} + \frac{3}{6} + \frac{1}{6} = \frac{8}{6} \qquad 2 + 3 + 6 = 11$$

$$11 + \frac{8}{6} = 11 + 1\frac{2}{6} = 12\frac{2}{6} = 12\frac{1}{3}$$

Remember that to convert the improper fraction to a mixed number, you do the division:

$$6\overline{)8} \quad \begin{array}{r} 1 \\ \hline 8 \\ -6 \\ \hline 2 \end{array}$$

So $\frac{8}{6} = 1\frac{2}{6}$

Another Way to Add Mixed Numbers

Remember that an improper fraction can name the same amount as a mixed number. If you turn your mixed numbers into improper fractions with a common denominator, you can add them easily.

$$2\frac{2}{3} + 3\frac{1}{2} + 6\frac{1}{6} =$$

$$\frac{8}{3} + \frac{7}{2} + \frac{37}{6} = \frac{16 + 21 + 37}{6} = \frac{74}{6} = 12\frac{2}{6} = 12\frac{1}{3}$$

Subtracting Mixed Numbers

There are several ways to subtract mixed numbers. Have a look at the problem and decide which way is easiest. You always need a common denominator for the fractional parts.

In the example below, the second fractional part is smaller than the first. You can subtract the fractional parts and the whole number parts without regrouping:

$$5\frac{2}{3} - 2\frac{1}{3} = \left(\frac{2}{3} - \frac{1}{3}\right) + \left(5 - 2\right) = 3\frac{1}{3}$$

In this second example, the denominators are different, but the second fractional part is still smaller than the first:

$$5\frac{5}{6} - 2\frac{3}{4} = 5\frac{10}{12} - 2\frac{9}{12} = \frac{10 - 9}{12} + 5 - 2 = 3\frac{1}{12}$$

Sometimes when you are subtracting, the fractional part you are subtracting from is too small. Then it can be easier to subtract improper fractions:

$$5 - 2\frac{3}{16} = \frac{80 - 35}{16} = \frac{45}{16} = 2\frac{13}{16}$$

It could be easier, especially if the whole numbers are large, to regroup the number you are subtracting from. You regroup by adding one of the wholes to the fractional part. In this same example

$5 - 2\frac{3}{16}$, you cannot take $\frac{3}{16}$ from 0.

Regroup 1 whole as $\frac{16}{16}$ so that there are sixteenths to subtract.

$$4\frac{16}{16} - 2\frac{3}{16} = \left(\frac{16}{16} - \frac{3}{16}\right) + \left(4 - 2\right) = 2\frac{13}{16}$$

When the fractions have different denominators, write the fractions with their LCD *first*, before you regroup, if you need to. In the problem $5\frac{3}{16} - 2\frac{11}{12}$ the LCD is 48.

Write the fraction with a common denominator.

$$\frac{3}{16} = \frac{9}{48} \qquad \frac{11}{12} = \frac{44}{48}$$

To subtract, you need to regroup $5\frac{9}{48}$. Add a whole to the fractional part:

$$5\frac{9}{48} = 4\frac{48}{48} + \frac{9}{48} = 4\frac{57}{48}$$

$$4\frac{57}{48} - 2\frac{44}{48} = \frac{57 - 44}{48} + 4 - 2 = 2\frac{13}{48}$$

Since you will not always need to regroup, write the fractions with their LCD first.

Multiplying Fractions and Whole Numbers

One way to multiply a fraction and a whole number is by repeated addition. You can think of $6 \times \frac{2}{3}$ as starting at zero and adding $\frac{2}{3}$ six times.

So

$$6 \times \frac{2}{3} = \frac{2}{3} + \frac{2}{3} + \frac{2}{3} + \frac{2}{3} + \frac{2}{3} + \frac{2}{3} = \frac{12}{3} = 4$$

Another way to think of multiplying a fraction and a whole number is taking part of the whole number.

The word *of* means the same thing here as the multiplication sign.

$$\frac{2}{3} \times 6 \text{ means } \frac{2}{3} \text{ of } 6$$

To find ⅔ of 6, divide 6 into 3 parts and then take 2 of them.

Divide 6 into 3 parts: 6 ÷ 3 = 2   Now take 2 of the 3 parts.

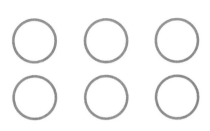 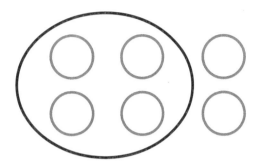

2 × 2 = 4. So ⅔ of 6 is 4.

Notice that ⅔ × 6 = 4 = 6 × ⅔. Multiplication is commutative; you will get the same answer whether you think of adding a fraction over and over again or taking part of a whole number.

You can use the following method to multiply a fraction and a whole number. Multiply the whole number and the numerator of the fraction, and write the product over the denominator. Write the product in lowest terms.

$$6 \times \frac{2}{3} = \frac{12}{3} = 4$$

Practise multiplying fractions and whole numbers in this way. Also practise writing a problem like 7 × ⅚ as repeated addition.

$$7 \times \frac{5}{6} = \frac{5}{6} + \frac{5}{6} + \frac{5}{6} + \frac{5}{6} + \frac{5}{6} + \frac{5}{6} + \frac{5}{6} = \frac{35}{6} = 5\frac{5}{6}$$

Practise solving a problem like finding ³⁄₇ of 56 in two ways. Remember that ³⁄₇ of 56 is the same as ³⁄₇ × 56.

A) Multiply: ³⁄₇ × 56 = ³ ˣ ⁵⁶⁄₇ = ¹⁶⁸⁄₇ = 24

B) Or to find ³⁄₇ of 56, divide 56 in to 7 equal parts. 56 ÷ 7 = 8. Now take 3 of the equal parts. 8 × 3 = 24. ³⁄₇ of 56 is 24.

Notice that in the first method , you multiply and then divide. In the second method, you divide and then multiply. You get the same answer either way.

Ratios and Probabilities

Ratio

A ratio is a way of comparing the size of two numbers. If a family has three dogs and two cats, the ratio of their dogs to cats is 3 to 2. You can write the ratio of their dogs to cats in a number of ways:

3 to 2   3:2 $\dfrac{3}{2}$

You read each of these ratios '3 to 2'. Notice that a ratio can be written as a fraction but we more often use a colon (:) in the middle. The fraction is like saying: 'There are one-and-a-half dogs to every cat.' You can write equal ratios the same way you write equivalent fractions, by dividing or multiplying both numbers of the ratio by the same number. Here is how you can write two ratios equal to the ratio 4:10 (4 to 10).

$$(4 \div 2) : (10 \div 2) = 2{:}5 \qquad\qquad 4 : 10 = 2{:}5$$
$$(4 \times 2) : (10 \times 2) = 8{:}20 \qquad\qquad 4 : 10 = 8{:}20$$

The ratio 2:5 is in lowest terms.

Practise writing equal ratios.

Solve for a:

$$8{:}21 = 24{:}a$$

You multiply 8×3 to get 24, so you must multiply 21×3 to get a.

$$a = 21 \times 3 \qquad\qquad a = 63$$

Also practise checking to see if two ratios are equal.

Does $5{:}9 = 10{:}14$?   You multiply 5×2 to get 10

You cannot multiply 9×2 to get 14   So $5{:}9 \neq 10{:}14$

The sign $\neq$ means 'is not equal to'.

Scale

A scale drawing uses a ratio, called its *scale*, to shrink or enlarge all the things it shows in the same way. For example, on a map of a city with a scale 1 cm = 2 km, each centimetre on the map represents two kilometres of actual distance in the city. The scale for that map is 1:200,000. A map is one kind of scale drawing; another example is a plan showing the rooms on a floor of a house.

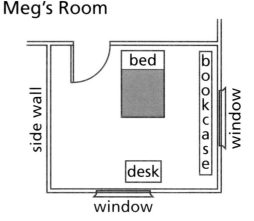

Meg's Room

side wall · bed · bookcase · window · desk · window

Scale 1:100

Meg has made a plan of her room, with the scale 1:100, which means 1 cm : 1 m.

length on the plan : actual length

1 : 100

1 cm : 100 cm

1 cm : 1 m

If her desk is 1 metre long, how long will it appear on the plan? Find a ratio equivalent to the scale.

length on the plan : actual length

1 cm : 100 cm

n cm : 100 cm

This is exactly what our scale tells us. 1 actual metre shows on the map as 1 cm. We do not need to do any more arithmetic. *n* is 1.

On her plan, the side wall is 4 centimetres long. How long is it actually? To find out, write the scale as a ratio, and then find an equivalent ratio to it.

length on the plan : actual length

1 cm : 1 m

4 cm : *n* m

You multiply 1 cm by 4 to get 4 cm, so you must multiply 1 m by 4 to get *n*.

n = 1 m × 4 = 4 m

The side wall is actually 4 m long.

To find a scale, write a ratio of a plan length to the actual length as a fraction in lowest terms. Here is an example:

On a plan, the length of a school playground is 2 centimetres. It is actually 50 metres long. What is the scale of the plan?

plan length : actual length

2 cm : 50 m

1 cm : 25 m

The scale of the plan is 1 cm : 25 m or 1 cm : 2,500 cm or 1:2,500.

Rates and Speed

A *rate* is a ratio between two different quantities. Here are some examples of rates: she was averaging 4 runs in each 6 balls when batting; he was getting 10 pence for every litre of juice he sold; the car was travelling at 100 kilometres per hour.

One very common rate is speed. Speed is a rate given in distance per unit of time. 100 kilometres per hour is a speed. You can abbreviate it to 100 km/h. Some other units of speed are miles per hour (mph) and metres/second (m/s).

Here are two formulae that relate distance, speed and time.

$s = D \div t$ Speed is distance divided by time.

$D = s \times t$ Distance is equal to the speed times the time.

The second formula tells you that you multiply the speed by the time spent travelling

at that speed to find the distance travelled. For example, an aeroplane travels at 550 mph for 4 hours. To find how far it has travelled, multiply: $D = 550 \times 4 = 2,200$. The plane has travelled 2,200 miles in 4 hours.

Sometimes speed is known per minute, or per second. If a train is travelling at 2 km/min, how long will it take to travel 86 km? Remember $D = s \times t$. The distance is 86 km and the speed is 2 km/min.

$$86 = 2 \times t$$

$$86 \div 2 = \quad t \qquad \text{(Use inverse operations.)}$$

$$43 = t \ \text{ or } \ t = 43 \qquad \text{It will take the train 43 minutes to travel 86 km.}$$

You can change distance per minute to distance per hour by multiplying the distance by 60. 2 km/min = 120 km/h.

You can also change distance per hour to distance per minute by dividing by 60. 90 mph = 1.5 miles/min, since 90 ÷ 60 = 1.5.

To find a speed, write the ratio of distance to a single unit of time. For example, if a train has travelled 195 miles in 3 hours, what was its speed? The train has travelled 195 miles: 3 hours. Divide by 3 to find the distance travelled in 1 hour.

$$\begin{array}{r} 65 \\ 3\overline{)195} \end{array} \qquad \text{The train has travelled at 65 mph.}$$

Finding a Percentage of a Number

There are 525 pupils at a primary school. 44% of them are in Year 5 or 6. How many pupils are in Years 5 and 6?

To solve this problem, you must find a percentage of a number: what is 44% of 525? To find a percentage of a number, change the percentage to a decimal and multiply.

Remember that 44% = 0.44. To find 0.44 of 525 you can multiply 0.44 × 525.

44% of 525 is 231.

There are 231 Year 5 and 6 pupils at the primary school.

$$\begin{array}{r} 525 \\ \times\ 0.44 \\ \hline 210.0 \\ 21.000 \\ \hline 231.00 \end{array}$$

Finding an Average

An *average* can give you an idea of how large a typical number in a set is. To find the average of a set of numbers, you add the numbers together and then divide by the number of addends. The number of addends will be the same as the number of items in the set.

For example, Mrs Tough wants to find the average number of questions out of 20 that Peter has got right on his last 5 tests. His scores have been 12, 12, 13, 15 and 17. She adds his scores:

$$\begin{array}{r} 12 \\ 12 \\ 13 \\ 15 \\ +\ 17 \\ \hline 69 \end{array}$$

Then she divides by the number of scores:

$$5\overline{)69.0} \quad 13.8$$

Peter has averaged 13.8 correct answers on his last five tests. Mrs Tough might round the average and say, 'Peter has been getting about 14 questions right out of 20.'

Another word for average is *mean*. Practise finding the average price of a litre of petrol in your local area if the various petrol stations sell it for £1.37, £1.42, £1.48 and £1.44 per litre.

Probability

Have you ever heard someone say there's a 'fifty-fifty chance' that something might happen? Do you ever describe the chances of something happening as 'one in a million'? Both of these expressions are ways of talking about probability. Probability is a measurement of how likely it is that a particular event will happen. A high probability means something is likely to happen but may not; a low probability means it probably won't but still could.

Suppose you have a black bag that contains three red apples and one green apple. If you reach into the bag and pick out one apple without looking, what is the probability that it will be a green apple? The probability is one in four because, of the four apples you might pick, only one of them is green. This probability can be written as a fraction: ¼. Or it can be written as a percentage: there is a 25% chance that you will pick a green apple. Probability can also be expressed as a decimal value between 0 and 1. A probability of 0 means that there is no chance of the event occurring. A probability of 1 means it is certain to occur. In our example, the probability of choosing a green apple is 0.25. What is the probability of choosing a red apple? Can you write that probability in each of the three different ways?

Now imagine that you have four red apples and no green apples in the bag: what is the probability of pulling out a green one? What is the probability of pulling out a red one?

Graphs, Functions and Word Problems

Pie Charts

Sometimes the best way to present mathematical information is to draw a graph. There are several different kinds of graph.

A *pie chart* is a circular graph, good for showing the relationship of different parts to a whole. It is usually divided into fractions or percentage. Pie charts can be used to show probability. For example, if a bag contains four red apples and two green apples, the probability of choosing a red or green apple can be shown on a pie chart, like this:

Here the shaded area represents the chances that an apple will be red (4 in 6); the unshaded area stands for the chances that an apple will be green (2 in 6). Looking at this graph, you can see why they are called pie charts. The chart looks like a pie cut into slices.

Pie charts can also be used in other way. The chart on the next page shows how the Brown family spent its income.

You can see straight away from the graph where the Brown family spent most of their

The Brown Family Income
Last Year (After Taxes)

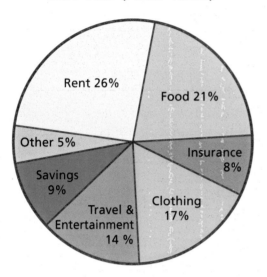

money and how much of their total income went on each area. If the Brown family had an income after taxes of £51,860 last year, how much did they spend on insurance? You find 8% of £51,860. 8% = 0.08

$$£\ 51,860$$
$$\times \qquad 0.08$$
$$\overline{£\ \ 4,148.80}$$

The Brown family spent £4,148.80 on insurance last year.

How much money did they save? How much money did they spend on food?

Bar Graphs

A *bar graph* is a good way to show the different sizes of amounts. Here is a table of data and a bar graph based on the numbers in the tables. *Data* are single facts or measurements that you are given as a starting point for calculations. The Latin word means 'things given'.

Player	Points
Sarah	24
Mary	19
Latisha	33
Flo	42
Samantha	31
Julia	29

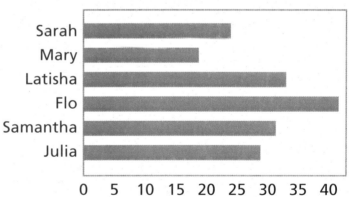

Points Scored by Each Player
on the Basketball Team

Down the left side of the graph we listed the players on the team. Along the bottom we listed numbers of points scored. Then we drew a series of bars to mark each player's total points. Lastly, we gave the graph a title.

You can see straight away from this chart that Flo is the top scorer on the team.

Line Graphs

Another kind of graph is the line graph. People often use line graphs to show how amounts or numbers change over time. The data below shows how the average maximum temperature in the Scottish city of Glasgow changed during the year.

January	5°	July	19°
February	7°	August	19°
March	9°	September	16°
April	12°	October	13°
May	15°	November	9°
June	18°	December	7°

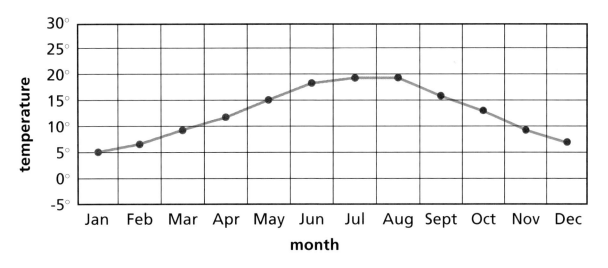

To make our line graph, we wrote the months along the bottom of the graph. Down the side, we put temperature intervals that would show the data clearly. We gave the graph a title and labels along the bottom and side. When you look at this line graph, you can see at a glance how the temperature rises in the summer and goes down in the autumn and winter.

Practise making your own bar graphs, line graphs and pie charts from tables of data. For each chart, you'll need to decide which kind of graph would be the best way to present your data.

Functions and Inverse Operations

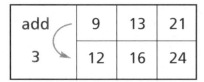

add	9	13	21
3	12	16	24

These tables show *functions*. These functions do the same thing to each number you put into them. For example, the first function adds 3 to each number in the top row to find the number that should go in the bottom row.

divide	26	57	16	3
by 2	13	28.5	8	1.5

multiply	6	22	5	11
by 7	42	154	35	77

Inverse operations can help you to see how functions work. For example, the inverse of the function *add 3* is the function *subtract 3*. If you add 3 to 9 and then subtract 3, you get back to 9 again. An inverse operation undoes the previous operation.

add	9	13	21	subtract
3	12	16	24	3

Addition and subtraction are inverse operations.

multiply	13	28.5	8	1.5	divide
by 2	26	57	16	3	by 2

Multiplication and division are inverse operations.

Practise filling in function tables like this one:

divide	16	27	10	18
by 4	4	6.75	?	?

Graphing Functions

You can make a graph of a function such as <u>add 3</u>.

add	0	1	2	3	4
3	3	4	5	6	7

Write each pair of numbers as co-ordinates. Then plot the co-ordinates as points on a grid using squared paper. Connect the points to show that they are on the same line. If these points are not on the same line, you have made a mistake.

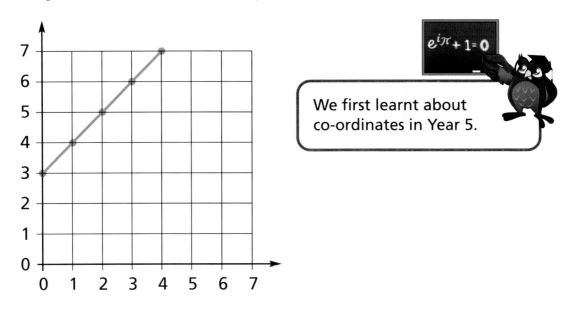

We first learnt about co-ordinates in Year 5.

Plot graphs of three more functions for practice. Here are the functions:

multiply by 2	0	1	2	3	4
	0	2	4	6	8

subtract 4	4	5	6	7	8
	0	1	2	3	4

divide by 2	0	2	4	6	8
	0	1	2	3	4

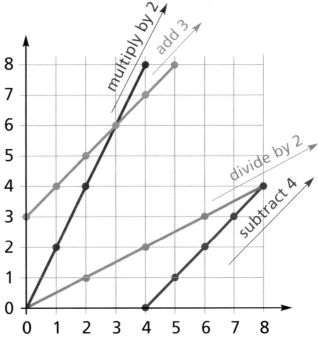

Writing and Solving Equations for Word Problems

You can write an equation for a word problem, using a variable like x or n to stand for an unknown number. Jennifer goes to the bookshop and buys a mystery and a romance for £8.90; the mystery costs £0.60 more than the romance. How much does each book cost?

Begin with a simple sketch. Draw line segments or bars that will help you write an equation. Be sure to be clear about what the variable or variables in your sketch represent. In the pictures below, r stands for the cost of the romance.

Next write an equation based on the picture. It is common not to include units in an algebraic equation. So, for now, leave out the pound sign and write your numbers as decimals:

$$r + (r + 0.60) = 8.90$$

Then solve the equation by finding what r is. Use inverse operations until r appears only once and by itself.

$r + r + 0.60 = 8.90$		
$(2 \times r) + 0.60 = 8.90$	$2 \times r$ is the same as $r + r$
$(2 \times r)\qquad = 8.90 - 60$	Remember, you can write $4 + 3 = 7$ as $4 = 7 - 3$
$2 \times r\qquad = 8.30$	
$r\qquad = 8.30 \div 2$	You can write $2 \times 4 = 8$ as $4 = 8 \div 2$
$r\qquad = 4.15$	

Now that you have done the calculations and solved the equation, you can restore the pound sign. The romance costs £4.15, and the mystery costs £0.60 more, or £4.75. You can check your answer by adding: £4.15 + £4.75 = £8.90.

Here is another example. Bill weighs three times as much as his dog Samuel. Together they weigh 92 kilograms. How much does each weigh?

1) As before, draw line segment *s* or bars to show the variable.

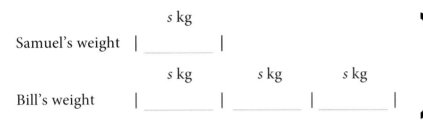

Samuel's weight

Bill's weight

92 kilograms in all

2) Set aside the units and write an equation.

$$s + (s + s + s) = 92$$

3) Solve the equation.

$$4 \times s = 92$$
$$s = 92 \div 4$$
$$s = 23$$

Finally, identify your units. Samuel weighs 23 kilograms. Bill weighs 3 × 23 kilograms, or 69 kilograms. You can check your answer by adding: 23 + 69 = 92.

Now you try one. Susan paid £20 for two hamsters and a goldfish. The goldfish cost £4. What did each hamster cost?

When solving word problems, bear in mind that the solution to your equation may sometimes be mathematically correct but not realistic as a solution for the original word problem. For example, suppose you wanted to find out how many buses are needed to transport the students in your school to a museum. There are 135 students, and each bus holds 30 students. Write an equation, where *b* stands for the number of buses you need:

$$b \times 30 \qquad = 135$$
$$b = 135/30 = 4.5$$

The maths says you need 4.5 buses, but since you can't travel in half a bus, you'll actually need 5 buses.

Geometry

Angles

Now let's learn some geometry. You remember that geometry is the study of points, lines and angles – and of the shapes and forms that can be constructed using points, lines and angles.

Whenever two lines, line segments or rays meet at a common point, they form an angle. The place where they come together is called a *vertex*.

You measure an angle by measuring the size of its opening in units called *degrees*. You can do this with a measuring tool called a protractor. First, place the protractor's centre on the vertex of the angle and the zero mark along one ray. Then you can read the number of degrees in the angle, where the second ray crosses the protractor. Angle EFG has a measure of 56 degrees. You write $\angle$EFG = 56°. The symbol ° stands for degrees.

You can also use a protractor to draw an angle with a certain measure. Use a ruler to draw a ray. Then place the protractor's centre on the end point and the zero mark along the ray. Mark a point at the right number of degrees, and draw a second ray from the vertex of the angle through this point.

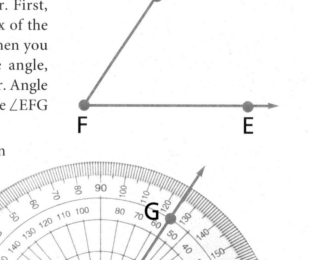

Kinds of Angles

A *right angle* has a measure of 90°. ∠BAD is a right angle.

An *acute angle* has a measure less than 90°. ∠BAC is an acute angle. Remember that acute angles are smaller than right angles.

An *obtuse angle* has a measure greater than 90° but less than 180°. ∠BAE is an obtuse angle. Obtuse angles are greater than right angles.

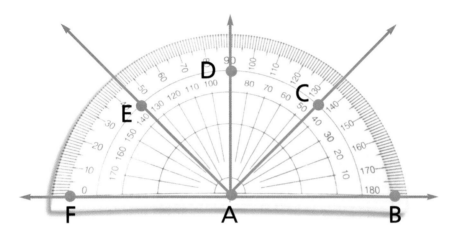

A *straight angle* is formed when its two rays are part of the same line. A straight angle has a measure of 180°. ∠BAF is a straight angle.

Practise drawing right, acute and obtuse angles using a protractor. Practise estimating how large some angles are, using right angles (90°) and straight angles (180°) as mental guides. For example, a 30° angle would have an opening about one-third as wide as a right angle.

Kinds of Triangles

Triangles have three interior angles. An *equilateral triangle* has three sides of the same length.

Triangle ABC is an equilateral triangle.

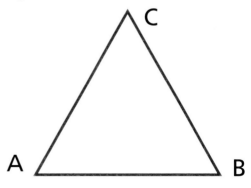

A *right-angled triangle* has one right angle. An *isosceles* [eye-SOSS-uh-lees] triangle has at least two sides of the same length.

Triangle DEF is a right-angled triangle.

Triangle GBS is an isosceles triangle.

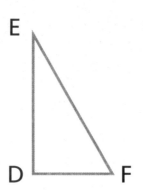

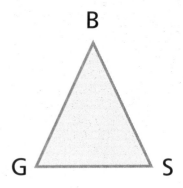

With some simple tools, you can construct a triangle with sides of a certain length. You'll need a ruler and a pair of compasses. A *pair of compasses* is a special tool that is used for drawing circles and parts of circles.

A pair of compasses

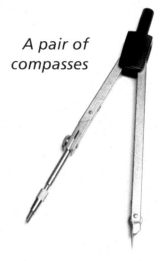

To construct triangle DGC with sides of 6 inches, 4½ inches and 3 inches, first draw a segment 6 inches long.

Label the endpoints D and G. Now, take your pair of compasses and expand it so the pencil point is 3 inches from the needle point. Place the needle point on endpoint D and guide the pencil point around to draw an arc (part of a circle) 3 inches from D. Drawing an arc 3 inches from D is like drawing part of a circle with centre D and a radius of 3 inches.

Now draw another arc, this time 4½ inches from G. Where the two arcs intersect, mark point C. Use your ruler to draw segments DC and GC and complete the triangle.

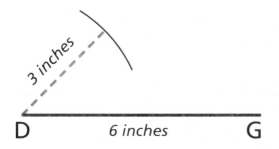

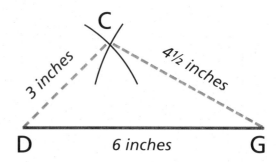

As you have a pair of compasses, you can use this method to construct equilateral and isosceles triangles. For example, construct an equilateral triangle with sides of 8 centimetres; construct two different isosceles triangles with sides of 5 centimetres and 7 centimetres.

Whenever two triangles are the same shape and size, they are *congruent*. These two triangles are congruent. ▶

If you were to copy the triangle on the right and rotate it, you could place it right on top of the triangle on the left, and you would see that the two triangles have the same shape and size. Try it!

These two triangles are not congruent: they do not have the same shape and size. ▶

Polygons

You know that a *polygon* is a closed figure made out of three or more line segments. Triangles are threesided polygons. Four-sided polygons are called *quadrilaterals*. In Year 5 we looked at some different kinds of quadrilaterals. A rectangle is a quadrilateral in which all the angles are right angles and the opposite sides are the same length.

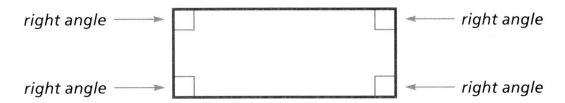

right angle ⟶   ⟵ *right angle*

right angle ⟶   ⟵ *right angle*

A *square* is a special kind of rectangle in which all four sides are equal in length.

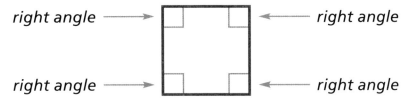

right angle ⟶   ⟵ *right angle*

right angle ⟶   ⟵ *right angle*

A *trapezium* is a quadrilateral in which only two of the four sides are parallel.

A *parallelogram* is a quadrilateral in which both pairs of opposite sides are parallel. They are also of equal length.

A *rhombus* is a special kind of parallelogram in which all four sides are of equal length.

The diagonals of a rhombus are perpendicular, and divide each other in half where they intersect.

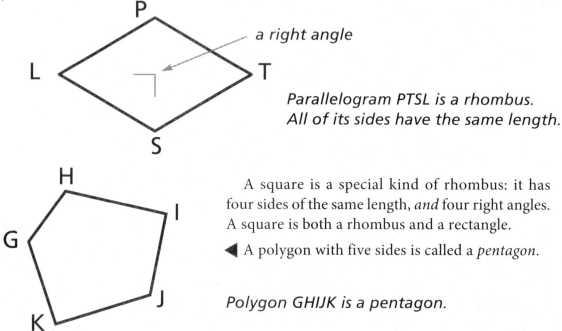

a right angle

Parallelogram PTSL is a rhombus. All of its sides have the same length.

A square is a special kind of rhombus: it has four sides of the same length, *and* four right angles. A square is both a rhombus and a rectangle.

◀ A polygon with five sides is called a *pentagon.*

Polygon GHIJK is a pentagon.

A polygon with six sides is called a *hexagon.*

A polygon with eight sides is called an *octagon.*

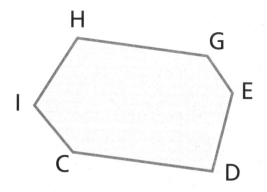

Polygon HGEDCI is a hexagon.

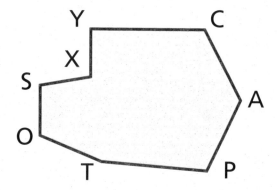

Polygon YCAPTOSX is an octagon.

A *regular* polygon has sides of equal length and angles of equal measure.

A regular triangle is also called an equilateral triangle and a regular quadrilateral is also called a square. A stop sign has the shape of a regular octagon.

Diagonals

A *diagonal* is a line segment that joins two vertices of a polygon but is not one of the sides of that polygon. A quadrilateral has two diagonals. How many diagonals does a pentagon have?

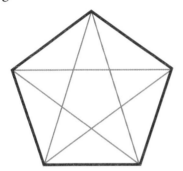 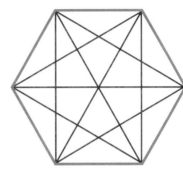

A pentagon has five diagonals. A hexagon has nine diagonals. How many diagonals does an octagon have?

Practise drawing in all the diagonals on a pentagon, a hexagon, a seven-sided polygon and an octagon. See if you can find a pattern.

Circles

Earlier you learnt how to draw a triangle using a pair of compasses. A pair of compasses can also be used to draw a circle. Simply keep the needle point fixed in one place and guide the pencil point all the way around until it ends where it began.

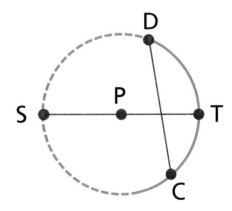

A line segment joining two points on a circle is called a *chord*. Segments DC and TS are chords of the circle with centre P.

273

The *diameter* of a circle is the length of a chord that passes through the centre of the circle. TS is both a chord and a diameter of the circle. A diameter is the longest possible chord of a circle. The *radius* is the distance from the centre of a circle to the circle. It is the same wherever you measure it and is always equal to half the diameter. PS is a radius of this circle, and so is PT.

An *arc* is a part of the circle. It has two endpoints on the circle.

The distance around a circle – or the distance travelled by the pencil end of the pair of compasses while drawing the entire circle – is called its *circumference*. You can measure the circumference of a circle (or of any other flat figure) by placing a piece of string along the circle and then measuring the length of the string that you used. You can also find the circumference of a circle using a formula.

arc DC

$$\text{Circumference of a circle} = \pi \times \text{diameter}$$
$$C = \pi \times d$$

The symbol π is a letter from the Greek alphabet. It is pronounced 'pie' and spelt out 'pi'.

π is a number: it is the number of diameter lengths there are in the circumference of a circle. For example, if you had pieces of string the length of the diameter, it would take you π number of these pieces of string to go all the way around a circle. You cannot write the number π exactly as a decimal, since the number goes on forever. To the nearest hundredth, π is 3.14. It would take a little more than three pieces of string the length of the diameter to go all the way around a circle.

Using the value 3.14 for π, practise finding the circumference of a circle. For example, find the circumference of a circle with a diameter of 13 centimetres. Round your answer to the nearest tenth of a centimetre.

Length of diameter

$$\begin{aligned}
C &= \pi \times d \\
&\approx 3.14 \times 13 \quad \text{(the symbol} \approx \text{means 'approximately equal to')} \\
&\approx 40.82 \quad \quad 40.82 \text{ rounds to } 40.8
\end{aligned}$$

The circumference of a circle with a diameter of 13 cm is approximately 40.8 cm.

Since the diameter of a circle is twice its radius, you can also write the circumference formula with the radius.

$$C = \pi \times 2 \times r \qquad \text{(r stands for radius)}$$

Practise using $C = \pi \times 2 \times r$ to calculate the circumference of a circle given its radius. Also practise using a pair of compasses to construct circles that have a certain radius.

Area

Remember that the area of a rectangle is its length times its width. The formula for the area of a rectangle is $A = l \times w$. So the area of a rectangle with sides 7 cm and 5 cm is 35 square cm, or 35 cm² ($7 \times 5 = 35$).

You can measure area in metric units or imperial units. Metric units are: square millimetres (mm²), square centimetres (cm²), square metres (m²) and square kilometres (km²). We also use Imperial units: square inches (in²), square feet (ft²), square yards (yd²) and square miles (miles²).

Suppose you wanted to paint a wall in your room that was a rectangle 10 feet long and 8 feet tall. Would a tin of paint that covers 100 ft² be big enough?

$A = l \times w$ (here the width is really the height of the wall)
$A = 10\text{ft} \times 8\text{ft}$
$A = 80\text{ ft}^2$
$80 < 100$, so you should have enough paint.

Now try a more difficult problem. Suppose you wanted to buy squares of fabric to make a small quilt. You want the quilt to be 13 square feet and each square to be 9 square inches. Each square costs 10 pence. How many squares will you need to buy?

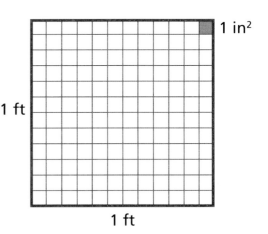

1 in²

1 ft

1 ft

The problem here is that some of your numbers are measured in square feet and others are measured in square inches. Before you can solve the problem you need to convert either the inches to feet or the feet to inches. Start by converting 13 square feet to square inches. If you know how many inches are in a foot, you can work out how many square inches are in a square foot. Since there are 12 inches in a foot, a square foot contains 12×12 square inches, or 144 square inches.

So if there are 144 square inches in 1 square foot, how many are there in 13 square feet? $13 \times 144 = 1{,}872$. 13 square feet = 1,872 square inches. The quilt has an area of 1,872 square inches. Now divide by 9 square inches to find how many squares are needed.

$$\begin{array}{r} 208 \\ 9\overline{)1{,}872} \end{array}$$

You will need 208 squares. At 10p a square, they will cost you £20.80.

$$\begin{array}{r} £ \quad 0.10 \\ \times\, 208 \\ \hline £\; 20.80 \end{array}$$

You can practise the same kind of question with **metric numbers**. For instance, how many square tiles measuring 10 centimetres on each side would you need to cover a wall that is 4 metres by 5 metres?

Finding the Area of a Triangle

To find the area of a triangle, you need to learn to measure the height of a triangle. Start by calling any side of the triangle its base. The **height** of a triangle is the perpendicular distance from the vertex opposite the base to the line containing the base. Here are examples of heights of triangles.

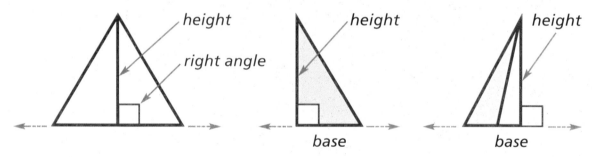

Practise drawing and measuring the heights of different triangles.

Study this rectangle. The area of rectangle PQST is 8 square centimetres ($4 \times 2 = 8$). Triangle OST is half of rectangle PQST: you can see that when you divide triangle OST into two right-angled triangles, there are two matching right-angled triangles left in rectangle PQST. Since triangle OST is half of rectangle PQST, the area of triangle OST must be half of 8 square centimetres, which is 4 square centimetres.

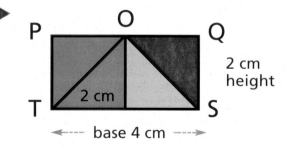

So you can find the area of triangle OST by multiplying its base (4 cm) by its height (2 cm), and then dividing by 2.

A = (4 × 2) ÷ 2
= 8 ÷ 2 = 4   The area of triangle OST is 4 cm²

You can find the area of any triangle by multiplying its base by its height and then dividing by 2.

Formula for the area of a triangle: $A = (b \times h) \div 2$

Practise finding the area of a triangle. For example, construct a triangle with sides of 6 cm, 7 cm and 8 cm, and draw its three different heights using each side as a base. (Notice that the heights all intersect each other at the same point.) Measure the heights in centimetres, and calculate the area of the triangle in square centimetres in three different ways.

Finding the Area of a Parallelogram

You can call any side of a parallelogram its base. The height of a parallelogram is the perpendicular distance from its base to the opposite side. The pictures below show you how to find the area of a parallelogram.

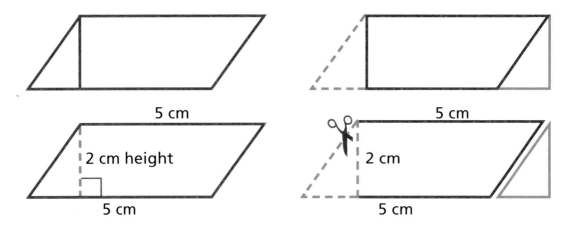

The parallelogram has the same area as a rectangle with the same base and height.

5 × 2 = 10. So the area of the parallelogram is 10 cm².

You can always find the area of a parallelogram in the same way, by multiplying its base by its height.

Formula for the area of a parallelogram: $A = b \times h$

Practise using this formula to find the area of parallelograms.

Finding Areas of Other Figures

Sometimes you have to find the area of a figure by dividing it into smaller areas that you know how to find. For example, you can find the area of this trapezium by dividing it into smaller areas. Here is one way.

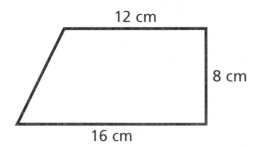

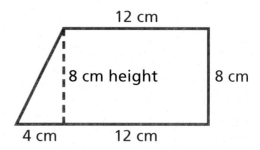

Divide the trapezium into a rectangle and a right-angled triangle. Find the area of each and add to find the total area.

Area of rectangle: $12 \times 8 = 96$

Area of triangle: $(4 \times 8) \div 2 = 16$

Add the two areas: $96 + 16 = 112$

The area of the trapezium is 112 cm²

See if you can find the area of the same trapezium by dividing it into two triangles.

Rectangular Prisms

So far the figures you have been working with have been flat, or *plane* figures. But it is also possible to use your geometry skills to measure three-dimensional shapes.

This figure is a rectangular prism. A rectangular prism has six faces that are rectangles, and twelve edges. Each edge is parallel to three other edges, and all four

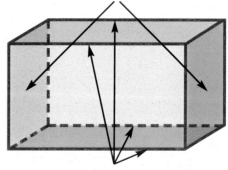

Opposite faces are congruent

Four edges are parallel and of equal length

of these edges have the same length. The opposite faces of a rectangular prism are congruent.

A *cube* is a special rectangular prism: all of its edges have the same length, and all of its faces are congruent. The illustrations below show a net, or what a cube would look like with all its surfaces opened out flat.

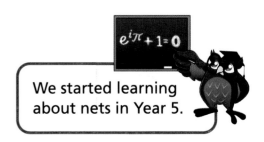

We started learning about nets in Year 5.

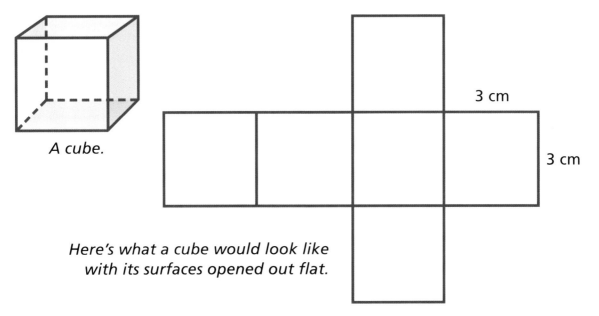

A cube.

3 cm

3 cm

Here's what a cube would look like with its surfaces opened out flat.

You can make a cube by making a copy of this page, cutting out the cross-shaped figure, and folding it along the lines so that all of the edges are touching each other. You can hold the figure together with tape.

Volume

Volume is measured in cubic units. Cubic units tell you how much space something occupies. Cubic units have three dimensions: usually length, width and height.

dimension

dimension

dimension

height

length

width

Some common cubic units are a cubic centimetre (cm³), a cubic metre (m³), a cubic inch (in³) and a cubic foot (ft³).

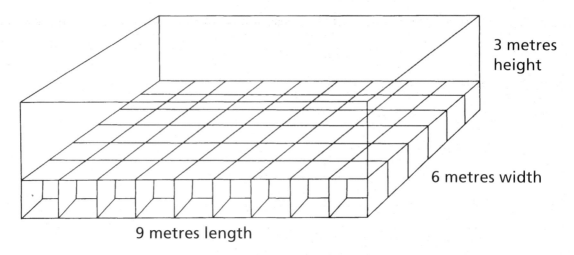

3 metres height

6 metres width

9 metres length

The volume of this rectangular prism is 9 × 6 × 3 or 162 cubic metres.

You can count by layers to find the volume of a rectangular prism.

On one layer you can fit 9 cubic metres along the length and 6 cubic metres along the width. You can fit 9 × 6 or 54 cubic metres on one layer. Since the prism is 3 metres tall, you can fit 3 layers of cubic metres. Altogether you can fit 54 × 3 or 162 cubic metres in the rectangular prism. Its volume is 162 cubic metres.

You can always find the volume of a rectangular prism by multiplying its length times its width times its height – even if the length, width and height are not in whole number units.

Formula for the volume of a rectangular prism: $V = l \times w \times h$

An easy way to remember this is as the area of its base ($l \times w$) times its height: the same formula gives the volume of a cylinder as well.

V = (area of the base) × height

For example, to find the volume of a box that has for its dimensions 4.3 cm, 3.6 cm and 3.9 cm, you multiply 4.3 × 3.6 × 3.9.

$$
\begin{array}{r}
4.3 \\
\times\ 3.6 \\
\hline
2.58 \\
12.90 \\
\hline
15.48 \\
\end{array}
$$

$$
\begin{array}{r}
15.48 \\
\times\ \ 3.9 \\
\hline
13.932 \\
46.440 \\
\hline
60.372 \\
\end{array}
$$

The volume of the box is 60.372 cm³

The volume of a box that is 4.3 centimetres by 3.6 centimetres by 3.9 centimetres is 4.3 cm × 3.6 cm × 3.9 cm. Its volume is 60.372 cm³. Notice that the word 'by' represents multiplication; to find the volume of a rectangular prism, multiply its three dimensions.

Volume and Surface Area

You can also find the *surface area* of a three-dimensional figure. The surface area is the area, in square units, occupied by all of the faces of a solid figure. Suppose you want to paint your toy box with a special bright blue paint. The paint comes in small tins that each hold enough paint to cover 0.5 square metres. If the box has a length of 40 cm, a width of 20 cm and a height of 30 cm, will one tin of paint be enough to cover it completely?

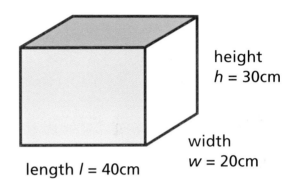

height
$h = 30cm$

width
$w = 20cm$

length $l = 40cm$

Remember that each face of a rectangular prism has an opposite congruent face. The top and the bottom are congruent. The area of each is $l \times w$. The front and back are congruent. The area of each is $l \times h$. The two sides are congruent. The area of each is $w \times h$.

Surface Area of a Rectangular Prism

SA = $(2 \times l \times w)$ + $(2 \times l \times h)$ + $(2 \times w \times h)$
top and bottom   front and back   two sides

SA = $(2 \times 40 \times 20) + (2 \times 40 \times 30) + (2 \times 20 \times 30)$
= 1,600 + 2,400 + 1,200
= 5,200

The surface area of the toy box is 5,200 square centimetres.

0.5 m² is
$0.5 \times 100 \times 100$ cm² = 5,000 cm².

5,200 > 5,000, so you'll need more than one tin of paint. If you decide not to paint the bottom of the box, will you still need more than one tin?

Practise finding the volume and surface area of rectangular prisms. Remember that you measure volume in cubic units and surface area in square units. For example, find the volume and surface area of a box with a length of 8 cm, a width of 6 cm and a height of 5 cm. Then find the volume and surface area of this box if each dimension is doubled.

By what number do you multiply the surface area of the box, when you double each of its dimensions? By what number do you multiply the volume?

Changing Imperial Units of Volume

If you know the equivalences among the imperial units of length, you can find the equivalences among the imperial customary units of volume.

There are 12 inches in 1 foot. There are $(12 \times 12 \times 12)$ in^3 in 1 ft^3

$$1{,}728 \text{ in}^3 = 1 \text{ ft}^3$$

There are 3 feet in 1 yard. There are $(3 \times 3 \times 3)$ ft^3 in 1 yd^3

$$27 \text{ ft}^3 = 1 \text{ yd}^3$$

Practise changing from one imperial unit of volume to another. For example, a van has 400 cubic feet of storage space. To the nearest cubic yard, how many cubic yards is that?

$$27 \text{ ft}^3 = 1 \text{ yd}^3$$

So to find how many cubic yards there are in 400 ft^3, divide 400 by 27.

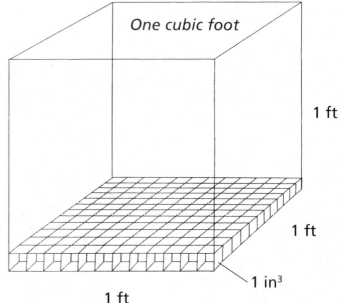

One cubic foot

1 ft

1 ft

1 in^3

1 ft

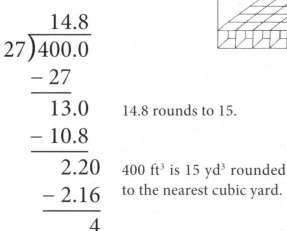

14.8 rounds to 15.

400 ft^3 is 15 yd^3 rounded to the nearest cubic yard.

Changing Metric Units of Volume

Changing units in the metric system is easy, because multiplying by ten and powers of ten is easy.

$$1\text{m} = 100 \text{ cm, so } 1 \text{ m}^3 = (100 \times 100 \times 100) \text{ cm}^3$$
$$= 1{,}000{,}000 \text{ cm}^3$$
$$1 \text{ cm} = 10 \text{ mm, so } 1 \text{ cm}^3 = (10 \times 10 \times 10) \text{ mm}^3$$
$$= 1000 \text{ mm}^3$$

How many cm^3 are in 3.23 m^3? $3.23 \text{ m}^3 = 3{,}230{,}000 \text{ cm}^3$ (multiply by 1,000,000).

How many cm^3 are in 237 mm^3? $237 \text{ mm}^3 = 0.237 \text{ cm}^3$ (divide by 1,000)

Notice that a metre is 100 times as long as a centimetre, but a cubic metre is 1,000,000 times as large as a cubic centimetre!

Volume and Capacity

Remember that metric units of capacity like litres and imperial units – such as gallons and pints – measure how much a container (for example, a bottle or a bucket) can hold. When you measure the capacity of a container, you are measuring the space inside the container, that is, the volume of the inside of the container. So units of capacity are also units of volume. For imperial units, there is no easy equivalence between units of capacity (such as fluid ounces) and units of volume (such as in^3). But in the metric system 1 litre = 1,000 cubic centimetres ($1 \text{ l} = 1{,}000 \text{ cm}^3$). Since $1 \text{ m}^3 = 1{,}000{,}000 \text{ cm}^3$, you also know that $1 \text{ m}^3 = 1{,}000 \text{ l}$.

Practise converting measures that are in cubic centimetres and cubic metres to litres. For example, $0.35 \text{ m}^3 = 350 \text{ l}$; $750 \text{ cm}^3 = 0.75 \text{ l}$; $800 \text{ m}^3 = 800{,}000 \text{ l}$.

Plotting Points on a Grid

In Year 5 you met the idea that you could use co-ordinates to tell where a point was on a grid. If you have an x-axis along the bottom of a page and a y-axis up the side, you can tell where a point is by a pair of numbers. The first number, x, is how far across. The second number, y, is how far up. Together, they make an ordered pair, which is a way of writing co-ordinates.

Look at quadrilateral ABCD. We are going to translate it, which is something else we first did in Year 5. If we add 3 to each x number and 4 to each y, we get new points which we call A'B'C'D' making a second quadrilateral. The co-ordinates are (5,9), (7,9), (6,8), (5,6).

We need some new terms. We say that A' ('A dashed' or sometimes 'A prime') is the image of A. The translation *maps* A onto its image A'. The same translation maps quadrilateral ABCD onto its *image* A'B'C'D'.

A translation means that you add or subtract the same amount to each point. As a consequence:

The original image and the new image after the translation are always congruent.

Both images are the same way up and the same way round.

Try plotting some images after some different translations.

We will start with another quadrilateral. JKLM (6,6), (7,8), (8,8), (9,6). What special sort of quadrilateral is that?

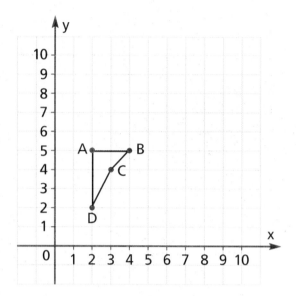

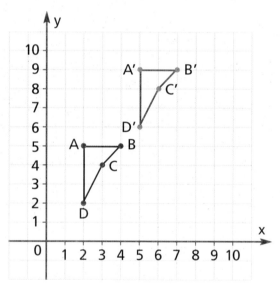

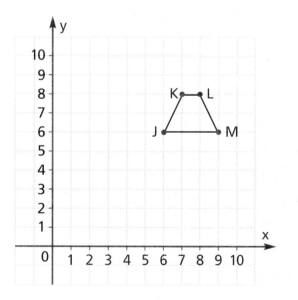

Translate JKLM 2 units to the left and 5 units down.

Work out the points of the image, point by point. You need to subtract 2 from each x value and 5 from each y.

For J, calculate 6 – 2 and 6 – 5. A table makes it clearer:

Point	(x, y)		Image	(x−2, y−5)
J	(6, 6)	→	J'	(4, 1)
K	(7, 8)	→	K'	(5, 3)
L	(8, 8)	→	L'	(6, 3)
M	(9, 6)	→	M'	(7, 1)

Check that each x is two less than it started and each y is five less. Draw the quadrilateral J'K'L'M' on your grid and check that the two shapes are congruent.

Now translate the new shape J'K'L'M'. Starting with the values from the chart above for J'K'L'M', move this quadrilateral left three units and up two units.

Point	(x, y)		Image	(x−3, y+2)
J'	(4, 1)	→	J"	(,)
K'	(5, 3)	→	K"	(,)
L'	(6, 3)	→	L"	(,)
M'	(7, 1)	→	M"	(,)

Draw quadrilateral J"K"L"M". We read " as 'double-dashed'.

Can you see a way of mapping JKLM to J"K"L"M" in only one step? Instead of two translations, we could have moved left by 2 + 3 and down by 5 – 2. Check it and see.

Negative Co-ordinates

Look at triangle EFG. It has co-ordinates (6,6), (7,8), (9,4). You need to translate it down 10 units.

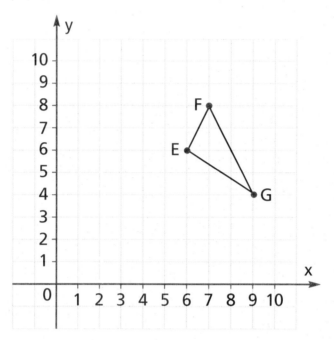

Complete the table:

Point	(x, y)		Image	(x, y−10)
E	(6, 6)	→	E'	(6,)
F	(7, 8)	→	F'	(7,)
G	(9, 4)	→	G'	(9,)

Have you noticed something about the y values for E'F'G'? They are negative numbers. We need to enlarge our grid to make room. Just as a number line can keep on past zero, so can x and y axes. They behave just like number lines. Here is our new grid:

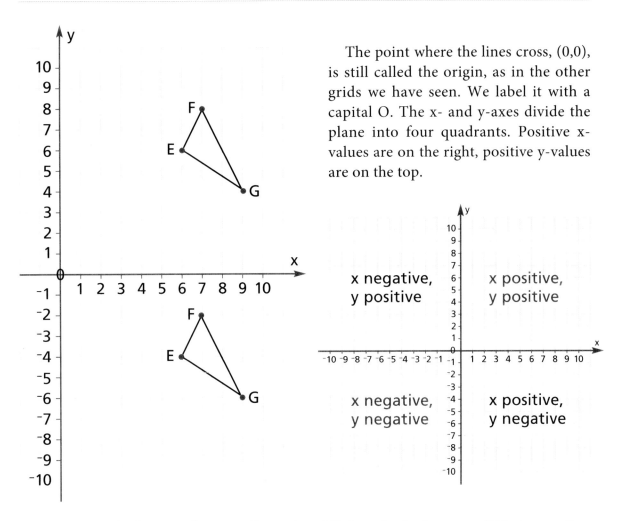

The point where the lines cross, (0,0), is still called the origin, as in the other grids we have seen. We label it with a capital O. The x- and y-axes divide the plane into four quadrants. Positive x-values are on the right, positive y-values are on the top.

It is time to look at another transformation. We have looked on page 214 at opposites, which are numbers the same distance either side of zero. A lot of mathematics follows from this idea but for now all we shall just consider changing the sign. That will make negative numbers into positive and vice versa.

Plot the irregular pentagon PQRST, with co-ordinates ($^-$2,0), ($^-$3,$^-$1), ($^-$3,$^-$3), (0,$^-$3), ($^-$1,$^-$1). The origin needs to go in the middle and the axes need to be at least five units in each direction. This should be in the bottom left of your graph, touching the axes. Next, calculate the points for P'Q'R'S'T', following these rules:

● Make x' the opposite of y.

● Make y' the opposite of x.

In other words, the new x is the old y with the sign changed. The new y is the old x with the sign changed.

Complete the table for all the points.

Point	(x, y)		Image	(⁻y, ⁻x)
P	(⁻2, 0)	→	P'	(0, 2)
Q	(⁻3, ⁻1)	→	Q'	(1,)
R	(⁻3, ⁻3)	→	R'	(, 3)
S	(0, ⁻3)	→	S'	(,)
T	(⁻1, ⁻1)	→	T'	(,)

Now plot the transformed pentagon on your graph. It should look like this:

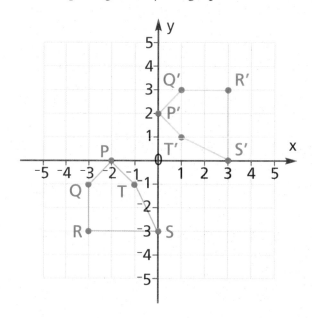

Draw a line midway between the two shapes. To draw it accurately, you can connect each point to its image with a line segment and find the points half way along each segment. Then connect them up with a line. If you look closely, you will see that all the segments between the points and their images are perpendicular to the mirror line. A point and its image are the same distance perpendicular to the line of reflection.

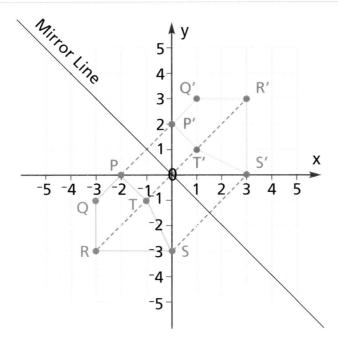

You have transformed PQRST with a *reflection* in that mirror line. The mirror line is now an axis of symmetry for the two shapes together. The shapes are still congruent and they are reflections of each other.

Try another one. Begin with triangle LMN, with co-ordinates (⁻3,1), (⁻4, 2), (⁻5, ⁻2). The line you will reflect it in is the x-axis, which happens to go through the triangle. Plot the points on the graph, then try plotting L'M'N' so that the image is a reflection in the x-axis. This time, the mirror line is horizontal, so you can tell that all the perpendicular segments between the points and their images will be vertical.

What this means is that you start at a point like L. You see how far it is from the mirror line, along a perpendicular line. For L it is 1 unit, crossing at (⁻3, 0). Then keep going an equal distance on the other side, 1 further unit. L' is therefore (⁻3, ⁻1). Work out images of the other two points in the same way.

For practice, choose some points, draw them on a graph and make a polygon by joining them up. Then reflect the whole shape first in the x-axis and then in the y-axis.

Sloping Mirrors

Mirror lines do not have to be always horizontal or vertical. Look at irregular hexagon CDEFGH. It needs to be reflected in two mirror lines. First reflect it in the one sloping upwards to make C'D'E'F'G'H'. Then reflect C'D'E'F'G'H' in the line sloping downwards to find C"D"E"F"G"H". To find the distance from the points to the mirror line, either use a ruler or count units. Notice how lines that are parallel to the mirror line are still parallel when reflected. Lines that are perpendicular stay perpendicular.

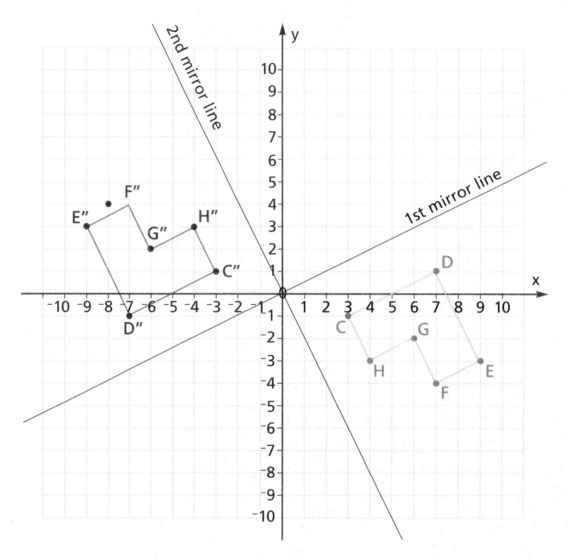

The image after both reflections is shown on the graph but you need to work out the stage in between, finding C'D'E'F'G'H'. After two reflections, is the shape the same way around or is it reversed?

Planes of Symmetry

If a shape can be folded in half so that both sides match, then it is symmetrical. The line of the fold is an axis of symmetry. If it can be folded many ways, then it has many axes of symmetry.

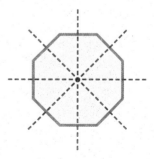

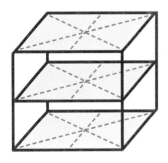

When thinking of three-dimensional symmetry, you need to consider whether each slice of the solid can have the same symmetry as one of the faces.

The answer for a cube is yes, because it has a regular section. Planes of symmetry pass all the way from the top face to the bottom face. It does not stop there. There are six faces and we have only thought about two. Each pair of opposite faces has its axes too that can be joined up to form planes. Three times four planes would give us twelve, except we must be careful not to count some twice. The plane half way up the cube, parallel to the top and bottom surfaces, includes an axis of symmetry for each of the four side faces. We cannot count it for both opposite pairs but only for one. That means that three planes have been counted twice.

Our final figures are:

4 axes on one side × 3 pairs of opposite faces − 3 planes counted twice

Altogether, a cube has nine planes of symmetry.

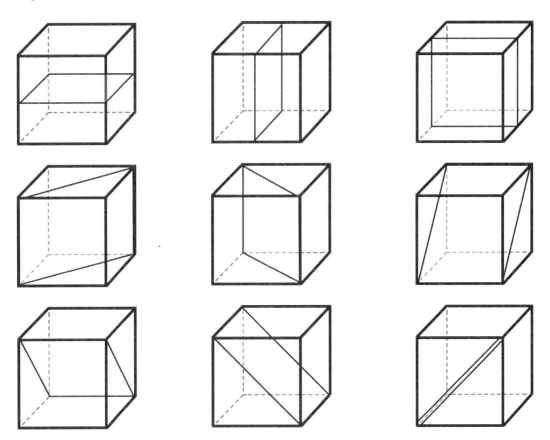

Next, think of a square-based pyramid, in which the triangular sides are equilateral. You know that an equilateral triangle has three axes of symmetry and a square has four. All the square's axes extend up to the apex and divide the pyramid symmetrically in two, so they form planes of symmetry. Those planes also pass through the vertical axes for each triangular face. That gives us four planes. As for the other axes of the triangles, they cannot divide the pyramid into two equal and symmetrical halves. There is only one square face and one apex. Only planes that bisect the apex and the base can be planes of symmetry.

The square-based pyramid has four planes of symmetry.

Angles

To get some more practice with a protractor, try these activities.

Draw a horizontal straight line, then draw a second line intersecting it.

Now take a protractor and measure the two angles above the line. Add the two angles together.

Repeat this a few times. Do you notice that you always get the same sum?

This is a general rule. Two angles that, when added together, form a straight line always sum to 180°.

Now mark a point on the paper and draw some lines ('rays' if you prefer) radiating from it.

Measure the angles between each pair of rays that are next to each other. Add them together.

As before, repeat this a few times and see whether you get the same answer each time. You should, because we have another rule: a set of angles that completely circles a point in a plane will always sum to 360°.

That rule also works if the angles are part of a polygon.

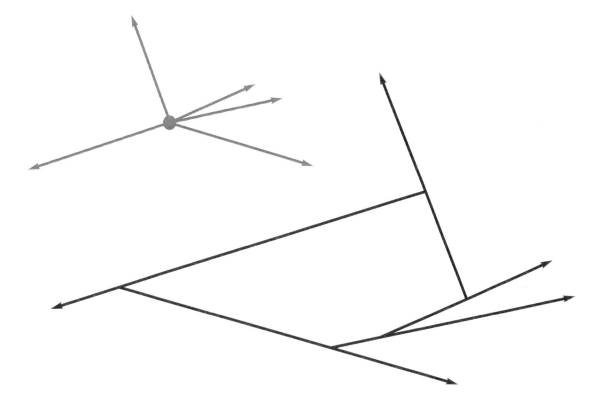

Do you see how each of the rays in the orange figure matches one in the red figure? In the red figure, they are the sides of a polygon, extended past the vertices. The angles between each ray and the next, outside the polygon, add up to 360°, just as the rays around a point did. When we close a polygon, we make a complete turn of angles outside it.

Now that you know those rules, you can work out many others if you like. The angles inside a triangle always sum to 180°. The angles inside a quadrilateral sum to 360°. Think of a square, which has four right angles of 90° each. Inside a pentagon, the angles sum to 540° and inside a hexagon, 720°. If an octagon has two more sides, what will its internal angles add up to?

Suggested Resources

What's Maths All About? by Alex Frith (Usborne) 2012

See Inside Maths by Alex Frith and Minna Lacey (Usborne) 2008

Mental Arithmetic, Books 1 and 2, by T R Goddard, J W Adams and R P Beaumont (Schofield & Sims) 1999, 2000

Junior Maths Book 3 by David Hillard (Galore Park) 2009

What's Maths All About? by Minna Lacey (Usborne) 2012

Practice in the Basic Skills, Books 3 and 4, by Derek Newton and David Smith (Collins) 2003

Be the Best at Maths by Rebecca Rissman (Raintree) 2013

Magnetic Tangrams: Explore the World of Tangram Pictures by Jon Tremaine (Barron's) 2009

Maths Dictionary by Carol Vorderman (Dorling Kindersley) 2009

Maths Made Easy Times Tables Ages 7-11 Key Stage 2 by Carol Vorderman (Dorling Kindersley) 2011

Science

Introduction

The pages that follow outline what Year 6 children should know about science. Students will be introduced to chemistry and atoms. They will also learn about the classification of living things, cells, plants, life cycles, the human body and the physical changes they experience as they enter adolescence. In addition, they will read brief biographies of four important scientists.

Parents and teachers can supplement this chapter with various science activities. Students who have studied the classification of animals will find trips to zoos more interesting. They will see how different animals in the zoo are grouped together and how species are linked by common features. Students who have studied plants and seeds may enjoy gardening, collecting leaves and seeds, and examining plant life with a magnifying glass. An inexpensive home microscope will allow children to see cells and other tiny structures, and a chemistry set (properly supervised) will allow them to perform some basic experiments. Many books collecting simple and safe science experiments are now available. You can find some suggested resources for the Year 6 student on page 345.

Hands-on scientific experience is so important that some educators have come to reject the very idea of teaching young children about science from books. But book learning should not be neglected altogether. It helps bring system and coherence to a young person's developing knowledge of nature and provides essential building blocks for later study. Book learning also provides knowledge not likely to be gained by simple observations; for instance, books can tell us about things that are not visible to the naked eye, like cells, eggs and sperm, hormones and atoms. Both kinds of experience, book learning and practical experience with science, are necessary to ensure that gaps in knowledge will not hinder later understanding.

Chemistry: **Matter and Change**

Atoms

Suppose you had a nugget of pure gold in your hands. With the right tools, you could cut the nugget in half. And you could cut one of the halves in half, too. But how long could you keep dividing like this? If you had very good tools, maybe even microscopic tools, could you keep going forever? Or would you eventually come up with a particle of gold so tiny that you could no longer divide it?

Many years ago, the ancient Greek philosophers wondered about this. Some philosophers claimed that you could go on dividing anything forever. Others thought there must be some limit, some particle so small that it cannot be divided. The philosopher Democritus thought that there must be such a particle and he named it *atomos*, which is Greek for 'indivisible'. That's where our idea of atoms comes from.

Although Democritus came up with the name *atom*, he couldn't prove that atoms exist. Atoms are much too small to see with the human eye or even with an ordinary microscope, and how can you study something that you can't see? Despite this difficulty, scientists now know a great deal about these basic building blocks of matter.

It turns out that atoms can be divided, but if you divide an atom of gold, it is no longer gold, and if you divide an atom of lead, it is no longer lead. So an atom is the smallest piece of a substance that retains the qualities and characteristics of that substance.

Atoms themselves are made of smaller particles, called *sub-atomic particles*. We learnt in Year 5 that these are called protons, neutrons and electrons. *Protons* have a positive (+) electrical charge. *Electrons* have a negative (−) charge. *Neutrons* have no charge: they are neutral. The protons and neutrons are located in the centre of the atom, called the *nucleus*, while the electrons swirl around them.

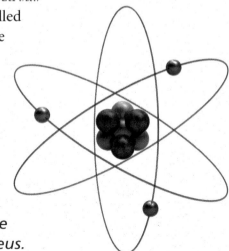

Atoms are too small to see but we can draw models. This lithium atom shows protons as red in the nucleus. They have positive charges. Electrons, with negative charges, circle the nucleus.

John Dalton

Although Democritus believed more than 2,000 years ago that atoms must exist, it wasn't until the 1800s that scientists investigated atoms in a scientific way. One of the earliest scientists to work on the subject was John Dalton (1766-1844). Dalton looked at the experiments done before his time and thought that Democritus might have been right: perhaps all matter really is made up of atoms. Scientists had already discovered that chemical reactions cannot break down certain substances, now called *elements*, into anything simpler. Gold is an element, and so are lead, silver, hydrogen and oxygen.

John Dalton

Dalton worked out that elements are composed of tiny particles called atoms, and that the atoms of each element are identical to each other, but different from the atoms of other elements. Even during dramatic chemistry experiments, the atoms themselves did not change, Dalton said; they just rearranged themselves.

The Parts of Atoms

Dalton's basic ideas proved to be correct, but it wasn't until the 1930s that scientists began to work out how atoms work. Several theories were proposed, and it was difficult to prove which one was right.

Scientists discovered that most of the mass of an atom is in its nucleus. The electrons surrounding the nucleus are much lighter. They discovered that the nucleus has a positive charge that exactly balances the negative charges on the electrons. Once scientists formed this picture of the atom's structure, they began to understand how chemical elements work.

Mendeleev and the Periods

By the late 1800s, scientists had identified most of the elements, from hydrogen, the lightest and most plentiful element in the universe, to lead and other heavy elements. But they did not understand why the elements interact with each other as they do.

A very important step in understanding elements was the discovery by a Russian chemist, Dmitri Mendeleev, that the properties of the elements repeated themselves at regular intervals, or periodically.

Mendeleev discovered that when you put the elements in horizontal rows, from lightest to heaviest, after a while you find another element that has similar properties to the first atom in the row. If you put the similar elements in vertical columns you can arrange all the elements in related groups.

Here is one such column:

element no.3 lithium

element no.11 sodium

element no.19 potassium

These three elements have many similar characteristics. They are all metals, which means that they are shiny and good conductors of heat and electricity; these particular metals are all soft, low in density and solid at room temperature. They can be hammered or drawn into different shapes. They also react with other substances in very similar and sometimes dramatic ways. It's much too dangerous for anyone to do at home, but if you were to place these elements on a pool of water, you would see that they float and jiggle around on bubbles of hydrogen that are created. Sometimes the hydrogen even burns or explodes!

Mendeleev made a chart of the repetitions he saw, and a version of his chart, called the *periodic table of the elements*, has been used ever since to show similarities and differences among the elements. Although no one doubted that Mendeleev had discovered something very important, it took many years to work out why the elements can be arranged this way.

Explaining the Periods

In the 1920s, Niels Bohr, a Danish scientist, proposed that what gives each element its distinctive characteristics and determines how it can combine with other elements is mainly one thing: the number of electrons in a single atom of the element. Scientists had already given a number to each element according to the number of electrons in a single atom. Lithium, the third element, has three electrons; sodium, the eleventh element, has eleven electrons and so on.

Bohr had the inspired idea that the electrons arrange themselves in something like shells, or energy levels, around the nucleus. When there were a certain number of electrons in a shell, that made the shell stable and complete, and another outer shell would form.

1 H Hydrogen	1 H Hydrogen	1 — Atomic Number H — Chemical Symbol Hydrogen — Name															2 He Helium
3 Li Lithium	4 Be Beryllium											5 B Boron	6 C Carbon	7 N Nitrogen	8 O Oxygen	9 F Fluorine	10 Ne Neon
11 Na Sodium	12 Mg Magnesium											13 Al Aluminium	14 Si Silicon	15 P Phosphorus	16 S Sulphur	17 Cl Chlorine	18 Ar Argon
19 K Potassium	20 Ca Calcium	21 Sc Scandium	22 Ti Titanium	23 V Vanadium	24 Cr Chromium	25 Mn Manganese	26 Fe Iron	27 Co Cobalt	28 Ni Nickel	29 Cu Copper	30 Zn Zinc	31 Ga Gallium	32 Ge Germanium	33 As Arsenic	34 Se Selenium	35 Br Bromine	36 Kr Krypton
37 Rb Rubidium	38 Sr Strontium	39 Y Yttrium	40 Zr Zirconium	41 Nb Niobium	42 Mo Molybdenum	43 Tc Technetium	44 Ru Ruthenium	45 Rh Rhodium	46 Pd Palladium	47 Ag Silver	48 Cd Cadmium	49 In Indium	50 Sn Tin	51 Sb Antimony	52 Te Tellurium	53 I Iodine	54 Xe Xenon
55 Cs Caesium	56 Ba Barium	57 La Lanthanum	72 Hf Hafnium	73 Ta Tantalum	74 W Tungsten	75 Re Rhenium	76 Os Osmium	77 Ir Iridium	78 Pt Platinum	79 Au Gold	80 Hg Mercury	81 Tl Thallium	82 Pb Lead	83 Bi Bismuth	84 Po Polonium	85 At Astatine	86 Rn Radon
87 Fr Francium	88 Ra Radium	89 Ac Actinium	104 Rf Rutherfordium	105 Db Dubnium	106 Sg Seaborgium	107 Bh Bohrium	108 Hs Hassium	109 Mt Meitnerium	110 Ds Darmstadtium	111 Rg Roentgenium	112 Cn Copernicium	113 Uut Ununtrium	114 Fl Flerovium	115 Uup Ununpentium	116 Lv Livermorium	117 Uus Ununseptium	118 Uuo Ununoctium
				58 Ce Cerium	59 Pr Praseodymium	60 Nd Neodymium	61 Pm Promethium	62 Sm Samarium	63 Eu Europium	64 Gd Gadolinium	65 Tb Terbium	66 Dy Dysprosium	67 Ho Holmium	68 Er Erbium	69 Tm Thulium	70 Yb Ytterbium	71 Lu Lutetium
				90 Th Thorium	91 Pa Protactinium	92 U Uranium	93 Np Neptunium	94 Pu Plutonium	95 Am Americium	96 Cm Curium	97 Bk Berkelium	98 Cf Californium	99 Es Einsteinium	100 Fm Fermium	101 Md Mendelevium	102 No Nobelium	103 Lr Lawrencium

Alkali Metal	Alkaline Earth	Transition Metal	Rare Earth	Basic Metal	Semi Metal	Non Metal	Halogen	Noble Gas

Here's a simplified periodic table. Can you find some of the elements you've been reading about?

Bohr was basically right. The chart below shows the number of electrons in the shells of lithium, sodium and potassium.

	Shell no. 1	Shell no. 2	Shell no. 3	Shell no. 4
element no. 3 lithium:	2	1		
element no. 11 sodium:	2	8	1	
element no. 19 potassium:	2	8	8	1

Can you see that the total number of electrons is the same as the number of the element? For example lithium is labelled as element no. 3 and it has two electrons in its first shell and one electron in its second shell. In total lithium has three electrons and it is element no. 3. Lithium, sodium and potassium all have a single electron in the outer shell of its atoms. It's that single electron that gives the element many of its chemical and electrical properties.

In general, all chemical reactions are determined by the electrons in the outer shells of atoms. Some elements, such as sodium, can give away an electron easily. Other elements like oxygen can take on electrons easily. That's why these types of elements tend to come together, one giving electrons, one taking electrons, to stabilise the outer shells of both kinds of atoms.

sodium atom

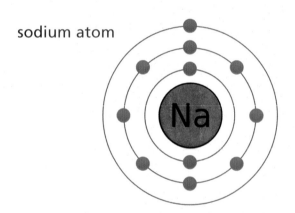

Sodium is the eleventh element on the periodic table. It has 11 electrons – two in its inner shell, eight in its middle shell and one in its outer shell. It can give off the single electron in its outer shell easily.

oxygen atom

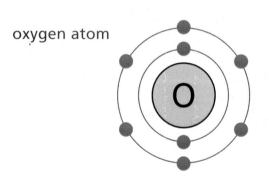

Oxygen is the eighth element in the periodic table. How many shells and how many electrons does an atom of oxygen have?

Elements and Abbreviations

There are more than one hundred known elements. Scientists often refer to these elements using a set of abbreviations known as chemical symbols. It is easier to write a chemical symbol than writing out the full name of an element. Some symbols have a single capital letter. Most others have two letters, the first a capital and the second a small letter. Many are easy to remember because they correspond with the first few letters or sounds of the English names:

H = Hydrogen   N = Nitrogen   Si = Silicon

He = Helium   O = Oxygen   Cl = Chlorine

C = Carbon   Al = Aluminium

Some other abbreviations are a little harder to remember because they are based on the Latin names of the elements:

Abbreviation	Latin name	English name
Fe	ferrum	Iron
Cu	cuprum	Copper
Ag	argentum	Silver
Au	aurum	Gold

Can you find these elements on the periodic table on page 299? Can you find elements that are in the same vertical column, called a group?

Metals and Non-Metals

Two important categories of elements are metals and non-metals. About two-thirds of the elements are metals. Lithium, sodium, potassium, iron, copper, silver, lead and gold are all metals. Carbon, oxygen, hydrogen and chlorine are some non-metallic elements.

This medal is made from element 47 on the periodic table. Can you work out what element that is?

How is a metal different from a non-metal? Metals are usually shiny and *malleable*, which means they can be beaten into different shapes. Metals are also usually *ductile*, which means they can be stretched out into wires. Finally, most metals *conduct* electricity – that is, they allow electricity to flow through them. Some metals are better conductors than others. Silver and copper are very good conductors of electricity. Since copper is less expensive than silver, it is often used in electric wires and motors.

Molecules

If the atoms of the elements always stayed by themselves, nothing much would happen. There would be no chemical reactions – and no life.

A *molecule* is created when two or more atoms join together – either atoms of different elements or atoms of the same element. For example, you know that humans need oxygen to survive. The oxygen in the air you breathe is actually in the form of molecules, that is, as two oxygen atoms joined together. The symbol for oxygen is 'O' and the double oxygen molecule can be represented like this:

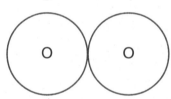

The way chemists show a normal molecule of two oxygen atoms is by the symbol O_2. The number means that there are two atoms of oxygen together in a molecule. Sometimes, though, lightning bolts can cause this oxygen molecule to break up into its individual atoms.

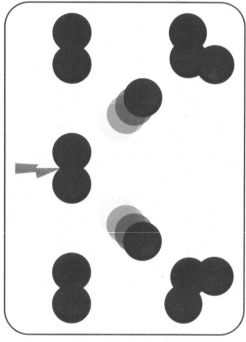

Forming O_3 ozone from O_2 oxygen

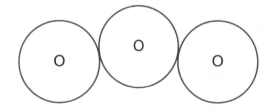

Chemists show an ozone molecule by writing O_3. Sometimes you can smell ozone after a thunderstorm. Because ozone is unstable, many ozone molecules break apart after a while, and regular oxygen molecules (O_2) form again.

Compounds

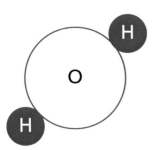

Compounds are molecules made up of atoms of different elements. Here is the scientific formula for the most important compound in the world: H_2O. That is the chemical formula for water. The way you say this formula is 'H-two-O'. It means that

two hydrogen atoms are joined with one oxygen atom to make one molecule of water. Here is one way to show a water molecule.

Another famous compound is carbon dioxide, or CO_2. Carbon dioxide is made up of two atoms of oxygen joined to one atom of carbon. Carbon dioxide is a colourless, odourless gas. Your body is a carbon dioxide factory. Every time you exhale, you breathe out millions of molecules of carbon dioxide. Some of this carbon dioxide is used by plants for a process called *photosynthesis*. Plants, in turn, give off oxygen needed by human beings.

Physical and Chemical Changes

Scientists distinguish between two kinds of changes that can happen to a substance. A *physical change* alters the properties or the appearance of a substance but does not change what it is made of. If you saw a piece of wood in half, you have made a physical change: the wood is still the same stuff, but now it's in two pieces. If you kick a football through your neighbour's window, you will physically change the windowpane, but the pieces of glass on the floor will still have the same chemical make-up. When water freezes it is still made up of the same H_2O molecules, but its physical properties change from a liquid to a solid.

In a *chemical change*, the atoms and molecules of the reacting substances are rearranged to create new substances. All the original atoms are still present, but there are new molecules with different properties and different chemical formulas. If, instead of cutting a piece of wood, you burn it, you change the wood in a chemical way. The molecules of the wood are transformed into different substances, including carbon dioxide, water vapour and carbon. Rust is another example. You may have noticed that iron rusts when it gets wet. When iron combines with oxygen, a chemical reaction takes place and a compound called iron oxide, or rust, is created.

This family is using the chemical reaction we call fire *to keep their feet warm!*

The chemical formula for table salt is NaCl. You can say it either 'N-A-C-L', or 'sodium chloride', which is what the letters stand for. Scientists can make NaCl by joining together HCl (hydrochloric acid) with NaOH (sodium hydroxide) when these substances are dissolved in a water solution. In these solutions, the atoms have either gained or lost electrons, which gives them an electrical charge. These charged atoms are called *ions*. When HCl and NaOH are combined, a chemical reaction takes place, in which the ions get new partners. The result will be table salt and water. Chemists write a chemical equation to show what happened:

$$HCl + NaOH \longrightarrow NaCl + H_2O$$

The chemical reaction is stated as follows: hydrochloric acid plus sodium hydroxide yields (makes) sodium chloride plus water. Notice that this equation is something like a mathematical equation. All the elements on the left side still appear on the right, but the sodium atom (Na) has joined the chlorine atom (Cl), and the first hydrogen atom has combined with the OH to make H_2O. This shows us that no atoms disappear and no new ones are created.

Chemical changes are essential for life. When your body processes the food you eat, it uses chemical reactions that give off the energy you need to do everything you do. It's this chemical energy that keeps you breathing and keeps your heart pumping blood through your body. Without chemical energy, there could be no life!

Classifying Living Things

Why Classify?

If someone asked you how to find apples in the supermarket, you'd probably send her to the fruit and vegetables aisle or tell her to look near the oranges and watermelons. Where would you tell a friend to look if he wanted to borrow a pair of your socks? You'd tell him to look in the drawer where you keep your socks.

Grouping things that are alike makes it easier for us to find them and easier to add similar new things to the group. Would you find frozen chips in the crisp aisle in a supermarket? No, because although chips and crisps have potatoes as ingredients, frozen chips, unlike crisps, need to be in a freezer. So we put these products in different places in the shop.

We group things together or separate them according to certain similarities or differences. When we group things together because they are alike in certain ways, we are *classifying* them.

If you go to school, you and your fellow students are probably grouped in a Year 6 class. You are placed in that class because you are the right age for Year 6. Within your class, you could think of other classifications, like boys and girls, or those who walk to school and those who come on the bus. There are many ways to divide people and things into classes, and it's important to remember that there is generally no single right way to divide up and name things. Still, *classes* and our names for them are very useful both for everyday life and for science. We *classify* and name things to make it easy to talk about them. In fact, we could not talk about most things without using classifications, because the very name we use for a thing is often the word for a whole class of things. A comfortable armchair and an upright wooden chair both belong to the class of things called 'chairs'.

Classifying Organisms

You've already read how chemists classify elements by their properties. Scientists who study living things, or *organisms*, also use classifications. One of the features scientists look at when they want to classify an organism is how it gets its food. Plants usually make their own food from sunlight, water and air, while animals do not. Animals can usually move themselves around, while plants cannot. Based on features like these, scientists have classified living things into large groups called *kingdoms*.

The first two kingdoms that scientists agreed on are the plant and animal kingdoms. Within these large kingdoms we can classify organisms into smaller groups. For instance, we put all flowering plants in one large group and all non-flowering plants into another. We put all animals that have hair and give milk into one class and all animals that have feathers and beaks into another.

> Carl Linnaeus worked out how to classify plants and animals. You can read about him on page 338.

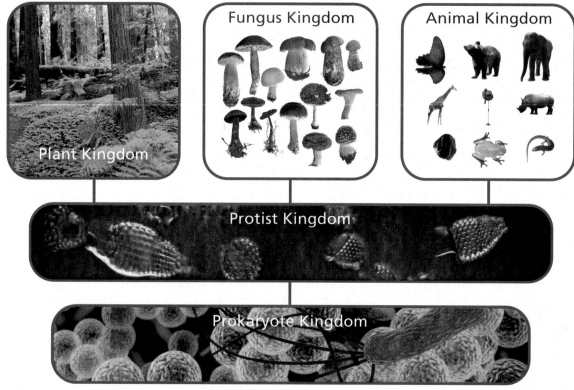

Five kingdoms of organisms

Once the microscope was invented and we could see more creatures, the classifier's job became more difficult. Scientists discovered many new organisms that seemed to be neither plants nor animals and needed new classifications. Their observations led to the naming of three new kingdoms: the *fungus* [FUN-gus], *protist* [PRO-tist] and *prokaryote* [pro-CARRY-oat] kingdoms. To see why scientists thought these microscopic organisms couldn't be classified as plants or animals, we need to learn about cells.

> We learnt about microscopes and the man who developed them in Year 3.

A light microscope works by shining light through a slide and magnifying it with lenses.

Cells

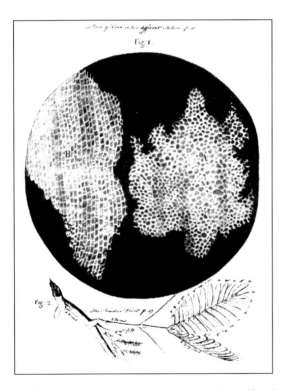

Cells are the tiny building blocks that make up all living things. There are many different types of cells and they are so small we can see them only with a microscope. Cells were discovered over 300 years ago when an English scientist named Robert Hooke was looking through his microscope at thin slices of cork – the material from the bark of the cork tree that can be used to seal bottles. Hooke noticed a regular pattern of small, boxlike squares in the cork, which reminded him of little rooms. He named these *cells*, after the Latin word for room, *cella*. When scientists developed even stronger microscopes, they were able to study the insides of cells and see various structures. Let's look at a picture of a cell and learn what its parts do.

Robert Hooke drew the cork cells that he saw under his microscope.

The Parts of a Cell

The *cell membrane* is a thin covering around the cell that separates it from its surroundings, a bit like a skin. The cell membrane helps give the cell its shape and controls what goes into it (food, water and oxygen) and out of it (waste). Inside the cell is the *cytoplasm* [SY-toh-plaz-um], a jelly-like liquid that surrounds all the other cell parts. Inside the cytoplasm is the *nucleus* [new-KLEE-us], the cell's control centre. The nucleus is surrounded by the nuclear membrane that controls what goes into and comes out of the nucleus. The nucleus contains all the instructions for running the cell. Sometimes cells need to make new cells; they need to reproduce. To reproduce, a cell splits into two cells. But before the cell splits, the instructions in the nucleus are copied and the two copies separate to form two nuclei, so that each new cell has a nucleus with a copy of the cell's instructions.

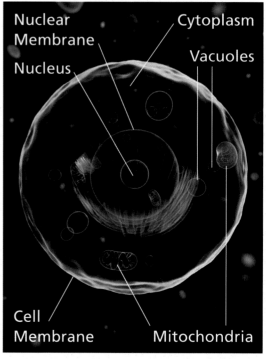

A cell and its parts as they might look under a powerful microscope.

Also inside the cytoplasm are tiny *organelles*, small structures that carry out the chemical activities of the cell. These organelles include *vacuoles* [VAK-you-oles], that store food, water or wastes, and *mitochondria* [my-toh-KONN-dree-uh], that help to break down food and release energy the cell can use.

Living *versus* Non-living

How do we know if something is alive? Sometimes it's easy: you know that you are alive and a rock is not. But sometimes it's hard to tell. What about a cloud, a fire or a tiny virus? Scientists say all living things do six activities. They take in nutrients, use energy to do work, reproduce, grow, get rid of wastes and react to outside changes. Is a cloud alive? What about a fire? Do you think cells inside living organisms are alive? Why, or why not? Can one cell be a living organism?

The cells in both plants and animals, though they may differ in shape and size, have the features you've been reading about: a cell membrane, cytoplasm, a nucleus, a nuclear membrane, vacuoles and mitochondria. As hard as it may be to believe, the cells that make up our body have all these things in common with the cells in a blade of grass!

Different Kinds of Cells

Cells are many different shapes depending on the special jobs they do. Muscle cells are long and thin so that they can relax or contract and move the body. Red blood cells are tiny, round and flat so that they can pass through blood vessels and bring oxygen to other cells. Cells in a tree trunk are long and thin and form tubes to transport food and water up and down the tree. The cells on the surface of a plant's leaves are flat and tightly connected to form a type of 'skin' that keeps water in.

In complex organisms like human beings, cells are often organised into tissues, organs and systems. A *tissue* is a collection of similar cells that work together. If you feel your upper arm, you touch skin tissue. If you flex a muscle, you can feel muscle tissue under the skin.

Tissues that do similar things work together to make *organs*, like the heart, the stomach or the brain. Organs can work together to form *systems*. For instance, the stomach, the large intestine and the small intestine are all organs that are parts of your digestive system. All of these tissues, organs and systems are built from cells.

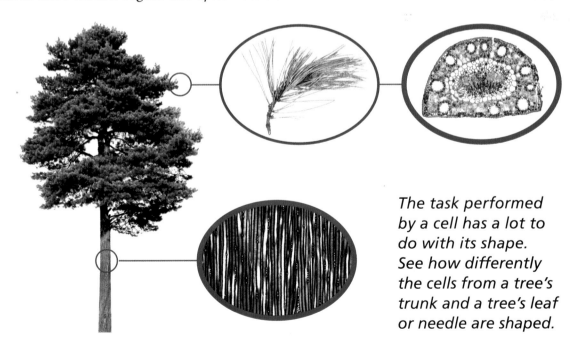

The task performed by a cell has a lot to do with its shape. See how differently the cells from a tree's trunk and a tree's leaf or needle are shaped.

309

How Plant Cells Differ from Animal Cells

Plant cells have two additional parts that animal cells don't have. Unlike animal cells, plant cells have *cell walls*. The cell wall is a sturdy layer around the cell membrane that supports and protects the cell. The cell wall helps the plant cell to be stiff when it has enough water and cytoplasm inside, and this helps the plant to remain upright. Robert Hooke was looking at the cell walls of tree bark cells when he made his discovery. The inside of the cells had died and dried up, leaving the pattern of 'boxes' that he saw.

Another structure that plant cells have that animal cells don't have is the *chloroplast* [KLO-roh-plast]. Chloroplasts contain chlorophyll [KLOR-oh-fill], a green substance that traps the energy from sunlight, enabling plants to make food in a process called *photosynthesis*.

Remember that one of the basic differences between plants and animals is that plants usually make their own food while animals don't. Animals have to find food themselves, they can't make it. It's the chloroplasts that allow plants to make their own food.

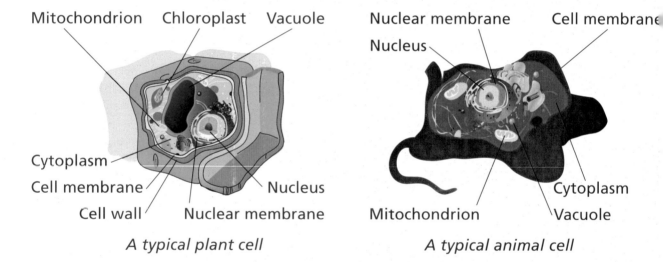

A typical plant cell

A typical animal cell

Fungi

If you have ever seen a mushroom, you've seen a fungus. If there were different kinds of mushrooms on display in the supermarket, you probably saw several kinds of fungi [FUN-gee]. Fungi were once thought to be part of the plant kingdom because they have cell walls and produce spores (which plants also produce). But they were separated into a distinct kingdom because they get their energy not from sunlight but by breaking down material from dead plants and animals. The mushrooms you can buy at the supermarket are created by colonies of fungi that feed on decaying plant material. From time to time, the fungi send

This fungus is growing on a log in the forest and it looks a bit different from the mushrooms you see in the supermarket.

up mushrooms. When they are mature, or fully grown, the mushrooms release millions of tiny spores, which are cells with a protective coat. The wind blows the spores to distant places, where they start new fungus colonies.

The yeast that makes bread rise is a type of fungus. So is the green mould that forms on bread when it is exposed to moist air. And so is the white, powdery mildew that can appear on houseplants and in moist places.

One of the most exciting fungi known to scientists is Pilobolus, also known as 'the shotgun fungus'. Pilobolus grows on cow manure. When the fungus is ready to spread its spores, its cap explosively pops off and flies through the air, sometimes travelling up to six feet!

Protists

The fourth kingdom is the protists. Some protists are so tiny they are only one cell. They can be seen only with a microscope. Others are quite large. Some protists have animal features, others have plant features, and still others have features of both! For years, scientists were confused about how to classify these organisms. Finally, scientists decided that these organisms should make up their own kingdom.

Protists that are single-celled and that act like animals are called protozoans [proh-toh-ZOH-unz]. *Proto* means 'early' in Greek and *zoan* means 'animal'. Protozoans can move around. They can also capture food they find in their environment. Some are found in fresh water, some in salt water. Some live in soil, and some live inside other organisms.

One protozoan you may have heard about is called an amoeba [uh-MEE-buh]. An amoeba is a blob-like protozoan that is one large cell. It can stretch its body around tiny organisms that it wants to eat. Once the prey is surrounded, the amoeba brings it inside its one-celled body. This forms a vacuole, in which the prey is digested.

Other protists are plant-like and are called algae [AL-gee]. Some of these are single cells and some have many cells. You may have seen algae growing as a film on top of a pond or lake. Seaweed, or kelp, is also a type of algae. These organisms photosynthesise and their cells contain chloroplasts.

Euglena [you-GLEE-nah] are single-celled protists that have both plant and animal features. Like plants, euglena contain chloroplasts, but, unlike plants, euglena can move around. Euglena can make food through photosynthesis, but when there is no sunlight, they can eat bacteria or other protists.

This picture, taken with an electron microscope, shows a single, ciliated protozoan – a kind of protist. The protist is covered with cilia, tiny hair-like projections that help the organism to swim in liquids.

Prokaryotes

Prokaryotes (formerly called monerans) are small, single-celled organisms that are very simple. Until high-powered microscopes were developed, scientists thought that prokaryotes were very small protists, and they had a difficult time classifying them. But once they could see prokaryotes more clearly under high-powered microscopes, scientists found that they have a very important characteristic that puts them in a group by themselves: prokaryotes have no cell nucleus! The material normally found in a cell nucleus is clumped together, but has no nuclear membrane around it.

Prokaryotes are also called *bacteria*. They have both a cell wall and a cell membrane. They are classified according to their shape: some are long rods or capsules, some look like spiral tubes and some are spherical. They get their food from other organisms or from decaying matter. They are found just about everywhere: in the air, water and soil, and even inside other organisms, including you!

Some bacteria cause diseases. (Perhaps you've taken medicine to get rid of a bacterial disease like tonsillitis or bronchitis.) Other bacteria are very useful to life. Like fungi, they help to break down decaying material so that nutrients are free to be used by plants. Certain types of bacteria are necessary for proper digestion in humans. Scientists have even been able to develop bacteria that 'eat' oil and help to clean up oil spills.

Cyanobacteria are prokaryotes found in water or soil. They photosynthesise but they do not have chloroplasts; instead, their chlorophyll is contained in membranes spread throughout the cell. Cyanobacteria used to be called blue-green algae. About half of them are bluish-green, but the rest are other colours, including red! Cyanobacteria are the

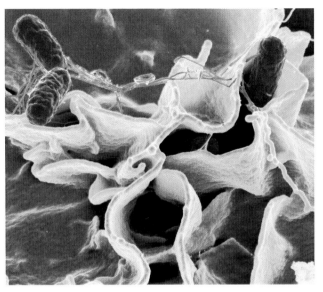

beginning of the food chain for many animals that live in water. They also produce oxygen in the water and in the air we breathe.

The classification on page 306 shows all prokaryotes in one kingdom. However, a growing number of scientists divide prokaryotes into two kingdoms, called Eubacteria ('true bacteria') and Archaebacteria ('ancient bacteria'). This is an area where ideas about classification are changing rapidly as scientists learn more about these tiny organisms.

The red Salmonella typhimurium prokaryotes, seen under an electron microscope and magnified many times their actual size, are invading the yellow human cells.

Taxonomy

Scientists first classify living things by placing them in one of the kingdoms. But these are very large categories, so scientists have divided them into a series of smaller groupings:

> **Kingdom**
>> **Phylum (plural: phyla)**
>>> **Class**
>>>> **Order**
>>>>> **Family**
>>>>>> **Genus (plural: genera)**
>>>>>>> **Species**
>>>>>>>> **(Variety)**

Each kingdom can contain several phyla, and each phylum can contain several classes, and so on. (You can remember these categories, in the correct order by size, by memorising the sentence 'King Philip came over for good spaghetti'.)

Here's how scientists would classify a collie dog:

Kingdom: Animalia (an animal)

Phylum: Chordata (an animal with a type of internal skeleton)

Subphylum: Vertebrata (a vertebrate, an animal with a backbone)

Class: Mammalia (a mammal, an animal that is warm-blooded, has hair, and makes milk)

Order: Carnivora (a carnivore, or meat-eater)

Family: Canidae (a group with dog-like characteristics)

Genus: Canis (a coyote, wolf, or dog)

Species: familiaris (a domestic dog)

Variety: collie (a specific breed of dog)

Can you see how this description gets more specific as it goes along? It begins by classifying the collie as an animal and then says that it's not just any kind of animal, it's an animal with a backbone. Gradually, more and more details are introduced and the description 'closes in' on the exact kind of animal. This system of classifying living things is called taxonomy.

Did you notice that there is one extra stage in the classification of the collie? In addition to phylum and class, this classification also includes a subphylum. Some phyla are divided into subphyla, which are then divided into classes.

Genus: canis; Species: familiaris; Variety: collie

Latin Names

When taxonomy was just getting started, Latin was a language spoken by educated people in many different countries. It enabled a Frenchman, an Englishman and a Dutchman to communicate with one another. So the early taxonomists used Latin. Today scientists still use Latin names so that everyone will know which plants and animals they are talking about.

When scientists want to specify an animal, they don't usually list all the categories it belongs to. It would not be very convenient to refer to a dog as an *Animalia Chordata Vertebrata Mammalia Carnivora Canidae Canis familiaris*. Scientists usually use only the genus name and species name. So the scientific name for a dog is *Canis familiaris*. We always capitalise the genus and never the species name. This system was devised by Carl Linnaeus, whom we will read about on page 338.

Meet the Vertebrates

One thing the taxonomic description of a collie tells you is that collies are vertebrates. That's another way of saying that collies have backbones. In fact, most of the animals you see at the zoo are vertebrates. Fish,

> We learnt about invertebrates in Year 4. They don't have any backbone!

amphibians, reptiles, birds and mammals are five different groups of vertebrates.

A fish is a vertebrate that lives in water and uses gills to get oxygen from water. Its body temperature is the same as the temperature of the surrounding water, so we say that it is 'cold-blooded'. Most fish are covered with small scales. Most of them also lay soft, jelly-coated eggs. Salmon, trout and tuna are different kinds of fish.

Amphibians are also vertebrates, and they also cannot adjust their body temperature. They live part of their lives in the water and part on land. (The word amphibian means 'living in two places'.) Amphibians have gills and live mostly in water when they are young, but most of them develop lungs when they grow up. Frogs and salamanders are amphibians.

Reptiles are vertebrates that hatch from eggs and breathe with lungs. The eggs have a hard shell to protect them and keep them from drying out. Like fish and amphibians, their body temperature depends on the temperature of their surroundings. Snakes, lizards and turtles are all reptiles.

This lizard is a reptile.

Birds are warm-blooded vertebrates, which means that they always keep their body at a certain warm temperature. To do this, they release heat when they break down

315

food. Birds have lungs, as well as feathers and wings. Most birds can fly, but a few, like ostriches and penguins, cannot. Most birds build nests in which to lay their hard-shelled eggs.

Mammals are another class of warm-blooded vertebrates. They breathe with lungs and usually have hair on their bodies. Female mammals produce milk to feed their babies. Human beings are mammals, and so are dogs, kangaroos, giraffes and lions.

With most animals, it's not hard to guess what kind of vertebrates they are. But a few are tricky. For instance, what category would you guess whales and dolphins belong in? Did you say fish? That's a logical guess, but have you ever noticed that both whales and dolphins come to the surface a lot and blow out big puffs of air? That's because whales and dolphins have lungs, not gills. They are warm-blooded and feed their babies milk. That means they are mammals, not fish!

This zebra and her foal are both mammals.

Plants

Plants and Photosynthesis

Animals like whales and dolphins and human beings have to eat food to keep their energy levels up. Plants, on the other hand, are able to make food from carbon dioxide and water, using sunlight energy.

All plants (as well as some types of prokaryotes and protists) contain *chlorophyll,* a molecule that makes some or all of their cells appear green. The word *chlorophyll* comes from two Greek words – *chlor*, meaning 'green', and *phyllo*, meaning 'leaf'. In fact, chlorophyll can be found in other green parts of a plant besides the leaves. Protists and prokaryotes containing chlorophyll have no leaves. But all of these organisms use chlorophyll to trap the energy they need to make food. The process they use to make food is called *photosynthesis.*

Photo means 'light'. *Synthesis* means 'putting together'. So photosynthesis means 'putting together with light'. Organisms that contain chlorophyll combine water and carbon dioxide using energy from sunlight. The end products of photosynthesis are sugars, which the organisms use for food, and oxygen gas.

How is this done? Where do the water and carbon dioxide come from, and where do the oxygen and sugars go? Let's start by finding out how water and carbon dioxide get into a celery leaf.

Photosynthesis in a celery plant

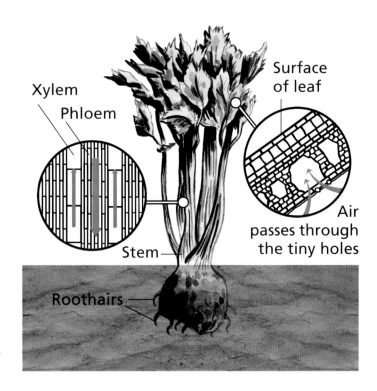

Step One: *Transporting Water and Nutrients:*

Cars, buses and underground trains are all means of transport we use to move from one place to another. Many plants transport things inside them, too, in order to make and store food. Look at the drawing of a celery plant. The plant takes in water and nutrients from the soil through tiny hairs on its roots. The water and nutrients are transported through the root hairs to the roots, and then up the stem (or 'stalk') of the celery through tubes arranged in bundles.

There are two types of tubes in plants: *xylem* [ZYE-lem] and *phloem* [FLOW-em]. Xylem tubes carry water and nutrients from the soil up the stem to the leaves where most photosynthesis occurs. Phloem tubes carry sugars from the leaves to every part of the plant that is not green (like the roots, trunk and flowers) and also to the growing tips and the fruits.

Step Two: *Light Energy from the Sun:*

Look at the cross section of the celery leaf, as seen through a microscope, in the illustration. Note the layer of cells just below the top surface of the leaf. These cells contain chloroplasts, where chlorophyll is found. Sunlight shines through the top of the leaf, and the light energy is trapped by the chlorophyll and stored in special molecules for later use.

Step Three: *Carbon Dioxide from the Air:*

In this step, food is made. Air passes in through tiny holes on the bottom surface of the leaf called *stomata*. (A single hole is called a stoma; many holes are called stomata.) Carbon dioxide from the air reaches the cells where chlorophyll has trapped energy from sunlight. This energy causes a chemical reaction that combines water and carbon dioxide to make oxygen and sugars.

Step Four: *Back to the Transport System:*

The sugars created in the leaves are transported down the celery plant in phloem tubes, to be stored as sugar or very large molecules called starch in other parts of the plant. The plant's cells use this food later to grow and do work.

The sugars and starches stored in a plant are necessary for the plant to survive, but they can also make the plant taste good to humans and animals. Doesn't an apple taste sweet? That sweetness comes from the sugars the apple tree

An apple is sweet because the apple tree has stored sugars in the fruit.

Transporting Water: See for Yourself

Collect the following materials: a glass large enough to hold a stalk of celery upright, water, black ink, a stalk of celery with leaves, scissors, a magnifying glass or hand lens. Cut about an inch off the bottom of the celery stalk. Place the stalk upright in a glass. Fill the glass half full of water and add a few drops of black ink. Let the celery sit overnight. What do you observe the next day? Take the stalk out of the water and with scissors cut it above the water line. Observe the bottom end with the magnifying glass. What do you see?

stored in its fruit – sugars created by photosynthesis. Many plants – potatoes and maize, for example – change the sugar they make into starch before it is stored.

We eat many plants to get their stored sugar and starch. And just like plants, we convert this stored food into energy for our cells to do their work.

Vascular and Non-vascular Plants

Scientists divide plants into two categories: vascular and non-vascular. Most of the plants you are familiar with are vascular plants. Vascular plants have roots, stems and leaves. Inside the stems and leaves are xylem and phloem that allow water and nutrients to move through the plant. But other plants don't have these tube-like structures and can't move nutrients as well. These are the non-vascular plants.

Moss is an example of a non-vascular plant. A moss relies on photosynthesis just like a celery plant, but it has to make do without the transport network provided by stems and branches. Non-vascular plants are small and low to the ground, and they can grow only in moist places because they don't have roots that can carry water.

Life Cycles and Reproduction

The Replacements

All living things are born, grow during their lifetime and eventually die. Tadpoles are born, grow, change into frogs and eventually die, but female frogs lay eggs that will hatch into new tadpoles. Chicks hatch, grow to be adult chickens and eventually die, but hens lay eggs that hatch

> We first learnt about the life cycle in Year 3, and now we'll learn more about reproduction.

into new chicks, so the life cycle continues. What would happen if no new chickens were born to replace those that died? There would be no chickens in the world – they'd be extinct. To keep from dying out, all living things *reproduce* themselves. 'Reproduce' means 'to make again' or 'to make a copy'. Reproduction is the process of making again.

The cells in your body reproduce themselves and increase in number, which is how you grow. Every day, for example, some of your skin cells reproduce themselves and some of them die. As you grow bigger, your skin cells reproduce faster than they die, so your skin can continue to cover your whole body. As you grow taller, cells in your bones reproduce and make longer, thicker bones. When you become an adult, cells reproduce more slowly, so slowly, in fact, that at about age twenty you stop growing bigger. From then on, cells are created at about the rate they die, so the number of cells stays about even.

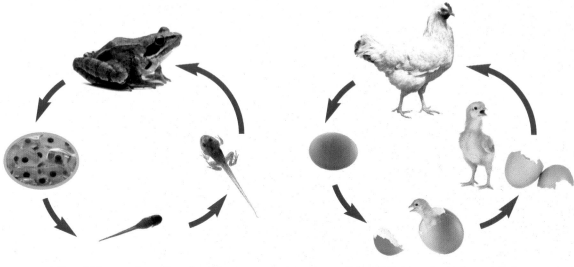

The life cycle of a frog   *The life cycle of a chicken*

Organisms reproduce in different ways. Some plants make seeds. Mushrooms and other fungi make spores. Frogs and chickens lay eggs. Dogs have litters of puppies. What about protists and bacteria? Let's read about two categories of reproduction: asexual and sexual.

Asexual Reproduction

One way that organisms copy themselves is through asexual reproduction. Asexual means 'non-sexual', that is, reproduction without using males and females. The organism simply copies itself through cell division.

Asexual reproduction can be very simple. Bacteria (the simplest of all organisms) and many protists reproduce by splitting. After making copies of their genetic material (the cell's set of instructions), bacteria simply split their single cell in half. Each half becomes a

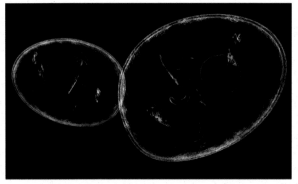

During asexual reproduction, cells duplicate their genetic material and divide into two cells.

new cell. Under the right conditions some bacteria can double their numbers every 20 minutes and quickly form colonies large enough to see without a microscope! That's why it's important to keep fresh food in refrigerators. Most food contains some bacteria, but not enough to make you ill. Cold temperatures keep bacteria from growing and dividing. However, if you leave some types of food out for too long, the bacteria will start reproducing until your food is full of millions of bacteria and is not safe to eat.

Mildews, moulds and mushrooms are fungi that reproduce by forming spores. Spores are single cells that are often protected by a hard covering. Spores drop off the parent and grow into fungi if there is enough water and food for them to live. On the other hand, most yeasts, which are single-celled fungi, reproduce by budding. A 'bud' forms on one side of the cell and eventually separates itself to form a new yeast cell.

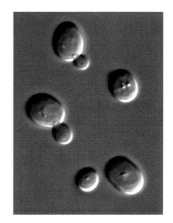

These yeast cells are reproducing by budding. Can you see how a small bud is forming on the side of the parent cell?

Asexual Reproduction in Larger Animals and Plants

Some plants and animals can reproduce themselves *asexually*. In plants, the most familiar example of such reproduction is called *cloning*, where a piece of the plant – a leaf or stem cutting – is put into some moist material, and a whole new plant forms – a new plant that is just like the parent. Some plants do this naturally, like strawberries that send out 'runners' or daffodil bulbs that divide in two underground. Only simple animals like sponges, flatworms and jellyfish reproduce asexually. Some simple animals just split in two, and some grow a new, smaller copy on their side that eventually falls off and grows on its own.

Most animals do not reproduce asexually. However, many animals have the ability to replace lost cells or even lost body parts. This is called *regeneration*. The amount of regeneration that can occur depends on the type of organism. You regenerate skin cells when you cut your finger and the wound heals. But if you cut off your whole finger, it won't grow back.

Other animals have a much greater ability to regenerate. Have you ever seen a starfish?

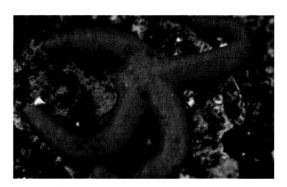

A starfish, or sea star, can regenerate amputated limbs.

A starfish can grow a whole new arm if one is cut off. The lost arm, if it still has a piece of the centre of the starfish, can even grow into a new starfish! When some kinds of worms are cut in half, each half grows into a new worm. Salamanders can regenerate a leg if they lose one. But the leg can't regenerate a new salamander. In general, more complex animals like salamanders and humans have a more limited ability to regenerate.

Axolotls are a kind of salamander.

Sexual Reproduction in Mosses and Ferns

Sexual reproduction requires special male and female cells to combine. These special cells are called *gametes* [gam-eats]. In sexual reproduction, male and female gametes join to form a fertilised egg.

Mosses, which you may have seen growing in shady spots, reproduce by making spores. Look at the drawing of the moss's life cycle. In the first step, shown on the lower right, a spore has just landed in a moist, nutrient-rich spot and germinated. Next it grows into a moss plant that is green and often forms a soft mat. After a time, something amazing happens. Buds near the tips of the moss plant begin making gametes. If the buds make gametes that are eggs, the moss plant is female. If the buds make gametes that can swim, called *sperm*, the moss plant is male. When a male and female plant are close enough together, and there is some water present, a male gamete (the sperm) swims to a female gamete (the egg) and fertilises it. This fertilised egg divides and grows into a stalk on top of the female moss plant. The cells continue to divide to form a capsule at the tip of the stalk and to form spores inside that capsule. When it is mature, the capsule bursts open and releases the spores. If the spores fall on moist ground, they germinate and the process starts all over again.

The life cycle of a fern is similar to that of a moss, but there are some differences. When the fern spore gets wet it germinates, turning into a tiny, heart-shaped plant that produces both male and female gametes. When these male and female gametes come together, the fertilised egg grows into a totally new and different plant that will become the large fern you can find in the woods. The leaves of a fern are called fronds. On the bottom of some of the fronds of a mature fern, there are special cells that produce capsules full of spores. These capsules burst open and release the spores to start the cycle again.

The life cycle of a moss

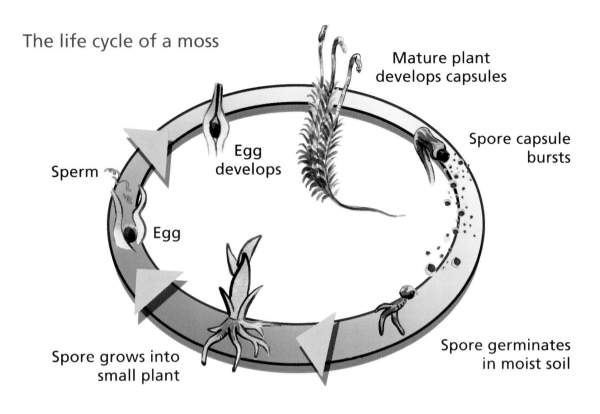

Mature plant
develops capsules

Spore capsule
bursts

Egg
develops

Sperm

Egg

Spore grows into
small plant

Spore germinates
in moist soil

The life cycle of a fern

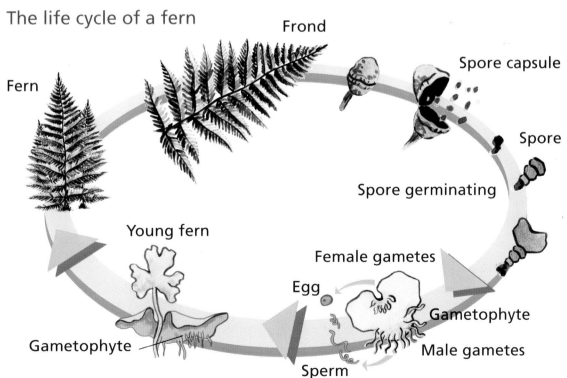

Frond

Spore capsule

Fern

Spore

Spore germinating

Young fern

Female gametes

Egg

Gametophyte

Gametophyte

Male gametes

Sperm

Conifer Seeds Are Naked

The male cones release pollen to the wind.

Most large plants reproduce by combining a male and female gamete to make a fertilised egg that grows into an *embryo* [EM-bree-oh]. This embryo, or baby plant, is protected inside a seed. Some of the simplest of these seed plants are the *conifers*, a name that means 'cone-carriers'. Have you wondered what a pine cone is for? It is the reproductive part of the pine tree.

If you can find a big pine tree, you may be able to see that there are both big and small cones on it. These two kinds of cones are usually found on the same plant. The small cone carries the male cells. That's because it doesn't take much space to store millions of tiny grains of pollen, each of which carries a male gamete.

Pollen from the male pine cone is carried by the wind and sticks to the larger female pine cone. Tubes grow from the grains of pollen to reach the eggs inside the female cone, and a male gamete joins with the egg to fertilise it. The fertilised egg then divides and grows into an embryo. In addition to the embryo, the seed also contains a supply of food on the inside and a seed coat on the outside. The seed coat keeps the embryo from drying out. The seed drops to the ground when the cone opens. If the soil is moist, the seed germinates, using the stored food to help the embryo grow. The embryo grows into a new tree if there is enough water plus enough nutrients in the soil.

The seed from a conifer is called a naked seed, because it has nothing on except its own seed coat. There is no fruit that surrounds it. Conifers belong to the group of plants called *gymnosperms*, which means 'naked seeds'.

Some pollen reaches the larger female cones.

Seeds of Flowering Plants Have Clothes

Most plants clothe the seeds they make with some sort of covering. The fruit of a cherry is the covering for the seed inside it. Tomatoes have seeds inside, and so do cucumbers, green peppers and oranges. All of these are fruits! You're probably more interested in the fruit than the seeds, but for the purpose of reproduction, the tomato or the orange are just coverings for seeds.

These plants with covered seeds are called *angiosperms*, which in Greek means 'covered seeds'. All these plants have one thing in common: they have flowers. The seed covers, hard or soft, big or small, sweet or sour, all come from the same place – a flower.

Flowers

Many plants you are familiar with, including most trees, shrubs, vines, grasses and garden plants, produce flowers. They can be as large and showy as sunflowers or as tiny as the flowers on a grass plant, but most flowers have essentially the same parts.

Let's look at a diagram of a typical flower on the next page to see how seeds are formed. Typically the flower is formed as a series of rings, one inside the other. The outer ring is made up of *sepals*, which are usually green and look like leaves attached to the stem at the base of a flower. Inside the sepals, the *petals* make the next ring. The colourful petals attract insects, which are often important for bringing pollen carrying the male gamete to the egg.

Inside the petals, in the centre of the flower, lie the reproductive parts. The *stamens* are the male reproductive organs. Each stamen has an *anther* on its tip, where millions of tiny pollen grains, each with a male gamete, are made. At the very centre of most flowers is the *pistil*, with the female reproductive organs. The pistil is a tube that leads down to the ovary with its egg or eggs.

What is an *ovary*? In Latin it means a 'place for eggs'. This place for the egg or eggs is completely protected, which is one of the great advantages of a flower. Sometimes, when there is just one egg, the ovary is called an *ovule*, which means 'small ovary'. For instance, when there is just one seed inside a fruit, you know it came from a single ovule. When there are several eggs, then there will be several ovules inside a larger ovary. And later when that ovary develops into a fruit, there will be several seeds inside, as in a tomato, orange, or apple.

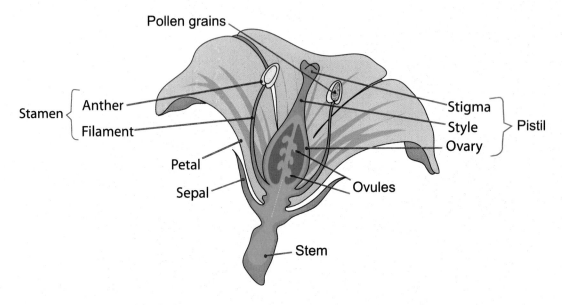

A typical flower and its parts

Flower Fertilisation

The first step of flower fertilisation is *pollination*, the movement of pollen from the anther to the sticky top of the pistil. But how does the pollen make that trip? Insects or birds are responsible for pollinating many flowers. But wind and rain also help. Look at the bee in the picture. When the bee sips nectar from the flower, it also picks up some pollen that sticks to its back or legs. When it visits another flower to get more nectar, the pollen can fall off and stick onto the pistil.

In the second step of fertilisation, a tube grows out of the pollen grain that is stuck to the pistil. A pollen tube cannot grow unless the pollen comes from the same kind of plant as the pistil it lands on. Inside the pollen tube is the male gamete. The tube grows down the pistil and into the ovule at the bottom.

In the last step, the male gamete joins the egg cell in the ovule, and fertilisation occurs. The fertilised egg cell begins to divide and form an embryo, or young plant. The ovule grows into a seed coat that protects what is now the seed. As the seed forms in the parent plant, the flower changes. The sepals and petals die and fall off, while the ovule or ovary grows into a covering or fruit – into beans or berries or tomatoes or the hard shells of nuts.

The covering protects the seed or seeds inside it and also helps to scatter the seed. These coverings are often juicy and nutritious. Animals eat fruits, but they often do not digest the seeds. When the seeds pass through the animal's body, they may end up in a new location where they can germinate. If the fruit falls from the parent plant but is not eaten, it starts to decay and the seed is uncovered. This allows the seed to reach the soil, where it can germinate and grow into a new plant.

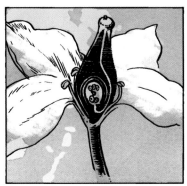

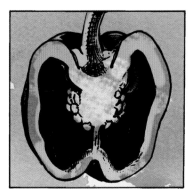

The stages of reproduction in a flowering plant: pollination, fertilisation, ovary begins to grow as flower petals die, ovary continues to grow, mature fruit or vegetable houses seeds for next generation.

Plant Development

What happens to a seed once it reaches the soil? Let's look at the development of a plant. The photographs on the next page show the outside and inside of a conker, which is a horse chestnut seed. When it is cut open, you can see the young plant or embryo inside. Notice the large area where food is stored. This is called the *endosperm*; it contains food for the young plant – and also for animals, including humans. We eat many seeds, though not conkers. This food keeps the embryo alive and helps it to germinate and grow until it is big enough to make its own food. See the seed coat? It protects the seed and keeps it from drying out.

When a seed falls to the ground, it is sometimes pushed into the soil by heavy rainfall. Certain seeds are buried by animals, like squirrels that want to eat them later. When seeds are planted in moist soil, they absorb water. This softens the seed coat and makes the inside of the seed swell up and burst through the seed coat. If temperatures are warm enough, the cells of the embryo inside the seed begin to divide and the embryo grows. The tiny embryo continues to use the stored food inside the seed to grow and breaks through the seed coat. The embryo sprouts roots and is now a new plant. This sprouting of the new plant is called *germination*.

The roots of the new plant take in water and minerals from the soil that the plant uses to grow. As the stem grows upward, leaves appear. Leaves help the plant to make its own food by photosynthesis, which helps the plant grow into an adult plant. Later, the adult plant develops flowers, the flowers develop seeds, and the cycle begins again.

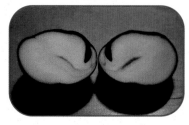

Inside the tough coating of a conker is a delicate embryo, ready to grow.

Examining a Bean Seed

Materials: One bean seed, a cup of water, one magnifying glass

Method: Soak the bean seed in water overnight. Remove the seed from the water and examine the soaked bean seed. Remove the seed coat and note its thickness. Carefully separate the two halves of the bean seed with your fingernail. Can you find the embryo inside? Draw a picture of the inside of your seed. Can you find the stored food?

Stages of germination in a seed.

The growing embryo breaks through its seed coat and sprouts roots. The roots grow bigger, pushing the new plant above ground. The plant grows leaves that help it make its own food as an adult. This one could grow into a neem tree.

Monocots and Dicots

There are two kinds of flowering plants: *monocots* and *dicots*. Grass is an example of a monocot. If you plant a grass seed and water it, in a few days a single seed leaf will break out of the seed and push its way through the soil. This seed leaf is called a *cotyledon* [cot-illy-don]. Because each grass seed produces only one cotyledon, grass is called a *monocotyledon*, or *monocot* for short. (The word 'monocotyledon' means 'one-seed leaf'.) If you plant a bean seed, it will send up two seed leaves. That's why bean plants are classified as dicots, or plants with two seed leaves.

There are other differences between monocots and dicots, too. The total number of flower parts on a monocot is often a multiple of three. So a monocot flower might have three petals, or six, or nine. By contrast, the total number of flower parts on a dicot is often a multiple of four, like eight or twelve, or a multiple of five, like ten or fifteen.

MONOCOTS

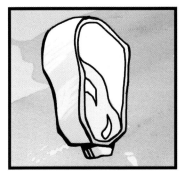
One cotyledon

Long narrow leaves with parallel veins

Flower parts usually in multiples of three

DICOTS

Two cotyledons

Broader leaves with net-like veins

Flower parts usually in multiples of four or five

This diagram shows some distinguishing features of monocotyledons and dicotyledons.

Monocots usually have long narrow leaves, with veins running parallel to one another. Dicots tend to have broader leaves with veins that look like nets.

Grains like wheat, maize and rice are all monocots, as are some flowers, like lilies and tulips. Most fruits and vegetables are dicots, as are many garden flowers.

Reproduction in Animals

Most animals reproduce sexually. Just as plants produce male and female gametes, so do animals. In animals, the male gametes, or *sperm*, are produced in special organs called the *testes*, while the female gametes, or *eggs*, are produced by *ovaries*. In some simpler animals – earthworms, for example – the sperm- and egg-making organs are in one creature. But in most animals, male and female gametes are made by separate male and female individuals.

If the sperm and egg join outside the bodies of the parents, the process is called *external fertilisation*. When the sperm and egg join inside the body of the female, as with humans, it is called *internal fertilisation*. (See page 326.)

Have you ever seen a film of fish spawning? *Spawning* is a form of external fertilisation. During spawning, female fish and male fish come very close together in the water. The female releases her eggs into the water and the male releases his sperm. The sperm swim to the eggs and fertilise them.

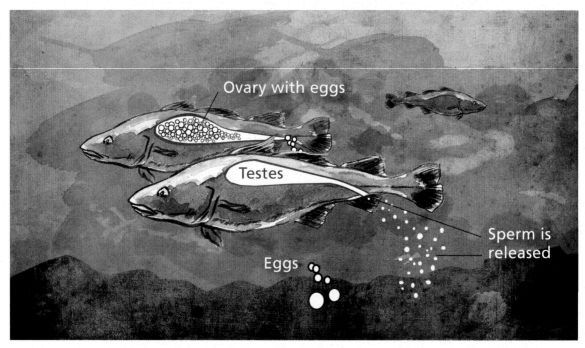

Ovary with eggs

Testes

Sperm is released

Eggs

During spawning season, adult fish release eggs and sperm into the water, where fertilisation takes place.

Egg — Ovary

Birds and also mammals like horses and humans reproduce by internal fertilisation. The female releases an egg from her ovary, and it travels down a tube that leads from the ovary. During mating, the male releases sperm inside the female. The sperm travels to the tube where the egg is located and fertilises it. If no sperm joins an egg, it is unfertilised, and it leaves the female's body.

Development of the Embryo

Once the egg is fertilised, it is called a *zygote* [ZYE-goat]. The zygote begins to divide and grow, and after several days or weeks, depending on the animal, it becomes an embryo. An embryo, remember, is a developing organism. In most mammals, the embryo develops inside the mother's body in an organ called the uterus [YOO-ter-us}. The zygote travels down the *Fallopian tube* from the ovary and attaches to the wall of the uterus. The developing embryo gets its food and water from the mother. In the later stages of development, the embryo is called a *foetus*. When it has developed enough to live outside the mother's body, the *foetus* is born.

The amount of time it takes an animal to develop before birth depends on the species. Horses take eleven months to develop inside their mothers. Sheep take only five months. It takes a human embryo nine months to develop.

Have You Ever Seen a Koalaroo?

What makes a species? Scientists use information about reproduction along with other information to classify organisms into smaller and smaller groups. One very important group is called a species. For species that reproduce sexually, members of a species usually mate and produce offspring only with other members of the same species. For example, when a female koala bear mates and produces a baby koala bear, we know that her mate must have been a male of the same species. Koala bears do not and cannot mate with kangaroos and produce young; that means koalas and kangaroos are different species. And that's why you've never seen a koalaroo!

Care and Growth of Young

Different species have different ways of looking after their young. Fish do not take care of their young at all. Nor do sea turtles. Female sea turtles lay 50 to 100 eggs in a hole in the sand and then return to the ocean. Their young hatch, crawl out of their nest, and crawl to the sea with no protection or help from their mothers. Before reaching the ocean they are often eaten by hungry gulls or crabs. If they do reach the water, they may be swallowed by hungry fish. But because the sea turtle lays so many eggs, there is a chance some of them will survive.

A newly hatched turtle has to find its own way to the sea.

Other newborn animals are cared for by one or more parents until they can survive on their own. Usually, birds tend their young until they are old enough to fly. Lion cubs stay with their parents for about four years, until they are old enough to defend themselves and to find food. Humans stay with their parents even longer.

Growth Stages

The development of an organism from birth through reproduction to death is called the *life cycle*. Usually there are noticeable stages of development during an organism's life cycle. During the life cycle of a horse, reproduction occurs inside the mother when egg and sperm unite, and an embryo develops. The embryo grows into a foetus, which looks almost like a full-grown horse in miniature. Soon after birth, when he can stand, the young foal drinks milk from his mother's teat. After a year, the foal no longer needs his mother's

Fertilisation and much of the development of the young horse takes place within the mother's body.

milk and eats grass beside her. In four years it is a mature horse.

The Human Body

Human Growth Stages

Humans also show stages in their growth. You developed into an embryo and then a foetus inside your mother's uterus. When you were a newborn baby, also called an infant, you were bottle-fed or you drank breast milk. You grew and developed fairly rapidly until, when you were about a year old, you learnt to walk. Between the ages of eight and seventeen, most of you will experience a period of rapid growth, and your bodies will begin changing as you reach *puberty*, the age at which you become capable of reproducing. By age twenty-one, you will stop growing. At about forty, your metabolism will begin to slow down, and at sixty or later, you will reach old age.

Toddler   *Child*   *Teen*   *Young adult*   *Adult*   *Middle Age*   *Old Age*

Adolescence and Puberty

The period of growth and change in the human body that occurs between eight and seventeen is known as *adolescence* [add-oh-LESS-ense]. During adolescence, powerful chemicals called hormones are released into the bloodstream from glands in your body. These hormones cause physical, mental and emotional changes. The process usually begins earlier in girls than it does in boys.

As an adolescent, you may experience an increase in your appetite; you may be hungry all the time. You may also require more sleep at night. Some people experience a very rapid change in height and weight, sometimes called a 'growth spurt'. Their muscles and bones get larger, and their favourite clothes don't fit anymore. They may feel awkward, because their hands and feet are growing faster than the other parts of their body.

Girls start to develop breasts, and their hips begin to round out. Boys' shoulders widen, and their voices change, sometimes cracking as they begin to deepen. Both boys and girls grow hair under their arms and around their genitals. These changes are normal and they happen to every human being, though there is variation in the age at which people begin adolescence.

The Human Reproductive System

The changes in a person's body during adolescence are in preparation for *puberty*, the time when male and female humans are able to produce children. Human reproduction is very similar to reproduction in other mammals. In females, an egg cell is released each month from one of two ovaries. The egg then passes into one of the *Fallopian* [fall-OH-pee-an] tubes, where it could be fertilised by sperm from a male. If it is not fertilised, it passes into the uterus and then out of the body along with the lining of the uterus. The uterus lining and egg pass through the *vagina* on their way out of the body. This monthly process of shedding the egg and the lining of the uterus is called *menstruation* [men-stroo-AY-shun] from the Latin word *mensis*, meaning 'month'.

How does the sperm reach the egg in the Fallopian tube? First we need to learn about the male reproductive organs. Sperm are produced in the *testes* [tes-tees], egg-shaped glands that are contained in a pouch of skin, the scrotum, which hangs below the penis. The sperm travel through tubes in the testes in a whitish fluid called *semen* [sea-men]. When the male is sexually aroused, the semen exits the male's body through the *urethra*, a tube in his penis.

During sexual intercourse, the male places his penis inside the female's vagina. The semen shoots out of his penis and into her vagina, and the sperm swim toward her uterus. After reaching the uterus, they swim toward the Fallopian tubes, where one sperm cell breaks through the egg's outer covering and then fuses with the egg and fertilises it.

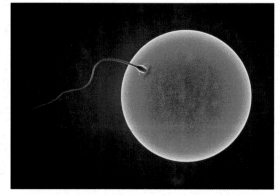

The moment of union between a sperm and an egg.

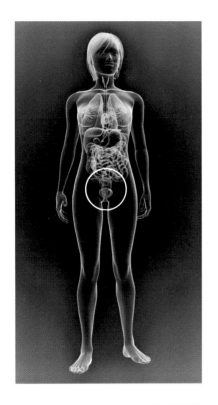

The reproductive parts of a human female

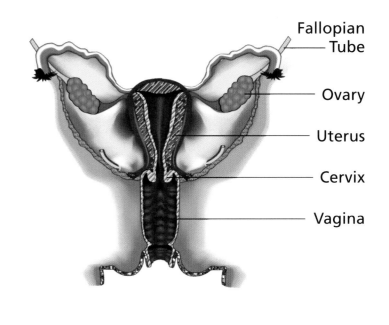

Fallopian Tube

Ovary

Uterus

Cervix

Vagina

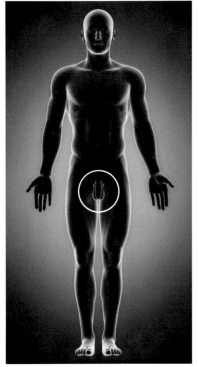

The reproductive parts of a human male

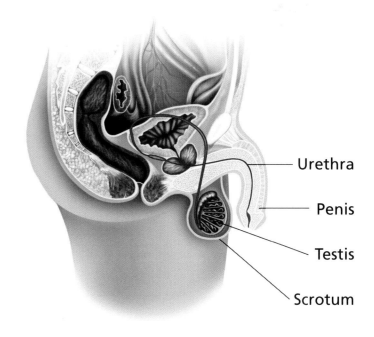

Urethra

Penis

Testis

Scrotum

If the egg is fertilised, it develops into a zygote, which travels down the fallopian tube and implants itself in the wall of the uterus. Once this happens, we say the woman is pregnant. In the uterus, the zygote grows into an embryo and further develops into a foetus. The foetus grows inside the mother for nine months until it has developed enough to live in the outside world. At that point, the mother's uterus pushes the foetus out of her body. The process of pushing the baby out is called *labour* and *delivery*. Sometimes the baby is delivered by *caesarean section*, an operation in which a cut is made in the abdomen and the uterus and the baby is removed through this incision.

Once it is born, a human baby needs constant care and attention. Human infants need an adult to take care of them, to feed them and keep them safe.

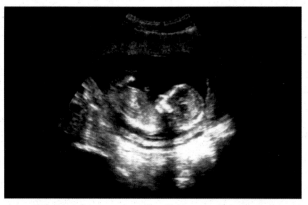

This ultrasound picture shows a baby in its mother's womb. You can see the baby's foot and head.

A mother with her baby ▶

The Endocrine System

Earlier you learned that the changes that take place during puberty are caused when glands inside the body secrete hormones into the bloodstream. Humans have two different kinds of glands: *duct glands* and *ductless glands*. Duct glands secrete their products outside the body or directly into the digestive system. Sweat glands are an example. When you run around or play sports, your sweat glands secrete perspiration outside your body to help keep you cool.

◀ *Sweat glands help keep us cool when we exercise.*

Ductless glands also secrete chemicals, but they secrete them inside the body. They secrete hormones that travel through the blood stream, carrying chemical messages to various parts of the body. These ductless glands are also known as *endocrine* glands, and together they make up the endocrine system.

Meet the Glands

The *pituitary gland* is a tiny gland located at the bottom of the brain, near where the brain meets the spinal cord. It is sometimes called the 'master gland', because it secretes hormones that tell the other endocrine glands what to do. The pituitary also secretes the hormone that makes you grow, as well as the hormones that trigger the beginning of puberty.

The *thyroid gland* is located in the front of the neck, just below the larynx, or voice box. It secretes a hormone that controls the rate at which the body burns energy and uses food.

The *pancreas* is located behind the stomach. It is divided into two parts. One part has ducts, while the other is ductless. The part with ducts releases chemicals that help the digestive system to break down food. The ductless part secretes hormones into the blood, including the hormone *insulin*, which regulates how the body uses sugar.

When a person's pancreas does not produce enough insulin, that person has a disease called *diabetes*. Fortunately, diabetes can be treated. Some diabetic people give themselves insulin injections to make sure their blood sugar levels don't get too high.

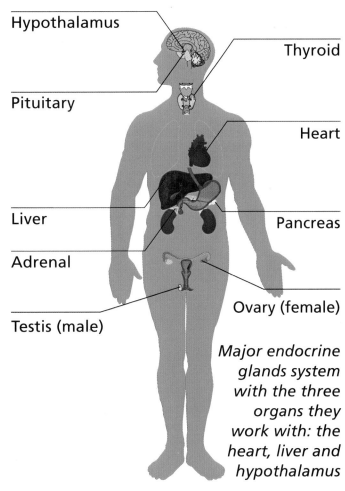

Major endocrine glands system with the three organs they work with: the heart, liver and hypothalamus

The *adrenal glands* are small glands located above the kidneys. They give off a hormone called *adrenaline* that speeds up the heart and allows blood to flow more rapidly to muscles and the brain. If you've ever become scared or angry and felt your breathing and heart rate speed up, you've experienced what people call an 'adrenaline rush'. This is your body's way of getting you prepared for an emergency situation in which you will need extra energy or courage, like trying to win a race or perform in the school play.

The Lives of Famous Scientists

Carl Linnaeus (1707–1778)

Earlier you learnt how scientists classify living things and give them special scientific names, using the Latin language. The man who did more than anyone else to develop this system of classification was the Swedish scientist Carl Linnaeus.

Carl Linnaeus

Linnaeus was born in 1707. His father and grandfather were priests and they hoped that Carl would follow in their footsteps. However, from an early age young Carl was more interested in plants than religion. In his mind, however, religion and nature were closely connected. He believed that God had created the world and all the plants and animals in it, so by studying these wonderful creations, he was learning about God.

Linnaeus went to school to become a doctor. This allowed him to learn even more about plants, because many medicines came from plants. He began travelling around gathering unusual plants. Once he had a large collection, he set about organising it. In the process, he developed a new, improved way of classifying plants.

In 1735, Linnaeus published the work that made him famous. It had a Latin name: *Systema Naturae*, which means *The System of Nature*. In this book he laid out a classification system for all living things.

Linnaeus gave the various species he identified two names, a *genus* name and a *species* name. The genus name was more general. For instance, both the lion and the tiger were members of the genus *Felis*, which is Latin for 'cat'. But the lion was *Felis leo*, the tiger *Felis tigris*. Linnaeus also developed larger categories called orders, classes and kingdoms. Do you know which species you belong to? It is *Homo sapiens*. *Homo* is the Latin word for human being; *sapiens* is the Latin word for wise. You are *Homo sapiens* because you are a person who can think about yourself and the world around you. Although scientists have adapted Linnaeus's system over the years, much of it is still used today.

Linnaeus became a professor at Uppsala University in Sweden. He made expeditions to different parts of Scandinavia, collecting plants and animals to study. He had some very enthusiastic students who travelled all over the world collecting specimens for him: one student went to the American colonies, another to Japan. Two visited Australia and the South Pacific with Captain Cook. Each time a student returned to Sweden with exotic plants and animals, Linnaeus had additional material to make his book bigger and better. By the time Linnaeus died, *The System of Nature* had expanded to fill several volumes and his collection of specimens was enormous. This collection was sold to an English botanist called Edward Smith, who brought it to London where he established the Linnean Society of London in 1788. The Society continues the work of Carl Linnaeus by making his collection and library available for scientists to study.

Sir Humphry Davy

Sir Humphry Davy (1778-1829)

Do you know the names of the three main areas of science? We call them physics, chemistry and biology. They are all 'science', but they tell us about the world we live in in different ways.

In Year 4 we read about Sir Isaac Newton who discovered the theory of gravity and the laws of motion. He was therefore known mainly as a *physicist*. Because he was regarded by many people as the greatest scientist who had ever lived, many people thought of physics as the 'Queen of the Sciences'. At the beginning of the nineteenth century, a young man called Humphry Davy decided that he wanted to be to chemistry what

Isaac Newton had been to physics. He thought that chemistry was the most important of the sciences.

Humphry Davy was born in Penzance in Cornwall, where his father was a woodcarver. When he left school he was sent to an apothecary-surgeon to be trained. (An 'apothecary' is what we call a chemist, and in those days chemists also performed surgery on people.) However, before he had finished his training, Davy was asked to join a group of people who had set up a laboratory in Bristol to investigate the properties of different gases and to find out how they could help sick people.

Davy decided that the only way to know what effect gases have on people would be to breathe them in himself and then make notes of how he felt. He very nearly died after breathing carbon monoxide, which is poisonous, but he found that when he breathed nitrous oxide (also known as laughing gas) he felt light-headed and cheerful. He noticed that his response to pain was not so great, and he wrote up his experiments to suggest that nitrous oxide could be used as an *anaesthetic*, to relieve the pain of people having operations.

The young Davy was then offered a job at the Royal Institution in London, which had only recently been set up to help farmers to produce more food. Davy began to give lectures on chemistry which were so popular that Albemarle Street, where the Royal Institution still has its building, had to be turned into a one-way street on lecture nights so that horse-drawn carriages would be able to drop off and collect their wealthy owners! Davy was made professor of chemistry for the Royal Institution at the age of only 22. He was able to isolate several elements that had not been known before, including potassium, sodium, calcium and magnesium. What pattern do they make in the periodic table on page 299?

When Davy was conducting an experiment with nitrogen trichloride, he caused an explosion and injured himself. He needed an assistant to help him with his experiments while he recovered, so he hired a young man called Michael Faraday. Faraday had trained as a bookbinder, but he educated himself by reading the books he was binding. He had attended some of Davy's popular lectures at the Royal Institution, so he made beautifully illustrated notes of these and bound them into a book, which he sent to Davy. Michael Faraday would become another great scientist and he would spend the rest of his life working in the laboratory of the Royal Institution, which you can still visit.

> We read about Michael Faraday in Year 5.

In 1815 Davy was asked if he could do something about the terrible explosions in mines, which were killing many people. The explosions occurred when a gas known as 'marsh gas' or 'firedamp' (we call it natural gas or methane) came into contact with the candles the miners carried to work by. Davy found that methane only explodes at high temperatures, so he had the idea of enclosing the flame of the candle inside a tube with tiny perforations in it. By the time the gas had passed over the surface of the metal, it had cooled down and did not explode. Davy refused to patent his discovery, which meant that people could use it free of charge. Soon it was being used in mines all over the world, and Humphry Davy was regarded as a great benefactor of the human race because of the lives his invention had saved. He was made a baronet, which means that he was called Sir Humphry and his wife was called Lady Davy. This was the highest honour awarded to a scientist at that time. He became President of the Royal Society and was regarded as the leading scientist of his generation for the rest of his life.

Dorothy Hodgkin (1910 – 1994)

Science is a fascinating subject, and in the books in this series we have read about many famous scientists whose wonderful discoveries have changed the way in which we live. Some students find science so interesting that they decide they want to make it their career. Have you ever thought about that?

Several of the famous scientists we have been reading about have been women, but for a long time it was difficult for a woman to become a scientist, because people used to think that science was a man's subject. One woman who was determined not to let this stand in her way was Dorothy Hodgkin.

Dorothy Hodgkin's portrait was painted by Bryan Organ.

Dorothy Hodgkin was born in 1910 in Egypt, where her father was an archaeologist. When World War I broke out in 1914, she was sent back to England to go to school, and after the war her parents returned as well, living at Beccles in Suffolk. Dorothy went to a small primary school where she had her first lessons in chemistry, being taught how to grow crystals of several chemicals. 'I was captured for life,' Dorothy wrote in her autobiography, 'by chemistry and by crystals.'

A crystal is a piece of something that is the same all the way through. It is arranged regularly, like a stack of bricks or like tightly packed marbles in a box. At the very smallest level, even the atoms or molecules are in the same arrangement. That is what decides what shape the crystal will be. You know some crystals already. Grains of sugar and salt are crystals. So are glass, snow and ice. So is a diamond! If you cut a big diamond into lots of small diamonds, they will all have the same shape, because of their crystalline structure.

> We looked at some beautiful snowflakes in Year 1.

When Dorothy went to a mixed secondary school, she was told that only the boys were allowed to study science. She protested until she was allowed to continue with her science course. Her teachers must have been glad that they let her, because Dorothy went to study at Oxford University, specialising in crystals.

If you can make a crystal, you can tell something about the arrangement of the atoms from the shape of the crystal. The atoms are too small to see but you can see the crystal. Dorothy used x-rays to look more closely at crystals and used an early computer to calculate the angles. Her computer was much, much slower than anything we use now so she had to ask it the right questions.

Dorothy worked with other scientists who were investigating the use of penicillin. It was already known that penicillin was very effective at fighting infections, but no one knew its structure, so it could not be manufactured. Dorothy wanted to crystallise it, but it was very hard to create a crystal of penicillin. Eventually she managed to obtain a sample and to work out the structure of penicillin.

She was later able to do the same thing for insulin. That is a chemical made in a person's pancreas to reduce the amount of sugar in the blood. You can see where the pancreas is in the body on page 337. Dorothy and her team spent a whole weekend in their laboratory building a model of the insulin molecule, which was very complicated.

Insulin crystals

Her work with crystals made Dorothy Hodgkin one of the most famous scientists in the world. The Royal Society awarded her its highest honour, the Copley Medal, and she is still the only British woman to have won the Nobel Prize for Science.

Sir Tim Berners-Lee (1955 – present)

Have you ever used a computer or a smart-phone to access the Internet? And have you ever wondered why website codes start with *www*? The answer is that we owe this wonderful technology to the genius of Sir Tim Berners-Lee, a British computer scientist who devised the World Wide Web.

Tim was born in London in 1955. His parents were mathematicians who worked on the very first commercial computer, the Ferranti Mark 1. When he was a boy, he loved trainspotting, and he began to learn about the basics of electronics by playing with a model railway. When he was older he went to Oxford University to study physics. In his spare time he used an old television set to make his very own computer.

He graduated with a first-class degree and started working at Plessey, a telecommunications company. His job was to create *software* which is the coding that goes into computers, rather than the physical nuts and bolts.

Next Tim started working at CERN (the European Organisation for Nuclear Research), a huge laboratory for studying small particles like atoms and electrons, which you met on page 296. Tim's fellow scientists worked in different towns and different countries and he wanted to be able to share ideas quickly, so he came up with *hypertext*. In hypertext, clicking one set of words (a link) would take his colleagues to another set of words. This system, called ENQUIRE, worked like a giant internet dictionary.

It wasn't until 1989 that Berners-Lee and Robert Cailliau proposed to make a universal hypertext system, the World Wide Web. This would use a computer language called Hypertext Markup Language, which we know as 'HTML'. You type an HTML address when you want to access a website. Berners-Lee also came up with the idea of *browsers*, which are programs we use to 'read' HTML such as Internet Explorer or Mozilla Firefox. He made his invention freely available to everyone, because he wanted people to be able to communicate with each other more easily.

The web is not the same as the Internet. Instead, the web is an *application* – it uses the internet like a car uses roads, or a hair-drier uses the electricity grid. Berners-Lee imagined that his system would be available throughout the world for communicating and developing ideas. In 1994 he set up the World Wide Web Consortium (W3C) which aims to improve the web's ability to deliver its full potential. He also founded the World Wide

Web Foundation in 2009 to promote free technology access, social power and democracy across the world.

He is often called the Father of the Web and Queen Elizabeth knighted him in 2004 in recognition of his great achievement. He appeared at opening ceremony of the 2012 London Olympics, in which he worked on an old computer and tweeted: 'This is for everyone'.

Sir Tim Berners-Lee unveiled a plaque near his home to mark his great achievement.

Suggested Resources

Books

Super Science: Human Body by Rob Colson (Franklin Watts) 2013

How to Build a Human Body by Tom Jackson (Scholastic) 2013

How to Make a Universe with 92 Ingredients by Adrian Dingle (Scholastic) 2011

What's Chemistry All About? by Alex Frith and Lisa Gillespie (Usborne) 2012

The Way Science Works by Robin Kerrod (Dorling Kindersley) 2008

Who Split the Atom? by Jillian Powell (Franklin Watts) 2011

Essential Life Science: Cells by Richard Spilsbury (Raintree) 2014

Variation and Classification by Melanie Waldron (Raintree) 2013

What Makes Me Me? by Robert Winston (Dorling Kindersley) 2010

Science Experiments by Robert Winston (Dorling Kindersley) 2011

See Inside Science by Alex Frith (Usborne) 2006

Online Resources

At-Bristol Science Centre: www.at-bristol.org.uk

Glasgow Science Centre: www.glasgowsciencecentre.org

Museum of the History of Science, Oxford: www.mhs.ox.ac.uk

Natural History Museum London: www.nhm.ac.uk

Royal Institution Christmas lectures: www.richannel.org/christmas-lectures

'Invigorate, bringing science to life' at the Royal Society: www.invigorate.royalsociety.org/

Science Museum, London: www.sciencemuseum.org.uk/on-line/energyhall/section6.asp shows an animated version of Boulton and Watt's steam engine

ThinkTank, Birmingham Science Museum: www.thinktank.ac

Illustration and Photo Credits

American School, (19th century), *Prospectors panning for gold during the Californian Gold Rush of 1849* (coloured engraving), Private Collection / Peter Newark Western Americana / The Bridgeman Art Library: **101 (b)**

Catherine Ashmore, photographer, 'Food, Glorious Food', from the 2008 production of *Oliver!* at the Theatre Royal, Drury Lane © Cameron Mackintosh Ltd: **204**

Ark Royal Launch, Tyne and Wear Archives and Museums: **96 (a)**

Aubrey Beardsley, *Le Morte d'Arthur*: **29, 30, 31, 32 (a & b), 33, 34**

Mark Beech: **38 (a & b), 40 (a & b), 42 (a & b), 48, 51, 53, 54, 57, 59, 60 (a-c), 61, 62, 63 (a & b), 81 (b), 101 (c), 201, 203, 207**

Quentin Blake, *Little Red Riding Hood and the Wolf* from *Revolting Rhymes* © Quentin Blake / AP Watt at United Agents on behalf of Quentin Blake: **12**

Sandro Botticelli (1444/5-1510), *The Birth of Venus*, c.1485 (tempera on canvas) Galleria degli Uffizi, Florence, Italy / Wikimedia Commons: **170**

British Library © The British Library Board: **95 (c), 178**

K. T. Bruce, 'The Sixteen performing the music of Renaissance composers at Christ Church, Oxford, as part of their annual Choral Pilgrimage': **192**

Buckingham Palace, 'The Queens Piper' © Buckingham Palace Press Office: **127 (c)**

Sir Edward Coley Burne-Jones (1833-98), Illustration for *Works of Geoffrey Chaucer*, 1896 © British Library Board: **178**; *The last sleep of Arthur in Avalon*, 1881-98 (oil on canvas), Museo de Arte de Ponce, Puerto Rico / Wikimedia Commons: **179**

J. C. Buttre, 'Portrait of Frederick Douglass', 1855, from Fredrick Douglass, *My Bondage and My Freedom*, New York and Auburn: Miller, Orton & Mulligan, 1855 / Wikimedia: **103 (a)**

Richard Carlile (1790–1843), *Peterloo Massacre*, 1819 (print), Manchester Library Archives: **143**

A. B. Clayton, *Inaugural Journey of the Liverpool and Manchester Railway*, 1830 (oil on canvas), Wikimedia Commons: **133**

Paul Collicutt: **68, 69, 72, 73, 74 (a & b), 100, 126, 317, 323 (a & b), 329 (a & b), 330, 332 (b)**

Library of Congress Prints and Photographs Division Washington, *The Room in the McLean House, at Appomattox C.H., in which Gen. Lee surrendered to Gen. Grant*, 1865, Library of Congress / Wikimedia Commons: **107**

George Cruikshank: **138**

George Cruikshank/Paul Collicutt, 'Oliver asking for more' from *Oliver Twist*, 1837-39: **27**

Declan Doherty (photographer), Kieran Quinn as Bottom with the fairies in the An Grianán Theatre Production of *A Midsummer Night's Dream* by William Shakespeare, directed by David Grant. July 2008: **195 (b)**

Gustave Doré, 'The New Zealander', from *London: A Pilgrimage*, 1872: **9**

Gustave Doré / Paul Collicutt, illustrations from *The History of Don Quixote*: **18, 19, 20**

Albrecht Dürer (1471-1528), *Self Portrait with Gloves*, 1498 (oil on panel), Prado, Madrid, Spain / Giraudon / Wikimedia Commons: **174 (b)**

Jan van Eyck (c.1390-1441), *The Portrait of Giovanni Arnolfini and his Wife Giovanna Cenami (The Arnolfini Marriage)*, 1434 (oil on panel), National Gallery, London, UK / Wikimedia Commons: **167 (a)**

Flickr Creative Commons: **82 (a)** (photo by Gary Craig), **84** (photo by Charlie McLean), **85** (photo by Norman Richards), **88 (b)** (photo by Alistair Bradbury / www.lakedistrictwalks.net), **89 (b)** (photo by Stephen Woodcock), **91** (photo by Ian McLoughlin, Blackpool), **115** (photo by Dipak Gohil), **168** (photo by Darren Milligan), **180** (photo by Andreas Wüthrich), **181 (a)** (photo by Yogi Johnson), **191** (photo by Tony Evans), **194** (photo by Sam Scholes), **344** (photo by Maggie Jones)

A. S. Forrest, illustration from *Our Island Story* by H.E. Marshall, Galore Park in association with Civitas, 1905/2005: **108**

Piero della Francesca (c.1415-92), *The Flagellation of Christ*, c.1463-4 (tempera on panel), Galleria Nazionale delle Marche, Urbino, Italy / The Bridgeman Art Library: **166**

James Gillray (1757-1851), *A Voluptuary Under the Horrors of Digestion*, 1792 (print), British Museum Images © Trustees of the British Museum: **125**

Edward Goodall, *Cottonopolis*, 1852, Wikimedia Commons: **129 (b)**

Andrew Carrick Gow (1848-1920), *St. Paul's Cathedral: Queen Victoria's Diamond Jubilee, June 22nd, 1897*, Private Collection / © Look and Learn / The Bridgeman Art Library: **155**

Benozzo di Lese di Sandro Gozzoli, (1420-97), *The Journey of the Magi to Bethlehem*, the right hand wall of the chapel, c.1460 (fresco), Palazzo Medici-Riccardi, Florence, Italy / The Bridgeman Art Library: **167 (b)**

Catherine Green: **79 (a)**

Roger Grainger: **198**

John Atkinson Grimshaw (1836 - 1893), *Blackman Street, London*, 1885 (oil on canvas), Wikimedia Commons: **8**

Jean Haagen & Alexander Roslin, *Carl Linnaeus*, 1775/copy 1905 (oil on canvas), by permission of the Linnean Society of London: **338**

Francis Hayman (1708–1776), *Robert Clive and Mir Jafar after the Battle of Plassey, 1757*, c.1760 (oil on canvas), National Portrait Gallery / Wikimedia Commons: **147**

Auguste Hervieu, illustration from *The Life and Adventures of Michael Armstrong the Factory Boy* by Frances Trollope, 1840: **139**

William Hogarth (1697-1764), *An Election Entertainment*, 1754-55, by courtesy of the Trustees of Sir John Soane's Museum: **142 (b)**

Henry Howard, *Sir Humphry Davy*, 1803 (oil on canvas), reproduced by permission of The Athenaeum Club: **339**

The Illustrated London News, 'The Sepoy revolt at Meerut', 1857: **148**

Philip James de Loutherbourg (1740-1812), *Coalbrookdale by Night*, 1801 (oil on canvas), Science Museum / Science and Society Picture Library: **131**

Rudyard Kipling (1865-1936), 'The Cat That Walked by Himself' from *Just So Stories*, 1902: **165**

Edwin Henry Landseer (1802-1873), *Monarch of the Glen*, 1851, National Museum of Scotland, Edinburgh, Scotland © National Museums Scotland: **127 (a)**

Emma Lennard: **4 (b), 5 (a-c), 299**

Edwin Longsden Long (1829-1891), *Uncle Tom and Little Eva*, 1866 (oil on canvas), London / Wikimedia Commons: **103(b)**

William Lucas, *Birthplace of the Locomotive*, 1861 © Science Museum / Science & Society Picture Library: **135**

Eduard Magnus (1799-1872), *Felix Mendelssohn*, 1846 (oil on canvas), Museum fur Geschichte de Stadt Leipzig, Germany / Wikimedia Commons: **195 (a)**

Tommaso Masaccio (1401-28), *The Trinity*, 1427-28 (fresco), Santa Maria Novella, Florence, Italy / Wikimedia Commons: **164 (b)**

Text Credits and Sources

Music

Index